THE OXFORD BOOK OF
LOCAL VERSES

THE OXFORD
BOOK OF
LOCAL VERSES

Chosen, and with an Introduction, by
JOHN HOLLOWAY

Oxford   New York
OXFORD UNIVERSITY PRESS
1987

Oxford University Press, Walton Street, Oxford OX2 6DP

Oxford New York Toronto
Delhi Bombay Calcutta Madras Karachi
Petaling Jaya Singapore Hong Kong Tokyo
Nairobi Dar es Salaam Cape Town
Melbourne Auckland
and associated companies in
Beirut Berlin Ibadan Nicosia

Oxford is a trade mark of Oxford University Press

British Library Cataloguing in Publication Data
The Oxford book of local verses.
1. English poetry
I. Holloway, John, 1920–
821'.008 PR1174
ISBN 0-19-214149-X

Library of Congress Cataloging in Publication Data
The Oxford book of local verses.
Bibliography: p.   Includes indexes.
1. Manners and customs—Poetry.   2. English poetry.   3. English poetry—England.
4. England—History, Local—Poetry.   5. Great Britain—History, Local—Poetry.
6. Anonymous writings, English.   7. Popular literature—Great Britain.   8. Folk poetry, English.
9. Inscriptions, English—Great Britain.   10. Great Britain—Social life and customs—Poetry.
I. Holloway, John, 1920–.
PR1195.M24086 1987   821'.008   86–18039
ISBN 0-18-214149-X

Set by Rowland Phototypesetting Ltd.
Printed in Great Britain by
Richard Clay Ltd.
Bungay, Suffolk

FOREWORD AND ACKNOWLEDGEMENTS

THE county locations given in the 'Index of Localities' (p. 334) are according to the pre-1974 divisions into counties. These correspond to the divisions followed by the sources used in preparing this book, and any other system seemed likely, in the long run, to create more difficulties than it avoided. Counties are not mentioned for places where the county is probably well known to all. Sources of verses are as given in the Notes, and what is said about this in the Introduction, p. ix, should be borne in mind. In one or two cases, where there are several villages of the same name and the source used is not explicit, an element of uncertainty remains.

I gratefully acknowledge the help given me by the *Times Literary Supplement* in publicizing my request to be sent inscribed verses, and express my thanks to all who responded. I was unable to include all the verses sent me, but the names of those whose contributions have been included are mentioned, with gratitude, in the Notes. I also gratefully acknowledge help of one kind or another from J. Diggle, H. H. Erskine-Hill, R. Palmer, and the staffs of several libraries but particularly, for unfailing considerateness and patience, that of the University Library Reading Room at Cambridge. To Richard Jeffrey I am greatly indebted for many corrections and improvements to the Notes. My chief debt is to my wife, to whom this book is dedicated.

CONTENTS

INTRODUCTION

A N anthology of verse should be a source of pleasure and interest, in the first place, through the poems in it, read one by one and for their own sake. If the individual poems do not offer such rewards, the anthologist could better employ his time than in anthologizing. But for all that, this book is not a miscellany of rewarding poems; it has pursued pleasure and enlargement of experience within the range of certain guiding ideas now to be made plain.

The word 'local' is used here as it is used in such expressions as 'local stone', 'local cooking', or 'local superstitions'; or as C. V. Lean used it for one section of his great work *Collectanea*: 'local proverbs'. 'Local verses' therefore does not mean verses about places or the specific events that happened in them. If it did, many famous poems, Spenser's 'Prothalamium' and Milton's 'Lycidas' among them, would demand inclusion, and the enterprise would be quite other than it is. Some of the verses included are indeed about localities or local events, simply because every poem is about something. But that is by the way. The criterion of their inclusion has been something else. Local superstitions are sometimes about local places, and sometimes not; and the same is true of local verses, as the phrase is used for this book.

Because of this, the most obvious category of 'local verses' is made up of the verses which have been literally and physically inscribed on some material object that stands, or has stood, in a particular place. Hence the verses inscribed on village crosses, or on the walls or windows of houses, or on fountains, sundials, or churches (whether on tombstones or elsewhere), or on wells, caves, or trees, or other things of such kinds. There is in fact a great wealth of such verses across the length and breadth of England, many of them of notable merit, and almost all of them much less well known than they deserve. Some such verses are inscribed on objects which, one may suppose, will never be moved. But it is easy to take too much for granted. A large and ornate funeral monument like that on which no. 219 of the verses below was inscribed would seem a good candidate for permanence and for not being moved. In fact, it has been transported from the church in one Norfolk hamlet, and re-erected in another.

From such examples one comes to realize that there is no rigid boundary between the movable and the immovable; and with that in mind, I have gone on from verses inscribed on buildings or tombstones, to those on church bells, clocks (and so watches), ceramics, silverware, and also cutlery and small ornaments in a few cases; or written into parish registers, or visitors' or other books on the flyleaf or elsewhere, or, occasionally, preserved in legal documents or as their unofficial equivalent. In general, the test has been, that the poet's intention was simply to be read by those who came into contact with one particular physical object: not to compose something for which the natural thing would be publication in a volume of poems, and embarkation upon the whole voyage of printing, study, reprinting, dissemination, and in the end the celebrity that can result from that. These verses were simply not sent out originally, one might say, upon the journey which in the end takes a poem (or so at least the writer is entitled to hope) into 'English Literature'.

What has been said so far, however, indicates only one part of the enterprise. Nothing would be easier than to compile a full-scale anthology (more than one, indeed) of verses inscribed only literally and in the way I have discussed; but to do only that would not show the real range and variety of a kind of verses and verse-making within which there is a real continuity. Of that continuity, verses inscribed in the literal sense make, as it were, only one part of a continuous spectrum. Being inscribed literally upon some particular localized object (like, say, a fountain or a village cross) is not very different from being, as one might put it, inscribed on the collective memory of some particular locality. Verses inscribed in stone in a fixed place become, to a greater or lesser extent, a permanent part of a certain local cultural environment. Two lines from the epitaph inscription which is no. 292 in this book were at one time 'obliterated on the instructions of the incumbent, but preserved, as now printed, in local memory'. Twenty-five years later, in a church a hundred miles away from the first one, the epitaph was used again. This time, incumbents were either less demanding or less observant, and the lines preserved elsewhere in local memory are still preserved in the stone.

The case is rather similar with verses, whether sung, or recited when occasion called for it, which are known by heart, passed on 'in performance', and lodged permanently in the minds of those who live in a certain locality. Number 124 here is a bell-ringers' verse that stands, or stood, upon the wall of the bell-ringers' room; but chaos would soon have resulted if the ringers had not also known it more or less by heart. Number 85, on the other hand, is a song that the Brighton fishermen who sang it must have known by heart, whether or not they also wrote it up on the wall of their boatyard. Number 381 is a verse physically inscribed on a piece of Staffordshire pottery, and refers to willow-pattern ware. Number 174, almost the same verse, is recorded as having been current in Dorset 'to familiarize a child with the design' of willow-pattern china. Number 109 is inscribed on a well in Dorset, but is exactly the same kind of verse, half charm half prayer, as the verses recited in many parts of England (see for example nos. 371, 372, 435) in order to have sight in a dream of one's future husband. The Wiltshire song about the hornet (no. 179) is quite different in content from the verses said to have been inscribed on stone at Clement's Inn, London (nos. 9, 10), but the purpose of each—to ridicule the rapacity of lawyers—was the same.

One may illustrate these continuities in another way. One country parson composes a poem for his gardener (no. 270); another writes an epitaph for his clerk (no. 145) and this is in due course inscribed on the clerk's tombstone. Another versifies a local legend in ballad form (no. 377). Another local writer does the same, but in amateurish literary verses (no. 429). Yet another, again a country parson, has some of his own verses inscribed above the parsonage door (no. 116). Lastly, a celebrated poet, also a parson, turns local charms into verses, or writes minuscule poems in the genre of the village charm (no. 143). The names of the first four of these are forgotten, the fifth is 'Hawker of Morwenstow', the sixth is Herrick. All this makes one more example of the continuity-in-variety which this book explores.

With such examples in mind one sees it is right, in order to represent the full range of 'local verses', to include not only local charms, but also weather rhymes, children's games, and some of the many songs for those festivals and celebrations which used once, in devout agricultural communities, to articulate the round of the year. With them come rhymes about farming practice, or verses that some localities have doubtless remembered and treasured, so as to pour scorn, good-humoured or otherwise, on neighbouring places. Number 367, the sarcastic 'Letter H's Petition' and the retort to it, are of that kind, and so are the 'Loppi'ton Bar' verses (no. 376). At the same time, it seems unduly narrow to anthologize what has sometimes been called 'the Common People', but leave unnoticed how their conventionally more educated contemporaries enjoyed much the same humour about their own not very different local affairs. Hence the epigrams about Adelphi and the Athenaeum (nos. 4, 5), the two Oxbridge epigrams, the one capping the other (no. 225) or the Blackburn newspaper poem about a young ladies' tea-party which was very much the middle-class equivalent of the Hertfordshire village girls' May-Day beer-promenade (nos. 220, 478). I have also noticed (though for the most part leaving ballads aside, as the genre is well enough known) verses like the election songs (no. 446), the hilarious verse speech for the Hereford centenarian morris dancers (no. 375), the lampoon about the striking bell-ringers (no. 126), a local poem about the dubious beauties of Harwich (no. 223), and the rhymes of a 'village bard' of Silkstone, Yorkshire, on the relative merits of Silkstone coal and Dublin whisky (no. 421).

Not all such verse is ironical, as may be seen in no. 379, the beautiful lines, by an almost unknown writer, to the 'unknown stream'; or—more literary but still by someone who has not begun to make the journey into 'English Literature'—the suave Horatian pastiche of no. 87. So, when they came my way and fitted naturally into the groups of verses that little by little were taking shape, I have also included a handful of striking pieces, on a variety of subjects, by 'local' poets: those who have never had more than a local reputation. Eccles's restrained but riotous 'Deein be Inches' (no. 441) is an example which in the present climate of opinion may find a warm welcome or perhaps a hot reception.

In this whole field there are no naturally sharp boundary-lines, though nothing would be easier than to prescribe such at the price of empty tidiness, exclusion of good verse, and loss of a sense of the whole. One should notice, for instance, that much the same verse, minor variations aside, may well have been inscribed on physical objects in several different places. Number 523 is recorded in the source I have used as 'often written in a book', and no. 534 as 'a common tavern notice'; no. 91, on the church clock at Bidborough, Kent, may be seen also, in fairly similar form, in Chester Cathedral. These are merely specific examples of a trend that has been common enough. Certain epitaphs, including some which one must suppose to have been by very ordinary people, became widely popular. Likewise with weather rhymes and seasonal verses. I have not included such verses, unless my source has related them to a particular locality, except in the last section of the book, by way of an appendix; but many of the verses which I have given for this or that locality will have occurred, often with variations, elsewhere as well. Just as 'local stone' does not mean something geologically unique, so 'local verses' are not necessarily confined to one locality and one alone.

Perhaps this is the place also to note how the present book is not the magisterial, multi-volume work of comprehensive scholarship which, given a substantial private income and half a lifetime of leisure, it would be an enjoyable thing and a major literary service to compile on the spot, village by village, over the whole extent of the country. It should therefore be borne in mind that texts are based upon the versions given in the sources cited in the Notes (pp. 313–33). These sources are, in large part, relatively obscure local histories, guidebooks or travel books, histories of schools or landed families, memorial books for town celebrations, or early collections of popular rhymes, proverbs, and country sayings. Scrupulosity of scholarship has been far from an invariable feature of such works; and I have encountered variations that some, though not all, might find surprising. Further investigation, especially by those able to pursue these matters *in situ*, would doubtless improve the texts of a number of the verses included here. Again, there may well be some who are ill-satisfied to find verses originating in an oral tradition taken from printed sources published before oral scholarship reached its present level of proficiency; this is a matter, however, not only of what is practicable, but of how interest may attach to some of the items included, precisely because they come from such sources—as do other verses composed by people with a local standing only. Written and oral have interacted over a very long time.

Only in a few cases (though these were indeed the beginning of the enterprise) have I drawn upon my own firsthand acquaintance with the inscriptions themselves, here and there over England. Nor, I am sorry to say, is there any guarantee that the verses given here are all still to be found in the places mentioned: only that they have been so recorded at this or that time in the past. Many inscriptions on permanent objects like buildings are located in the sources only in general or even vague terms, or have become illegible through the work of time, or have been removed or bowdlerized. I have allotted verses on Sunderland ware to the North-East, on Liverpool ware to the North-West, and so on, but often it is not possible to allot verses on small objects like chinaware, watches, etc., to any regional locality. The 'locality' of such a verse is the individual object upon which it has been written, and the life of which is, save for the interference of persons like myself, its own life.

A small number of verses inscribed literally upon objects, and for that reason included here, are by more or less famous writers. Where possible, as with Jonson's verses for the Apollo Room (no. 11) or Pope's epitaph for himself, I have included them among the regional sections into which the collection has been divided. Moreover, if it is of interest to see an epitaph by Pope, or Carew, or Crashaw, along with those by obscure anonymous writers, it is of interest to see Herrick's country charm-poems along with the anonymous charm-verses also from the West Country, or elsewhere—especially as Herrick seems to have based his verses upon this or that 'local superstition'. Likewise with Coleridge's epitaph for himself (no. 32), written only a few months before his death.

In this as it were outer circle of the collection I have included such poems as Hardy's bell-inscription verses, which are an ironical parody of the real thing, and Milton's celebrated 'Captain or colonel, or knight in arms' sonnet, though his editor describes the poet-author's reference to hanging it on the front door of his house as a 'poetic device'. After all, it has occasionally not been certain, from the sources used, whether this or that obscure and anonymous poem was inscribed in fact, or only written for that purpose. The hilarious lines 'On the burial of the leg of Henry Paget' (no. 501) are of that kind. Again, from time to time poems quite literally inscribed in a particular place were originally set there (e.g. no. 20) for a short time only. The verses by well-known poets have been included partly for purposes of comparison, and partly—what is surely of much interest and importance—to help fill out the complex continuity between the sub-literary (the 'of the People') and the literary itself.

At the end of the book come two ancillary sections. The collection as a whole covers England, and hence come the eight regional divisions. But as I have prepared it, a few verses have come my way from elsewhere that have been good, or much to the point for purposes of comparison, and I think that readers would wish not to be without them. Hence the section entitled 'Wales, Scotland, Ireland, etc.'. This section must be seen as an invitation to others to do systematically what is here only pointed to. Finally, some movable objects can reasonably be referred to this or that region of England; but for others knowledge is lacking and this cannot be done, and verses from these are included in the closing section of the book. As I suggested above, making a verse anthology is not an exercise in conceptual analysis, but in bringing worthwhile poems together in an orderly way. This is also why the sequence of the poems within each section has been decided by the interest and appropriateness of reading on from one poem to the next, all the way through, and not by divisions of kind or chronology.

Sometimes, verses inscribed in a specific locality acquire an added force and tellingness, as a result of time and the changes brought by time, in the particular places where those verses were given a localized existence. On W. B. Yeats's grave in Drumcliff churchyard stand the lines, for his poem 'Under Ben Bulben':

> Cast a cold eye
> On life, on death.
> Horseman, pass by!

That terse reference to a reader who would be mounted carried a wealth of social and also local meaning. Yeats meant his tomb to speak to his own people and to some extent to his own class. When those words were written, it would have been local farmers or gentry who would have been on horseback, and we find the words 'hard-riding country gentlemen' in the poem from which those words were taken. Today times have changed. Those people· will be in cars, and a tourist from some local riding-stables is the most likely person to be on horseback.

Again, on Edwin Muir's grave at the edge of a country churchyard that adjoins a panorama of rich East Anglian cornland, one may read the lines, from his poem 'Milton':

... his unblinded eyes
Saw far and near the fields of Paradise.

When Muir's tombstone was placed there, those lines were beautifully apt. Now, the vision of boundless harvest has been replaced, in the foreground, by the sight of a bypass thronged with traffic. Number 192 in the present collection, the grand panegyric to the triumphant power of steam, carved on a stone in the wall of a Fenland pumping-station, now carries ironic overtones of another kind. Most of the steam pumping-engines in the Fens have long ago been replaced, and the very building with that hubristic inscription to the power of steam became a repair shop, I am told, for the diesels that have supplanted it. This is the kind of irony, silent, and time-induced, that Shelley celebrates in his sonnet 'Ozymandias'. 'Look on my works, ye mighty, and despair!', the proud king had had inscribed upon his monument; but Time, the poet intimates, invites the proud of a later age, as they gaze upon the forgotten ruins of that spurious grandeur, to despair in a deeper sense.

Pope's astonishing epitaph for himself (no. 49, 'On One who would not be buried in Westminster Abbey'), a miracle of hauteur in the guise of succinct humility, delights us enough when we read it in his collected *Poems*; but its import rings out much more, as we contemplate it inscribed upon a modest tablet in a now suburban church. In much the same way, a traditional Catholic prayer (see no. 96) gains in poignancy when it is found scribbled on a paper in the purse of a murderer who died in prison.

Something needs to be said about the detail of the texts as they are printed here. Those who check them against some surviving original in a local churchyard, or wherever it may be, will sometimes, I believe, be surprised; as I have been when noticing substantial and inexplicable variations between one printed source and another. In such cases, one must use good sense, and remember that the purpose of the whole operation is as I said at the beginning of this Introduction. Needless to say, in the sources I have used there has often been some degree of modernization of texts; but it is clear that this has varied from case to case, and that it has very seldom been made explicit. In general, I have reproduced texts as I have found them, correcting obvious misprints or, very occasionally, adjusting punctuation in order to avoid some clear risk of confusion of the sense. I have modernized spelling where not to do so would have been distracting, and otherwise have left it alone.

To a greater or lesser extent, many of the verses collected here do for us what is done by more celebrated and 'literary' verse. They show us how poetry can emancipate itself—and therefore, can emancipate us with it—from the prosaic and pedestrian consciousness, and offer a strange invigoration, a vivid glimpsing of half-caught connections, through phrases and ideas that it brings together in a kind of revelatory energy. The mind is invited not to a tidy and limited knowledge, but to pause and to explore and to wonder.

> As I was going o'er misty moor
> I spied three cats at a mill-door   (no. 363)

is one example;

> Take her by the lily-white hand,
> Lead her cross the water . . .   (no. 221)

is another, and so is the strange

> Jesus was born in Bethlehem,
> Baptised in river Jordan, when
> The water was *wild in the wood* . . .   (no. 144)

In this last, corruption is easy to trace, though exactly how the original ran is open to doubt; but it is not the first time that confusion has resulted in poetry.

Such unexpected and thought-provoking linkages occur elsewhere. This is why no. 44, the catalogue of those in sanctuary at a certain date, in Westminster, though not of course composed as a poem, seems to read like a poem and to deserve inclusion. In no. 337, the boundaries down to hell and up to heaven, witnessed by biting on the 'white wax', leave one with the same sense of an order of things freer, stranger, and perhaps richer than the prosaic, the practical. Some of these verses take one further still. The whorish widow who rides into the manorial court backward on a black ram (no. 161), the girl who holds the 'even ash-leaf' so as to glimpse her future husband (no. 435), the farmer who sows his field when he hears the bird at night (no. 240), all seem to belong to a world that hints at us to consider whether our own is as everyday as we have thought: and to do that (though of course the strangeness of fantasy is one thing, and that of reality another) is one major function of true poetry.

Reading through these verses, one is also struck (not, needless to say, for the first time) by how widely the gift of poetic creativity must be spread, or at least must once have been spread, through the population: how much it has been the possession of ordinary people generally. What must be the earliest British example, or at least the earliest known to me, abbreviated to a cryptic terseness, is at Hexham. It was originally inscribed as an epitaph for a young soldier serving on the Roman Wall. In English it might run:

To the Gods and the Shades.
Flavinus.
Standard-Bearer. Petriana Horse.
White Troop. Age Twenty-Five
Service Seven.

Lies Here.[1]

No Horace or Virgil (see no. 49) would have needed to blush for that simple frontier epitaph. Among examples from the pages which follow one might mention the silver that 'did no service in the earth' (no. 100), the much-married old man (no. 408) who 'now lies under the grass so green' (whether the poet himself saw what his lines suggested about the greenness, one does not know), or the righteous who were to 'ride to glory', on the 'spiritual railway' (no. 216). None of those verses bears the marks of having been composed by someone belonging to a literary élite—by a 'poet'. Yet all of them, and many more besides, suggest that a gift for poetry is not the preserve of any élite. It at least can be, and has been, something about as widespread as having a singing voice or being able to draw. How far that remains true in the circumstances of our own time may be another matter; but in general, it would be surprising and anomalous if being able to create poetry were altogether a rare and exclusive gift, while being able to enjoy it were a widespread possession of people in general.

*   *   *

Such at any rate are among the thoughts I believe to be suggested by this book; and it also seems to cast doubt on the notion, endorsed both by those with no interest in popular poetry, and by those who champion it and incline to be supercilious about literary poetry, that the popular and the literary are two unrelated and contrasting things. The rollicking epitaph for the first Lord Wharton (no. 465) has, however, a genuine kinship with the parish clerk's grim humour about another marriage (no. 199), or the eloquent terseness of country epitaphs like no. 130 or no. 416. That parish clerk may never have rhymed before in his life, or since. His modest effort if anything encourages such a supposition. Bringing popular verses and more literary verses together, as has been done constantly in this anthology, has been done of set purpose: to invite reflection upon the nature of the boundary, or it may be the absence of boundary, between them.

In either case we can recognize, as we sense that what we read is true if modest poetry, a heightening and enriching of our experience which is

---

[1] J. Gibson, *Hexham and its Abbey* (1919), p. 73.

among the things that poetry brings. At the same time we sense how objects may be charged with meaning by their inscriptions, or verses enriched by being inscribed in some due and appropriate place, or by being truly the possession of a community. As the St Austell bells ring out their peals (no. 121), it adds to the experience of listening to know that in a figurative sense they ring out, also, their bold and moving mottoes, which taken all together prove to be a good eight-line poem. The weathercock at Olney (no. 258) turns, as it says itself, in silence; but eloquently for all that, once one knows the inscription on it. Bell and weathercock inscriptions are in fact everywhere; and it adds a little to the density and variety of one's experience, to have that in mind as one listens, even if in this or that case one does not know the words. There is something that one might call 'the poetry of location': a poetic gain through the physical embodiment of words that have taken root, as it were, among the objects, or, and just as much, the daily doings, of human society and its environment.

In a good many of these pieces, the reader will be gratified by some sudden and unforeseen turn in the meaning: helping one to a recognition that such abrupt and reassuring closeness to reality is among the things important in a great deal of verse. The Hertfordshire village girls (no. 220) call for a May morning drink of strong beer. The full force of that, alone, takes an instant or so to sink in; and only on second thoughts does it transpire how, for these charming young maidens, 'small beer' is going to be only a wretched second best. One is reminded of the dry, husband-hunting humour of no. 109. The climax of the Surrey harvest-home song (no. 82) is that not a single load of hay was overturned: the urban reader may reflect that this simple verse was nearer to the heart of the matter, as one of labour, of toil and skill, than he could have got for himself. Sometimes, one can clearly see where limited verbal skill has been compensated for by something of a larger awareness, a range of view to which one can oneself be blind. Number 234, on the Grimsby disaster, is better than some of the purely doggerel pieces that survive about the same event, partly because its closing stanzas, albeit modestly, open into something of that larger view.

One can also, however, find clear examples of skill – perhaps intuitive skill—with words, choice of metaphor, or rhythm; gifts definitely akin to what we admire in the 'poets of literature'. We encounter lines which have the sudden power of the Brighton fishermen's work-song, singing for a good catch of mackerel:

White may they be, like blossom on a tree

where metaphor and rhythm combine in no merely verbal exercise, because they illuminate, and in a strange and almost mystical sense integrate, reality itself: fish scales and fruit-tree petals are all one, fertility by land or by sea is the same. The light-hearted but on second thoughts profound oneness of 'luck' and 'love', expressed with moving reticence in the refrain of the gypsy song (no. 324), the huntsman who, now himself pursued by death, 'takes to earth' as his hunted foxes used to do (no. 65), the 'ashen ile' with which the husband 'anoints' his good-for-nothing wife (no. 228), the man of the Cole family whose epitaph calls him 'a Cole raked up in dust', to await rekindling on the 'Glorious Morning' (no. 134; the quotidian aptness of this will be lost on those who know nothing of open fires, and how to keep them in overnight), the sudden dazzling juxtaposition of corpse and Christ, 'lumpe' and 'lampe', in the Boston epitaph (no. 207), the haunting suggestiveness of no. 239, are all flashes of poetic imagination such as readers will long have admired elsewhere.

Sometimes also, these verses are moving and memorable through a kind of telling silence. The evocatively, disturbingly remote fills the imagination because it is left to be divined. This is so with the riddles, for example no. 369. Popular riddles go back to times before the Norman Conquest, as also do the country and village charms—there are Anglo-Saxon charm-verses against 'the stitch', and against nightmares. Elsewhere, the reader will find examples of the power of poetry to move us by displaying a kind of final simplicity: a sort of decisive selectiveness such as brings the essence of the old Sussex mill (no. 54) down to its ultimates of wood, iron, stone—and, in the decisive place in the verse, simply the wind itself.

Another thing that may catch the reader's attention is how many of these verses show keen emotion in poetry coming near not only to wit (as in no. 66, where the lifetime of disciplined and self-effacing service of the trained working dog is so succinctly recorded), but to broad humour and hearty laughter: as when the domestic servant Susan Jones, in her gifted poem about the Bagbury Ghost (no. 378), brings together the strange and supernatural, and the joyously ridiculous. Many indeed of the pieces in this collection confirm our knowledge that the pang of true emotion and the start of sudden laughter often come close together. Longinus said sublime emotion 'nudged the corner' of the everyday; and keen feelings are much given to nudging the corner of what tempts us to laugh. That is something we know from Chaucer or Shakespeare or Pope or Blake; and readers of this book will find something here of what they have found there.

Because this anthology is so largely an anthology of pieces by unknown obscurities, non-poets, 'Sunday poets', forgotten local poets, it ought to interest also in another way. It invites one to see it as of interest in excess of the direct pleasure it may bring in the reading, and in excess also of any light it may throw on the nature of poetry, or how it may reinforce the light we have already. What it reveals also, and greatly, is the nature of ordinary life, across the length and breadth of the land, and over the centuries. The mill, the workshop, the inn, the church and the churchyard, labour on the farm or at the forge or 'in service', hunting and sport, eating and drinking, love and love-making and the joys (and horrors) of marriage, child-bearing, schools, life and also death on the sea—all these are reflected here, and reflected in a distinctive way: as they have been recorded by men or women not in the first place poets and writers, but ordinary people who were plain and mostly anonymous units of ordinary life. They have remained in obscurity, unknown outside their own local part of the country; but their verses have remained, either as a real physical object and part of the physical surroundings of those with whom they lived, or as living on in the memories of their fellows and their descendants.

Sometimes—especially perhaps in the world of today—those verses have been lost, in some places if not in all. Last All Hallows' Eve a group of children came to the door of my house in a small town in the West Country. They were in bits and pieces of fancy dress and with their faces painted, and they asked for the gifts traditional on that day. But when I amiably said, as I got out my purse, 'Aren't you going to sing the song?' (thinking, needless to say, of perhaps another verse for this book), their gaiety rather faded away. 'We don't know it', they said a little ruefully. It was a moment not without its poignancy. They knew that by tradition there was a song, but not what it was. They had knowledge, but they knew it was no more than a fragment of what it might have been, and once would have been.

A few—and I must emphasize, no more than a few—of the poems and verses of all those ordinary men and women and children are gathered together here, so that others may enjoy, and perhaps also ponder, what they did, and so that we may keep in mind how widespread and deep-rooted has been, among our people, a sense of true and varied poetry. I say a few only of the poems and verses, because (to say nothing of certain recent collections which have touched on one or other part of this whole field) I am very much aware of how much remains to be done. The rhymes included here have been brought together, in the main, from a very large number of miscellaneous obscure works, most of them published long ago, and now more or less unknown to literary scholars, or at least to the large majority of them. This book, however, has gone to the press when the supply of good verse from such sources by no means seems to be coming to an end.

On the contrary. I believe that the somewhat out-of-the-way voyage of exploration which has been undertaken here lies more or less as much open as ever. The range and variety of material which awaits discovery, or rather rediscovery, and which deserves to become familiar to readers of literature, is the main reason why I have sought to avoid limiting the selection by rigid definition, categorization, or exclusion. Rather, I have sought to be open and flexible, so that this book will suggest how one kind of verse shades into another, how 'local' shades sometimes into more general, how the interests, and the poems, of countrymen and labourers could make a continuity with those of the more urban, middle-class, or learned; and in the end, how the popular and the literary make up one broad and open spectrum. It is when these things are recognized that the full interest of the whole field, and its full potentiality for further interest, will be adequately understood.

I
LONDON

1 *On a portrait of Queen Elizabeth at Hampton Court*

The restles swallow fits my restles minde,
In still revivinge, still renewinge wronges;
Her just complaintes of cruelty unkinde
Are all the musique that my life prolonges.

With pensive thoughtes my weepinge stagg I crowne,
Whose melancholy tears my cares expresse;
His teares in sylence, and my sighes unknowne,
Are all the physicke that my harmes redresse.

My onely hope was in this goodly tree,
Which I did plant in love, bringe up in care,
But all in vaine, for now to late I see
The shales be mine, the kernels others are.

My musique may be plaintes, my physique teares,
If this be all the fruite my love-tree beares.

2 *Inscriptions on conduits in the City of London*

(i) *in Cheapside for James I's progress through London on his accession*

Life is a dross, a sparkle, a span,
A bubble: yet how proud is man!

(ii) *Gracechurch Street*

All in this world's Exchange do meete,
But when death's burse-bell rings, away ye fleete.

3 *Found on a seat in Kensington Gardens, c.1844*

Poor Adam and Eve were from Eden turned out
As a punishment due to their sin.
But here after eight, if you loiter about
As a punishment you'll be locked in.

shales] shells

2 burse-bell] bell of the Exchange or Bourse. Death is ready to do business

3

4   *Verses on the building of Adelphi, London*

> 'Four Scotchmen by the name of Adams,
> Who keep their coaches and their madams,'
> Quoth John in sulky mood to Thomas
> 'Have stole the very river from us.'

5   *An epigram on the statue of Minerva outside the Athenaeum Club*

> Ye travellers who pass by, just stop and behold,
> And see, don't you think it a sin,
> That Minerva herself is left out in the cold,
> While her owls are all gorging within.

6   *Scratched by Hookham Frere on a window at Holland House, Kensington, 1811*

> May neither fire destroy nor waste impair
> Nor time consume thee till the twentieth heir,
> May taste respect thee and may fashion spare.

7   *Lines on Tom Doggett the actor, on a Lambeth window-pane, 1737 (see the note)*

> Tom Doggett, the greatest sly droll in his parts,
> In acting was certain a master of arts;
> A monument left—no herald is fuller—
> His praise is sung yearly by many a sculler.
> Ten thousand years hence if the world last so long
> Tom Doggett will still be the theme of their song.

8   *On an inn window, Fetter Lane*

> Should you ever chance to see
> A man's name writ on glass,
> Be sure he owns a diamond
> And his parents own an ass.

9 *Verses said to have been attached to the figure of a naked
'Moor' supporting a sundial in Clements Inn*

In vain, poor sable son of woe,
  Thou seek'st the tender tear;
For thee in vain with pangs they flow,
  For mercy dwells not here.
From cannibals thou fled'st in vain,
  Lawyers less quarter give:
The *first* won't eat you 'till you're dead,
  The *last* will do't *alive*!

10 *Two inscriptions on the Inner Temple Gateway, London*

As by the Templar's hold you go,
  The horse and lamb display'd
In emblematic figures show
  The merits of their trade.

The clients may infer from thence
  How just is their profession;
The lamb sets forth their innocence,
  The horse their expedition.

Oh! happy Britons, happy isle!
  Let foreign nations say,
Where you get justice without guile,
  And law without delay.

*

Deluded men, these holds forego,
  Nor trust such cunning elves;
These artful emblems tend to show
  The *clients*—not *themselves*.

'Tis all a trick; these all are shams
  By which they mean to cheat you:
But have a care—for *you're* the *lambs*,
  And they the *wolves* that eat you.

5

Nor let the thought of 'no delay'
    To these their courts misguide you;
'Tis *you're* the showy horse, and they
    The *jockeys* that will ride you.

11 *Ben Jonson (1573–1637); inscription over the entrance to the*
    Apollo Room, upstairs in the Devil Tavern, Fleet Street (?),
    London

Over the Door at the Entrance into the Apollo

Welcome all, who lead or follow,
To the Oracle of Apollo.
Here he speaks out of his Pottle,
Or the Tripos, his Tower Bottle:
All his Answers are Divine,
Truth itself doth flow in Wine.
Hang up all the poor Hop-Drinkers,
Cries Old Sym, the King of Skinkers;
He the half of Life abuses,
That sits watering with the Muses.
Those dull Girls, no good can mean us,
Wine it is the Milk of Venus,
And the Poets' Horse accounted.
Ply it, and you all are mounted;
Tis the true Phœbeian Liquor,
Clears the Brains, makes Wit the Quicker:
Pays all Debts, cures all Diseases,
And at once, three Senses pleases.
Welcome all, who lead or follow,
To the Oracle of Apollo.

12 *On a Chelsea figure of Shakespeare*

The cloud cap't towers and gorgeous palaces,
The solemn temples, the great globe itself,
Yea, all which it inherit, shall dissolve
And like the baseless fabric of a vision,
Leave not a wreck behind.

11 pottle] half-gallon   tripos] three-legged cauldron   skinkers] tapsters,
barmen   Phœbeian] of Phoebus Apollo

13 *A watch-paper verse used by Adams of Church Street,*
    Hackney; probably nineteenth-century

> Tomorrow, yes, tomorrow! you'll repent
> A train of years in vice and folly spent.
> Tomorrow comes—no penitential sorrow
> Appears therein, for still it is tomorrow.
> At length Tomorrow such a habit gains,
> That you'll forget the time that Heaven ordains,
> And you'll believe that day too soon will be
> When more Tomorrow's you're denied to see.

14 *Lines inscribed on John Clarke's 'Eureka' hexameter-making*
    machine, exhibited in London in 1845

> Eternal Truths of Character Sublime   .
> Conceived in darkness here shall be unroll'd.
> The mystery of Number and of Time
> Is here display'd in Characters of Gold.
> Transcribe each line composed by this machine,
> Record the fleeting thoughts as they arise;
> A Line, once lost, will ne'er again be seen,
> A thought, once flown, perhaps for ever flies.

15 *In St Leonard's Church, Streatham; for the two wives of*
    Thomas Hobbes, d. 1623, 1682

> Susannah late a lovely Lillye
>   Soon faded tho' she be,
> And Margarite an ancient Pearl,
>   Resolved to dust ye see
> Yet Lillye's roots shall spring again,
> And Pearl repayr'd with Christ to reign.

16 *Ben Jonson; epitaph for Salomon Pavey, a child actor in the*
    Queen's Revels Company

> Weepe with me all you that read
>   This little storie:
> And know, for whom a teare you shed,
>   *Death's* selfe is sorry.

'Twas a child, that so did thrive
    In grace, and feature,
As *Heaven* and *Nature* seem'd to strive
    Which own'd the creature.
Yeeres he numbred scarse thirteene
    When *Fates* turn'd cruell,
Yet three fill'd *Zodiackes* had he beene
    The stages jewell;
And did act (what now we mone)
    Old men so duely,
As, sooth, the *Parcæ* thought him one,
    He plai'd so truely.
So, by error, to his fate
    They all consented;
But viewing him since (alas, too late)
    They have repented.
And haue sought (to give new birth)
    In bathes to steepe him;
But, being so much too good for earth,
    Heaven vowes to keepe him.

17 *An inscription in St Mary Overie (i.e., Southwark
    Cathedral), London; the original is by Francis Quarles
    (1592–1644)*

Like to the damask rose you see,
Or like the blossom on the tree,
Or like the dainty flower of May,
Or like the morning of the day,
Or like the sun, or like the shade,
Or like the gourd which Jonas had,
        Even so is Man, whose thread is spun,
        Drawn out, and cut, and so is done.
The rose withers, the blossom blasteth,
The flower fades, the morning hasteth;
The sun he sets, the shadow flies,
The gourd consumes, and Man he dies.

16 Zodiackes] i.e. years   Parcæ] the Fates

8

18 *Verse will of Joshua West of Chancery Lane; 1804*

> Perhaps I died not worth a groat;
>   But should I die worth something more,
> Then I give that, and my best coat,
>   And all my manuscripts in store,
> To those who shall the goodness have
>   To cause my poor remains to rest
> Within a decent shell and grave.
> This is the will of Joshua West.

19 *Epitaph for the highwayman Claude Duval, born in*
   Normandy, 1643, hanged at Tyburn, 1670, and buried in
   Covent Garden church

> Here lies Du Vall: Reader, if Male thou art,
> Look to thy purse: if Female, to thy heart.
> Much havoc has been made of both; for all
> Men he made stand, and women he made fall.
> The second Conqueror of the Norman Race
> Knights to his arms did yield, and ladies to his face.
> Old Tyburn's glory, England's illustrious thief,
> Du Vall the ladies' joy: Du Vall the ladies' grief.

20 *Lord Herbert of Cherbury (1583–1648); epitaph for Sir*
   Philip Sidney, at St Paul's

> Reader,
> Within this church Sir Philip Sidney lies,
> Nor is it fit that I should more acquaint,
>   Lest superstition rise,
>   And men adore,
> Soldiers their martyr; lovers their saint.

21   *In the church of St Bartholomew the Great, Smithfield*

CAPTN JOHN MILLET MARINER 1660

Many a storm and tempest past
Here hee hath quiet anchor cast
Desirous hither to resort
Because this Parish was the Port
Whence his wide soul set forth and where
His father's bones intrusted are.

The Turkey and the Indian trade
Advantage by his dangers made;
Till a convenient fortune found,
His honesty and labours crown'd.

A just faire dealer he was knowne,
And his estate was all his owne
Of which hee had a heart to spare
To freindshipp and the poore a share.

And when to time his period fell
Left his kind wife and children well
Who least his vertues dye unknowne
Committ his memory to this stone.

22   *Epitaphs by Tennyson (1809–92)*

(i) *for the Arctic explorer Franklin, in Westminster Abbey*

Not here! The white North has thy bones; and thou,
   Heroic sailer-soul,
Art passing on thine happier voyage now
   Toward no earthly pole.

(ii) *for Caxton the printer, in St Margaret's, Westminster*

FIAT LUX (his motto)

Thy prayer was 'Light—more Light—while Time shall last!'
Thou sawest a glory growing on the night,
But not the shadows which that light would cast,
Till shadows vanish in the Light of Light.

23 *Dedicatory sonnet in the photograph album of the London Glaziers' Company; 1889*

When first our pious Ancestors besought
  Th' Eternal Power to give His blessed light,
They little deemed the precious boon they sought
  Would, in the future, by its subtle might
(By Skill directed, and by Science taught),
  Preserve 'Our Worthies' to our mortal sight,
E'en when, in fulness of their honoured age,
Their parts well played they quit Earth's troubled stage.
  Within this Volume, by the Mystic power
Of the Great Gift, our Motto humbly asks—
  They live again beyond this transient hour;
Their works completed, and perform'd their tasks.
    May they enjoy the day that knows no night,
    And in the shadow of their God, find perfect light.

24 *John Dryden (1631–1700), an epitaph on Sir Palmes Fairborne's tomb in Westminster Abbey*

Sacred
To the Immortal Memory of Sir Palmes Fairborne, *Knight, Governor of* Tangier; *in execution of which Command he was mortally wounded by a Shot from the* Moors, *then Besieging the Town, in the 46*th. *year of his Age.* October *24*th. *1680.*

Ye Sacred Relicks which your Marble keep,
Here undisturb'd by Wars in quiet sleep:
Discharge the trust which when it was below ⎫
Fairborne's undaunted Soul did undergo, ⎬
And be the Towns Palladium from the Foe. ⎭
Alive and dead these Walls he will defend,
Great Actions great Examples must attend.
The *Candian* Siege his early Valour knew,
Where *Turkish* Blood did his young hands imbrew.
From thence returning with deserv'd Applause, ⎫
Against the *Moors* his well-flesh'd Sword he draws; ⎬
The same the Courage, and the same the Cause. ⎭
His Youth and Age, his Life and Death combine, ⎫
As in some great and regular design, ⎬
All of a Piece throughout, and all Divine. ⎭

Still nearer Heaven his Vertues shone more bright, ⎫
Like rising flames expanding in their height,   ⎬
The *Martyr*'s Glory Crown'd the Soldiers Fight.   ⎭
More bravely *Brittish* General never fell,
Nor Genreal's Death was e're reveng'd so well,
Which his pleas'd Eyes beheld before their close,
Follow'd by thousand Victims of his Foes.
To his lamented loss for time to come,
His pious Widow Consecrates this Tomb.

25   *St Mary's, Battersea; for Sir Edward Wynton, d. 1636*

Alone, unarm'd, a tyger he oppress'd,
And crush'd to death the monster of a beast;
Twice twenty mounted Moors he overthrew
Singly on foot; some wounded, some he slew,
Dispers'd the rest. What more could Samson do?

26   *Westminster Abbey; for William Lawrence, d. 1621*

With diligence and trust most exemplary,
Did William Lawrence serve a Prebendary.
And for his paines now past, before not lost,
Gain'd this remembrance at his master's cost.

O read these lines againe; you seldome find,
A servant faithfull, and a master kind.

Short hand he wrote; his flowre in prime did fade.
And hasty Death Short-hand of him hath made.
Well could he numbers, and well mesur'd Land;
Thus doth he now that ground whereon you stand,
Wherein he lyes so geometricall:
Art maketh some, but thus will Nature all.

26 geometricall] 'laid out'

27   *Southwark Cathedral; epitaph for 'Lyonnell Lockier Dr. of Physick', d. 1672*

> Here Lockyer lies interr'd: enough, his name
> Speaks one hath few competitors in fame,
> A name so great, so gen'ral, it may scorn
> Inscriptions which do vulgar tombs adorn.
> A diminution 'tis to write in verse
> His eulogies, which most men's mouths rehearse.
> His virtues and his pills are so well known
> That envy can't confine them under stone.
> But they'll survive his dust and not expire
> Till all things else at th' universal fire.
> This verse is lost, his pills embalm him safe
> To future times without an epitaph.

28   *Epitaph for Robert Preston, drawer at the Boar's Head Tavern, Eastcheap, d. 1730; in St Michael's Church, Crooked Lane (later in St Magnus)*

> Bacchus to give the toping world surprise,
> Produc'd one sober son, and here he lies.
> Tho' nurs'd among full hogsheads, he defyd
> The charm of wine, and every vice beside.
> O reader, if to justice thou'rt inclined,
> Keep honest Preston daily in thy mind.
> He drew good wine, took care to fill his pots,
> Had sundry virtues that outweighed his fauts.
> You that on Bacchus have the like dependence,
> Pray copy Bob in measure and attendance.

29   *On a set of Lambeth ware plates (one line to each of six plates)*

> What is a Merry Man!
> Let him do what he can
> To Entertain his Guests
> With Wine and Merry Jests
> But if his Wife do frown
> All merriment Goes down.

30   *Beauchamp Tower, Tower of London; epitaph for a goldfinch*

> Where Raleigh pin'd, within a prison's gloom,
> I cheerful sung, nor murmur'd at my doom;
> Where heroes bold, and patriots firm could dwell,
> A goldfinch in content his note might swell:
> But death, more gentle than the law's decree,
> Hath paid my ransom from captivity.

Buried, June 23, 1794, by a fellow-prisoner
in the Tower of London.

31   *Sir Walter Raleigh (1552?–1618); 'the story runs' that he*
wrote the following on a flyleaf of his bible. Lines 1–6 are the
last stanza of his 'Nature that washed her hands in milk'

> Even such is Time which takes on trust
> Our youth, our joys, and all we have,
> And pays us but with age and dust;
> Who in the dark and silent grave
> When we have wandered all our ways
> Shuts up the story of our days.
>   And from which earth and grave and dust
> The Lord shall raise me up I trust.

32   *Coleridge's epitaph for himself, written 9 November 1833*

> Stop, Christian passer-by!—Stop, child of God,
> And read with gentle breast. Beneath this sod
> A poet lies, or that which once seem'd he.—
> O, lift one thought in prayer for S.T.C.;
> That he who many a year with toil of breath
> Found death in life, may here find life in death!
> Mercy for praise—to be forgiven for fame
> He ask'd, and hoped, through Christ. Do thou the same!

33 *From a seventeenth-century masque performed by the Grocers'*
    Company at the installation of the Lord Mayor of London; a
    song sung by 'the Planters, the Gardeners, and Pipers'

> This Wilderness is
> A place full of Bliss
> For caring and sparing
> We know not what 'tis;
> By the sweat of our brows,
> We do purchase our meat;
> What we pluck from the boughs,
> We do lye down and eat.

> *Chorus*
> We labour all day, but we frollick at Night
> With smoaking and joking, and tricks of delight.

> The Merchant that Plows
> On the Seas rugged Brows
> Submits all his hits
> To what Fortune allows:
> If she do but frown
> The trader is down;
> Till he comes to his Port he has nothing his
>   own.

> *Chorus*
> We labour all day, yet we frollick at Night
> With smoaking and joking, and tricks of delight.

> Of Fruits that are ripe
> We all freely can take;
> With Tongues and Bag-Pipe
> Jolly Musick we make:
> In our Pericraniums no mischief doth lurk;
> We are happier than they that do set us a work.
> We never are losers
> Whatever Wind drive;
> Then God bless the Grocers
> And send them to thrive.

Chorus

We labour all day, yet we frollick at night,
With smoaking and joking, and tricks of Delight.

34 *'The Alamode or ye Maidens Mode . Admir'd & Continued .
By ye Ape Owl and Mistris Puss'. Inscribed on a dish,
London or Brislington ware, 1688; a satire on some women's
fashions of the time*

I am ye owl that Stood In Feare
Of other Birds It doth appeare
But Being in this Dress I'le Vow
I dont Beleeve theyl Know me now.

I heare ye Clamors of ye Thron
Wherein they would run top-knots down
But yet alas alas al in Vain
For I this Mode will still maintain.　　(the Cat)

Top Knots and Night Vailes I declare
For Evermore I mean to Ware
This dress there's none that can excell
I see it doth be com me well　　(the Ape)

How, now you females of this age
I would not have you in a Rage
Although I doe present you heare
With what you have esteeme(d) deare
Top Knots and nigh(t) Vails you adore
But see by whom they now are wore

ye Cat she wears In perfect View
a Cornet & a Top Knot too,
ye very owl, that flyse by night
In this your Mode takes mouch delight
ye Reason this for in a Storm
this Vail will keep her shoulders warm

yᵉ very ape, Adors this Dress
& Cryes It up, Can he doe Less
But females yᵉ first found this pride
Pray tell me how can you Abide
to weare this mode against Controul,
When used by ape, nay cat and owl.

35 *Verses on the kaleidoscope (a London sensation of c.1820),
signed 'W.H.M.'*

The Kaleidoscope

Mystic trifle, whose perfection
Lies in multiplied reflection,
Let us from thy sparkling store
Draw a few reflections more:
In thy magic circle rise
All things men so dearly prize,
Stars, and crowns, and glitt'ring things,
Such as grace the courts of kings;
Beauteous figures ever twining,—
Gems with brilliant lustre shining;
Turn the tube;—how quick they pass—
Crowns and stars prove broken glass!

Trifle! let us from thy store
Draw a few reflections more;
Who could from thy outward case
Half thy hidden beauties trace?
Who from such exterior show
Guess the gems within that glow?
Emblem of the mind divine
Cased within its mortal shrine!

Once again—the miser views
Thy sparkling gems—thy golden hues—
And, ignorant of thy beauty's cause,
His own conclusions sordid draws;
Imagines thee a casket fair
Of gorgeous jewels rich and rare;—
Impatient his insatiate soul
To be the owner of the whole,

He breaks thee ope, and views within
Some bits of glass—a tube of tin!
Such are riches, valued true—
Such the illusions men pursue!

36   *Lines inspired by an ancient bone found at the Roman Camp*
'between Sydenham and Peckham'

Bonus! Bona! Bonum! which means, you know,
He-bone, she-bone, bone of the neuter gender.
Or by what name soever thou may'st go,
Bone of a certain age, tough bone or tender!
Art thou a rib of that illustrious Dane
Hight Sweyne by those old rogues who wrote his history?
Or part and parcel of some *other* swain?
Speak, if thou canst speak, and resolve the mystery!
Thou wert, aforetime, that which now thou art
(For certain things change not with changing time),
Haply, some hard, unyielding, *Bonypart*
Too stern for verse, too rigid for a rhyme,
So I'll betake me to mine ease again,
Restrain the muse, and lay aside my pen.

37   *'A Dialogue between the Old Black Horse at Charing Cross,*
and the New One, with a Figure on it in H[anover] Square';
    c.*1719*

In London late happen'd a pleasant discourse,
Twixt an Old English Nagg and a Ha—er Horse
No wonder my Friends, if plain English they speak,
For in (old) Æsops time, Horses spoke Heathen Greek.
                           Derry Derry down.

King Charles's black Nagg being tir'd of the Town,
From fair Charing Cross, one fine Evening stole down,
And trotting along t'wards the Fields for fresh Air,
He Spy'd a strange Beast up in H—er Square.
                           Derry, &c.

Marching up, he most Civilly greeted the Steed,
But soon found, he was not of true English breed,
And the Rider he thought, a much more Aukward thing,
For he look't like a Lout, and was dress'd like a King.

                      Derry, &c.

The Charing Cross Nagg, thus began; Brother Pad,
Tis enough sure to make any mortal Horse mad,
To see such a Rider bestride a poor Horse,
Were you Hag-ridden, sure you'd scarce be rid worse.

                      Derry, &c.

Quoth the poor harmless beast, my hard Lot I must bear,
And I but the Lot of these Three Kingdoms share;
For this Wretch on my Back has a Proverb on's side
Set a Begger on Horse back, to the D—l he'll ride.

                      Derry, &c.

You seem to have brought him Sr. many a long Mile
But *Englishmen* sure, will ne're think it worth while;
For this Creature to rule them, to send very far,
When my good Old Master, they never would bear.

                      Derry, &c.

We came from a poor little Town call'd Ha—er,
But Oh! had you seen us before we came over,
You'd say times mend with me, and this stupid Thief,
Since, I've eat good Oats, and his Worship good Beef.

                      Derry, &c.

H—er! O Pox, I remember that Name,
His Grandsire I think was King at Boheme,
My good natur'd Master, poor Man was undone,
By helping that Beggarly House to a Throne.

                      Derry, &c.

To a throne they were mounted, then as they desir'd
But all the whole Crew of them fairly retyr'd,
And tho' these poor Palatines, seem settled here,
Their Grand-fathers Fortune, 'tis hop'd they may share.

                      Derry, &c.

Says Charles's Black-Nagg, be ruled by me,
To Tyburn you now, being in the right Way,
Then carry him thither, and there let him Swing,
Or else pack him home, like a Dog on a string.
                    Derry, &c.

Put on his Bob-Wigg, Piss-burnt with the Weather
And his Grogerum Coat, in which he came hither,
With his Hoe in his hand, he will look very smart,
And so drive him back in an old Turnip Cart.
                    Derry, &c.

From fam'd *Charing-Cross*, they wou'd fain have me down,
In room of a *Hero*, they'd put up a Clown;
But still my old Master, I hope, will me stride,
When the *Devil* away with that Cuckold does ride.
                    Derry, &c.

So saying, in Wrath he march'd back to his station,
And left this advice, for the good of the Nation,
Since this H—er beast you'll not find worth your care
Let him go to Grass, and the man have his Mare.

38   *From a ballad of 1690, 'Upon the Stately Structure of Bow
     Church and Steeple', London*

          Look how the country Hobbs with wonder flock
          To see the City crest turned weather-cock!
          Which with each shifting gale veres to and fro,
          London has now got twelve strings to her Bow!
          The wind's south-east and straight the dragon ruffels
          His brazen wings to court the breeze from Brussels!
          The wind's at north! and now his hissing fork
          Whirls round to meet a flattering gale from York;
          Boxing the compass with each freshing gale;
          But still to London turns his threatening tayle.
          But stay! what's there? I spy a stranger thing;
          Our Red Cross brooded by the dragon's wing;
          The wing is warm; but oh! beware the sting!
          Poor English Cross, exposed to winds and weather,
          Forced to seek shelter in the dragon's feathers!
          Ne'er had old Rome so rare a piece to brag on,

---

37 piss-burnt] sunburnt

REMARKS: _____

_____

_____

_____

_____

_____

_____

_____

_____

_____

_____

_____

_____

_____

_____

_____

_____

PARKSIDE MEMORIAL CHAPEL, INC.

PARKSIDE MEMORIAL CHAPELS, INC.

BROOKLYN, N.Y.	FOREST HILLS, N.Y.	BRONX, N.Y.
2576 Flatbush Avenue	98-60 Queens Boulevard	1219 Jerome Avenue
(718) 338-1500	(718) 896-9000	(718) 588-7970
NASSAU COUNTY	NASSAU COUNTY	MONTICELL, NEW YORK
175 Long Beach Road	8000 Jericho Turnpike	195 Broadway
Rockville Centre, N.Y.	Woodbury, New York	(914) 794-1141
(516) 868-1616	(516) 868-1616	
BROWARD COUNTY, FLA.	PALM BEACH COUNTY, FLA.	DADE COUNTY, FLA.
(954) 472-2821	(561) 655-6844	(305) 864-3774

Rabbi's Record

Name...

Jewish Name...

Age..

Residence..

Date of Death ....

Interment at..

Surviving family ....

....

Date..............................Time.................................

Family at ....

....

Organizations affiliated with......................................

....

Services were conducted by:

Rabbi..

Telephone ....

A temple built to great Bell and the dragon!
Whilst yet undaunted Protestants dare hope
They that will worship Bell shall wear the Rope.
Oh, how our English chronicles will shine,—
Burnt Sixty-Six; rebuilt in Seventy-nine.
When Jacob Hall on his high Rope shows tricks
The dragon flutters; the Lord Mayor's horse kicks;
The Cheapside crowds and Pageants scarcely know
Which most to admire, Hall, Hobbyhorse, or Bow!
But what mad frenzy set your zeal on fire
(Grave citizens!) to raise immortal spire
On Sea-coal basis? which will sooner yield
Matter to burn a temple than to build!
What the coals build, the ashes bury! No men
Of wisdom but would dread the threatening omen!
To Royal Westminster next turn thy eye
Perhaps a Parliament thou mayest espy,
Dragons of old gave oracles at Rome
Then prophesy their day, their date, and doom!

39 *An 'Ode to the inhabitant of a well-known dirty shop in Leadenhall Street'*

Who but has seen (if he can see at all),
'Twixt Aldgate's well-known Pump and Leadenhall,
A curious hardware shop in general full
Of wares from Birmingham and Pontipool?
Begrim'd with dirt behold it's ample front,
With thirty years collected filth upon't;
See festoon'd cobwebs pendant o'er the door,
While boxes, bales and trunks are strew'd around the floor.
Behold how whistling winds and driving rain
Gain free admission at each broken pane,
Save where the dingy tenant keeps them out
With urn or tray, knife-case or dirty clout!
Here snuffers, waiters, patent-screws for corks;
There castors, card-racks, cheese-trays, knives and forks!
Here empty cases pil'd in heaps on high;
There packthread, papers, rope in wild disorder lie.
O say, thou enemy to soap and towels!
Hast no compassion lurking in thy bowels?
Think what the neighbours suffer by thy whim,
Of keeping self and house in such a trim?

The Officers of Health should view the scene,
And put thy shop and thee in quarantine.
Consider thou in summers' ardent heat,
When various means are tried to cool the street,
What must each decent neighbour suffer then,
From noxious vapours issuing from thy den.
When fell disease, with all her horrid train,
Spreads her dark pinions o'er ill-fated Spain,
That Britain may not witness such a scene,
Behoves us doubly now to keep our dwellings clean.
Say, if within the street where thou dost dwell
Each house were kept exactly like thy cell;
O say, thou enemy to brooms and mops!
How long thy neighbours could keep open shops,
If, following thee in taste, each wretched elf,
Unshav'd, unwash'd, and squalid like thyself,
Resolv'd to live?—the answer's very plain,
One year would be the utmost of their reign:
Victims to filth, each vot'ry soon would fall,
And one grand jail distemper kill them all.
Persons there are, who say, thou hast been seen
(Some years ago) with hands and face wash'd clean;
And would'st thou quit this most unseemly plan,
Thou art ('tis said) a very comely man,
Of polish'd language, partial to the fair,
Then why not wash thy face and comb thy matted hair;
Clear from thy house accumulated dirt,
New-paint the front and wear a cleaner shirt?

40   *Two verses for Bartholomew Fair, London*

(i) '*an Ancient Song of Bartholomew Fair*', dated *1655*

In fifty-five, may I never thrive,
    If I tell you any more than is true,
To London che came, hearing of the fame
    Of a Fair they call Bartholomew.

In houses of boards, men walk upon cords,
    As easie as squirrels crack filberds;
But the cut-purses they do lite, and rub away,
    But those we suppose to be ill birds.

40 che] I

22

For a penny you may zee a fine puppet play,
  And for two-pence a rare piece of art;
And a penny a cann, I dare swear a man,
  May put zix of 'em into a quart.

Their zights are so rich, is able to bewitch
  The heart of a very fine man-a;
Here's patient Grizel here, and Fair Rosamond there,
  And the history of Susanna.

At Pye-corner end, mark well, my good friend,
  'Tis a very fine dirty place;
Where there's more arrows and bows, the Lord above knows,
  Than was handl'd at Chivy Chase.

Then at Smithfield Bars, betwixt the ground and the stars,
  There's a place they call Shoemaker Row,
Where that you may buy shoes every day,
  Or go barefoot all the year I tro'.

(ii) by G. A. Stevens (1710–1784)

  Here were, first of all, crowds against other crowds driving
Like wind and tide meeting, each contrary striving;
Shrill fiddling, sharp fighting, and shouting and shrieking,
Fifes, trumpets, drums, bagpipes, and barrow girls squeaking—
'Come my rare round and sound, here's choice of fine ware!'
Though all was not sound sold at Bartelmew Fair.
Here were drolls, hornpipe-dancing, and showing of postures,
With frying black puddings, and opening of oysters;
With salt-boxes, solos, and galley folks squalling,
The tap-house guests roaring, and mouth-pieces bawling.
Here's 'Punch's whole play of the gunpowder plot,'
'Wild beasts all alive,' and 'peas pudding all hot.'
'Fine sausages' fried, and 'the Black on the wire,'
'The whole court of France,' and 'nice pig at the fire.'
Here's the up-and-downs, 'who'll take a seat in the chair?'
Tho' there's more up-and-downs than at Bartelmew Fair.
Here's 'Whittington's cat,' and 'the tall dromedary,'
'The chaise without horses,' and 'queen of Hungary.'
Here's the merry-go-rounds, 'Come who rides, come who rides, sir,'
Wine, beer, ale, and cakes, fire eating besides, sir,
The fam'd 'learned dog,' that can tell all his letters,
And some *men*, as *scholars*, are not much his betters.

41 *A famous London children's song*

London Bridge is broken down,
  Dance over my Lady Lee;
London Bridge is broken down,
  With a gay ladie.
How shall we build it up again?
  Dance over my Lady Lee.
Silver and gold will be stolen away,
How shall we build it up again?
Build it up with iron and steel,
  Dance over my Lady Lee;
Build it up with wood and clay,
  Dance over my Lady Lee.
Build it up with stone so strong,
Hurrah! 'twill last for ages long,
  Dance over my Lady Lee.

Then we must set a man to watch;
  Dance over my Lady Lee.
Then we must set a man to watch,
  With a gay ladie.
Suppose the man should fall asleep?
Then we must put a pipe in his mouth.
Suppose the pipe should fall and break?
Then we must set a dog to watch.
Suppose the dog should run away?
Then we must chain him to a post;
For London Bridge is broken down,
On Christmas Day in the morning.
  Dance over my Lady Lee.

42 *A verse catalogue of London seasonal feasts*

At Yule we wonten gambol dance to carol and to sing
To have good spiced sewe and roast and plum pie for a king:
At Easter-eve pan-puffes: Gangtide Cakes did holy messes bring:
At Pasque began our Morris and ere Pentecost our May,
Though Robin Hood, lyle John, Friar Tuck, and Marian deftly play,
And Lord and Lady gang til kirk with lads and lasses gay:
Fra' mass and e'ensong so good cheer and glee on every green
As save our walles, twixt Eames and Sibbes, like game was neere seen.

42 sewe] broth   Gangtide] Rogation Days (before Ascension Day)   lyle]
little   eames] uncles; friends, neighbours

At Baptist day, with cakes and ale, mid bonfires neighbours stood:
At Martinmas we turned a crab then told of Robin Hood,
Till after long time merk, when blest were windows doors and
    lights,
And pails were filled and hearths were swept 'gainst fairy elves and
    sprites
Rock and Plough Monday games shall gang with Saint feasts and
    kirk sights.

43   *Verses recited by the clerk at St Sepulchre's, London, outside
the condemned cell at Newgate Prison, the night before an
execution*

> All you that in the condemned hole do lie,
> Prepare you, for tomorrow you shall die;
> Watch, all, and pray, the hour is drawing near
> That you before the Almighty must appear;
> Examine well yourselves, in time repent,
> That you may not t'eternal flames be sent.
> And when St. Sepulchre's Bell tomorrow tolls,
> The Lord have mercy on your souls!
> > > Past twelve o'clock!

44   *A list of those in sanctuary at Westminster Abbey, 1532*

Inprimis John Gonne for the dethe of A mane in Westm' all moste xx
    yeres paste.
Willm Stafferton marchaunte for dett of longe continuance.
Thomas Barkysdale Clothyer for dett to diverse p'sons.
Richarde Lynne Coriere for dett. A poore man.
Thomas Wayte poynte makere and Alice hys wyffe for dett.
John Cowlarde mercer for dett.
Johane Hode upon suspicon of murdre.
Rauffe Sampson servyngmane for felony.
John Walett for dett. A poore mane.
Willm Vaughan Bakere for felony.
Richarde Lute Draper for dett.
John Parkyne Vintnore for murdre of ii sergeants of London, but a
    true . . .
Richard Vulstone for dett.
Sir James Whytakere preste for murdre.

44 poynte] tagged lace or cord (for fastening clothes)   Sir] the title of a priest who
had no university degree

Richarde Ade Grocere for dett.

John Huffa Goldsmythe for felony, this mane companyth w^t many suspecte persons.

Symon Hyde Barbore for felony, this maneys sone beinge w^t suspecte persons resortynge to hym and hys house.

Thomas Forde waterman for suspicion of felony.

Gyles Sowley Fyshmongere for dett.

John Albone Goldsmythe for suspicion of felony.

John ap Morgane Walshmane for ye dethe of a mane in Wales wher he was . . .

John Mylles gentylmane for dette.

John Andrew taylor for dett and recevinge and lodgynge of suspecte persones.

John Newington mercere for dett.

Stevne Hornere mercere for dett. A poore mane.

Morgane Albrey Walshmane for murdre.

Edward Brynnynhame for felony.

X'pofer Atkryke cappere for dett and suspicion upon a murdre.

Rowlande Hyde cappere for murdre. A poore mane.

Philippe Costrowe alias Crownslawe Iryshmane for felony.

John Lovell for felony of Robbynge of churches and other.

Petere Fenton for felony.

Rogere Poley for felony.

Morgane Foulke Flescher A yonge mane for murdre.

Marmaduke . . . for felony.

. . . Fartlawe for felony.

Willm Calverley for roberye comytted upon the sea.

John ap Howell for felony. A poore mane for stellynge of herrings.

Willm Saule taylor for dett.

Olyvere Kelly for murdre.

Thomas Hynde for murdre.

Richarde Gowre taylor for felony. A poore mane.

Degere Chonterell prentyce for conveynge of certayne of hys m^r goodes.

Symonde grene Colyere for felony.

. . . Holte servyngman for dett.

John Busyne Bochere for dett.

Willm Symson for Robbynge and spoylynge of diverse churches and other persons.

Roberte Hyll servyngmane for murdre.

Thomas Jenyns Bocher for dett.

X'pofer] Christopher (with *Xp* for Greek chi-rho as an abbreviation of *Christ*)
cappere] cap maker   m^r] master's

45 *Verses inscribed in a book in Newgate prison,* c.*1881*

> Goodbye, Lucy dear,
> I'm parted from you for seven long year.
>   Alf Jones.

*

> If Lucy dear is like most gals,
>   She'll give few sighs or moans,
> But soon will find among your pals,
>   Another Alfred Jones.

46 *Some English prisons: a rhyme scratched with a nail on the bottom of a dinner-can at Millbank prison*

> *Millbank* for thick shins and graft at the pump;
> *Broadmoor* for all laggs as go off their chump;
> *Brixton* for good toke and cocoa with fat;
> *Dartmoor* for bad grub but plenty of chat;
> *Portsmouth* a blooming bad place for hard work;
> *Chatham* on Sunday give four ounce of pork;
> *Portland* is worst of the lot for to joke in—
> For fetching a lagging there's no place like *Woking*.

47 *A Suffolk story, in a Cockney ballad of* c.*1850*

The Foundling of Shoreditch and the Ixworth Doctor

Come all ye Christian people, and listen to my tail;
It is all about a doctor was travelling by the rail,
By the Heastern Counties Railway (vich the shares I don't desire),
From Ixworth town, in Suffolk, vich his name did not transpire.

A travelling from Bury this doctor was employed,
With a gentleman, a friend of his, vich his name was Captain Loyd;
And on reaching Mark Tey station, that is next beyond Colchest-
Er, a lady entered into them most elegantly dressed.

---

46 shins] of beef   graft] work   laggs] convicts   toke] bread   fetching
a lagging] serving a sentence

She entered into the carriage all with a tottering step,
And a pooty little baby upon her bussum slep;
The gentleman received her with kindness and siwillaty,
Pitying this lady for her illness and debillaty.

She had a fust-class ticket, this lovely lady said,
Because it was so lonesome, she took a secknd instead;
Better to travel by secknd class, than sit alone in the fust,
And the pooty little baby upon her breast she nust.

A seein of her crying, and shiverin, and pail,
To her spoke this surging, the Ero of my tail;
Says ee, 'You look unwell, ma'am, I'll elp you, if I can,
And you may tell your case to me, for I'm a meddicle man.'

'Thank you, sir,' the lady said, 'I only look so pale
Because I ain't accustom'd to travelling on the Rale;
I shall be better presnly, when I've ad some rest;'
And that pooty little baby she squeezed it to her breast.

So in conversation the journey they beguiled,
Capting Loyd, and the medical man, and the lady and the child,
Till the warious stations along the line was passed;
For even the Heastern Counties' trains must come in at last.

When at Shoreditch tumminus at length stopped the train,
This kind meddicle gentleman proposed his aid again.
'Thank you, sir,' the lady said, 'for your kyindness dear;
My carridge and my osses is probbibly come here.

'Will you old this baby, please, vilst I step and see?'
The doctor was a family man: 'That I will,' says he.
Then the little child she kist—kist it very gently,
Vich was sucking his little fist, sleeping innocently.

With a sigh from her art, as though she would have bust it,
Then she gave the Doctor the child—wery kind he nust it;
Hup then the lady jumped hoff the bench she sate from,
Tumbled down the carridge steps, and ran along the platform.

Vile all the other passengers vent upon their vays,
The Capting and the Doctor sate there in a maze:
Some vent in a Homminibus, some vent in a Cabby;
The Capting and the Doctor vaited with the babby.

There they sate, looking queer, for an hour or more,
But their feller passinger neather on 'em sore;
Never, never back again did that lady come,
To that pooty sleeping hinfint, a sucking of his thum!

What could this pore Doctor do, bein treated thus,
When the darling baby woke, cryin for its nuss?
Off he drove to a female friend, vich she was both kind and mild,
And igsplained to her the circumstance of this year little child.

That kind lady took the child instantly in her lap
And made it very comfortable by giving it some pap;
And when she took its close off, what d'you think she found?
A couple of ten pun notes sewn up in its little gownd!

Also in its little close was a note, which did conwey,
That this little baby's parents lived in a handsome way:
And for its Headucation they reglarly would pay,
And sirtingly, like gentlefolks, would claim the child one day,
If the Christian people who'd charge of it would say,
Per advertisement in the *Times*, where the baby lay.

Pity of this baby many people took,
It had such pooty ways, and such a pooty look;
And there came a lady forrard (I wish that I could see
Any kind lady as would do as much for me.

And I wish with all my art, some night in *my* night-gownd,
I could find a note stitched for ten or twenty pound)—
There came a lady forrard, that most honorable did say
She'd adopt this little baby which her parents cast away.

While the Doctor pondered on this hoffer fair,
Comes a letter from Devonshire, from a party there,
Hordering the Doctor, at his Mar's desire,
To send the little Infant back to Devonshire.

Lost in apoplexity, this pore meddicle man,
Like a sensable gentleman, to the Justice ran;
Which his name was Mr. Hammill, a honourable beak,
That take his seat in Worship street four times a week.

'O Justice!' says the doctor, 'instrugt me what to do,
I have come up from the country, to throw myself on you;
My patients have no doctor to tend them in their ills,
(There they are in Suffolk, without their draffts and pills.)

I have come up from the country to know how I'll dispose
Of this pore little baby, and the twenty pun note, and the clothes;
And I want to go back to Suffolk, dear Justice, if you please,
And my patients wants their Doctor, and their Doctor wants his
    feez.'

Up spoke Mr. Hammill, sittin at his desk,
'This year application does me much perplisk;
What I do advise you is, to leave this babby
I' the parish where it was left by its mother shabby.'

The Doctor from his Worship sadly did depart—
He might have left the baby, but he hadn't got the heart
To go for to leave that Hinnocent, has the laws allows,
To the tender mussies of the Union House.

Mother, who left this little one on a stranger's knee,
Think how cruel you have been, and how good was he!
Think, if you've been guilty, innocent was she;
And do not take unkindly this little word of me,
Heaven be merciful to us all, sinners as we be.

48　*John Milton (1608–74); sonnet 'When the assault was
intended to the city', 1642*

Captain or colonel, or knight in arms,
　　Whose chance on these defenseless doors may seize,
　　If deed of honor did thee ever please,
　　Guard them, and him within protect from harms;
He can requite thee, for he knows the charms
　　That call fame on such gentle acts as these,
　　And he can spread thy name o'er lands and seas,
　　Whatever clime the sun's bright circle warms.
Lift not thy spear against the Muses' bow'r:
　　The great Emathian conqueror bid spare
　　The house of Pindarus, when temple and tow'r
Went to the ground; and the repeated air
　　Of sad Electra's poet had the power
　　To save th' Athenian walls from ruin bare.

II

SOUTH-EAST ENGLAND

Pope (1688–1744); epitaph by himself, 'for one who would not be buried in Westminster Abbey'; in Twickenham church, Middlesex

> Heroes and kings, your distance keep:
> In peace let one poor poet sleep,
> Who never flattered folks like you:
> Let Horace blush, and Virgil too.

50 *A verse from a song by Theo Marzial, once painted on a board beside the ferry-house at Twickenham*

> O hoi-ye, ho ho! you're too late for the ferry
>   (The briar's in bud, the sun going down),
> And he's not rowing quick, and he's not rowing steady
>   You'd think 'twas a journey to Twickenham town,
> O hoi and o ho! you may call as you will—
>   The moon is a-rising o'er Petersham Hill
> And with Love, like a rose in the stern of the wherry,
> There's danger in crossing to Twickenham Town.

51 *James Thomson (1700–48); lines formerly on a board in Richmond Park, Surrey*

Lines written on Richmond Park

>   Richmond, ev'n now,
> Thy living landscape spreads beneath my feet,
> Calm as the sleep of infancy—the song
> Of Nature's vocalists, the blossom'd shrubs,
> The velvet verdure, and the o'ershadowing trees,
> The cattle wading in the clear smooth stream;
> And, mirrored on its surface, the deep glow
> Of sunset, the white smoke and yonder church,
> Half hid by the green foliage of the grove—
> These are thy charms, fair Richmond, and through these
> The river, wafting many a graceful bark,
> Glides swiftly onward like a lovely dream,
> Making the scene a Paradise.

50 journey] ?day's travel

52 *On a signboard, Pembroke Lodge, Richmond Park (Thomson
is buried in Richmond parish church)*

Lines on James Thomson, the Poet of Nature

Ye who from London smoke and turmoil fly,
To seek a purer air and brighter sky,
Think of the Bard who dwelt in yonder dell,
Who sang so sweetly what he loved so well!
Think, as ye gaze on these luxuriant towers,
Here Thomson loved the sunshine and the flowers.
He who could paint in all their varied forms
April's young bloom, December's dreary storms.
To yon fair stream which calmly glides along,
Pure as his life and lovely as his song,
There oft he roved. In yonder churchyard lies
All of the deathless bard that ever dies!
For here his gentle spirit lingers still,
In yon sweet vale, on this enchanted hill,
Flinging a holier interest o'er the grove,
Stirring the heart to poetry and love.
Bidding us prize the favourite scenes he trod,
And view in Nature's beauties Nature's God.

53 *A 'fuliginous rebuke' to the steamer that plied in summer from
Queenhithe to Richmond*

A Legal Lament

Ye Richmond Navigators bold
   all on the liquid plain,
When from the bridge we envied you,
   with pleasure mix'd with pain,
Why could you be so cruel as
   to ridicule our woes,
By in our anxious faces turn-
   ing up your steamer's nose?

'Twas 'strange, 'twas passing strange, 'twas
   pitiful, twas wonderous
Pitiful, as Shakspeare says,
   by you then being under us,

To be insulted as we were,
   when you your chimney rose
And thought yourselves at liberty
   to cloud our hopes and clothes.

The same sweet poet says, you know,
   'each dog will have his day,'
And hence for Richmond we, in turn,
   many yet get under weigh.
So thus we are consoled in mind,
   and as to being slighted,
For that same wrong, we'll right ourselves,
   and get you all indicted.

54   *On an old Sussex (?) mill-post*

The windmill is a couris thing
Compleatly built by art of man,
To grind the corn for man and beast
That they alike may have a feast.

The mill she is built of wood, iron, and stone,
Therefore she cannot go aloan;
Therefore, to make the mill to go,
The wind from some part she must blow.

The motison of the mill is swift,
The miller must be very thrift,
To jump about and get things ready,
Or else the mill will soon run empty.

55   *Verses formerly inscribed on a tablet in the parish church at Battle, Sussex*

This place of war is Battle called, because in battle here,
Quite conquered and overthrown the English nation were;
This slaughter happened to them upon St. Celict's Day,
The year thereof (1066) this number doth array.

---

54 couris] curious   motison] motion

56   *Greenwich, Kent; inscription beneath the 16-foot-long lion,*
     figurehead on Anson's ship the Centurion

> Stay, traveller, awhile, and view
> One who has travelled more than you;
> Quite round the globe, thro' each degree,
> Anson and I have ploughed the sea.
>   Torrid and frigid zones have pass'd
>   And—safe ashore arrived at last—
> In ease with dignity appear,
> He in the house of Lords—I here.

57   *An inscription at the bowling green at Milton, near*
     Gravesend, Kent, by Frances Webb; to the memory of
     Alderman Nynn

> Full forty long years was the Alderman seen,
> The delight of each Bowler, and King of this Green,
> As long be remembered his art and his name,
> Whose hand was unerring, unrivalled his fame.
> His Bias was good; and he always was found,
> To go the right way, and to take enough ground,
> The Jack to the uttermost verge he would send,
> For the Alderman lov'd a full length at each end.
>
> Now mourn ev'ry eye that has seen him display,
> The Arts of the Game, and the wiles of his play;
> For the great Bowler Death, at one critical cast,
> Has ended his length, and close rubbed him at last.

58   *To the poet Shenstone (1714–63); on a votive tablet and urn*
     at Burford Lodge, near Dorking, Surrey

> To the bard of Leasowe's grove,
> Tears of silent tribute lend;
> Scenes like these he loved to rove,
> Nature's and the Muse's friend.

58   Leasowe] Leasowes, Shenstone's estate in Worcestershire

Tho' no more the path he guides,
Through the dell's embow'ring shade,
Still his spirit there presides,
Still his urn shall deck the glade.

59   *On a silver flagon, altar plate at Friern Barnet church,*
Middlesex (1655?)

This pott's for holy wine, this wine pure blood,
This blood true life, this life containes all good.
Not potts, but soules, are fitt to hold such wine,
Such blood, such life, such good, O Christ take mine.

60   *Verses for the new spire (covered with copper), Wingham*
church, Kent, 1793

In Seventeen Hundred and Ninety and three,
Richard Hodgman, of Folkestone, he coppered me,
And fixed on my Head a magnificent Vane,
Which discovers the way of the wind by the same.
'Twas the fifth day of August this work was begun.
With intent for to keep me from rain, wind, and sun,
But some seem to think that never would be done,
This matter by many had oft been discussed,
Which was the best clothing and which was the worst;
Some were partial to Copper, and some for lead,
And others said shingle will serve in its stead,
But I on that point will never trouble my head,
If you finish me well, for to make me secure,
So that I a hundred of years may endure.

61   *Verses found on the minister's porch at Wye, Kent, 1630*

The corne is so dear,
I dout mani will starve this yeare;
If you see not to this,
Sum of you will speed amis.
Our souls they are dear,

60 shingle] wooden tiling

37

For our bodies have some ceare.
Before we arise,
Less will safise.
Note. The pore there is more,
Then goes from dore to dore.
You that are set in place,
See that your profession you do not disgrace.
Well you know my name,
You must be wise in the same.
Signed—A.T. C.B. E.D. etc.

62 *Inscriptions on the bells of the parish church, Rye, Sussex*

To honour both of God and King
Our voices shall in concert ring.

May heaven increase their bounteous store
And bless their souls for evermore.

Whilst thus we join in joyful sound
May love and loyalty abound.

Ye people all who hear me ring
Be faithful to your God and King.

Such wond'rous power to music's given
It elevates the soul to heaven.

If you have a judicious ear
You'll own my voice is sweet and clear.
Our voices shall with joyful sound
Make hills and valleys echo round.

In wedlock bands all ye who join,
    With hands your hearts unite;
So shall our tuneful tongues combine
    To laud the nuptial rite.

Ye ringers all who prize
Your health and happiness;
Be sober, merry, wise,
And you'll the same possess.

63 *Epitaph for William Burnett, d. 1760; in St John the Baptist Church, Croydon*

What is man?—
To-day he's drest in gold and silver bright,
Wrapt in a shroud before to-morrow night;
To-day he's feasting on delicious food,
To-morrow, nothing eats can do him good;
To-day he's nice, and scorns to feed on crumbs,
In a few days, himself a dish for worms;
To-day he's honour'd, and in great esteem,
To-morrow, not a beggar values him;
To-day he rises from a velvet bed,
To-morrow lies in one that's made of lead;
To-day, his house, though large, he thinks too small,
To-morrow, can command no house at all;
To-day, has twenty servants at his gate,
To-morrow, scarcely one will deign to wait;
To-day, perfum'd, and sweet as is the rose,
To-morrow, stinks in every body's nose;
To-day he's grand, majestic, all delight,
Ghastly and pale before to-morrow night.
Now, when you've wrote and said whate'er you can,
This is the best that you can say of man!

64 *Epitaph for Rebecca Rogers, Folkestone, 1688*

A house she hath, it's made of such good fashion,
The tenant ne'er shall pay for reparation;
Nor will her landlord ever raise the rent,
Or turn her out of doors for non-payment.
From chimney money, too, this cell is free,
To such an house who would not tenant be?

65 *Epitaph for Thomas Johnson, huntsman, d. 1774; Charlton, Sussex*

Here Johnson lies; what human can deny
Old honest Tom the tribute of a sigh?
Deaf is that ear which caught the opening sound;

63 nothing eats] ?nothing he eats

Dumb that tongue which cheer'd the hills around.
Unpleasing truth: Death hunts us from our birth
In view, and men, like foxes, take to earth.

66 *Harefield church, Middlesex; Robert Mossenden, gamekeeper,*
d. 1744

> In frost and snow, thro' hail and rain,
> He scour'd the woods, and trudg'd the plain;
> The steady pointer leads the way,
> Stands at the scent, then springs the prey;
> The timorous birds from stubble rise,
> With pinions stretched divide the skies;
> The scattered lead pursues the sight,
> And death in thunder stops their flight;
> His spaniel of true English kind,
> With gratitude inflames his mind;
> This servant in an honest way,
> In all his actions, copied Tray.

67 *For Margaret Hawtree, 'an eminent midwife', d. 1734;*
Deptford, Kent

> She was an indulgent Mother, and the best of Wives,
> She brought into this world more than three thousand lives.

68 *Epitaph for Sarah Gundry, d. 1807; in the churchyard at*
Hendon, Middlesex

> Reader! She wander'd all the desert through
> In search of happiness, nor found repose
> Till she had reach'd the borders of this waste.
> Full many a flower that blossom'd in her path
> She stoop'd to gather, and the fruit she pluck'd
> That hung from many a tempting bough—all but
> The rose of Sharon and the tree of life.
> This flung its fragrance to the gale, and spread
> Its blushing beauties: that its healing leaves
> Displayed, and fruit immortal, all in vain.
> She neither tasted nor admired—and found

All that she chose and trusted fair, but false!
The flowers no sooner gather'd than they faded;
The fruit enchanting, dust and bitterness;
And all the world a wilderness of care.
Wearied, dispirited, and near the close
Of this eventful course, she sought the plant
That long her heedless haste o'erlook'd, and proved
Its sovereign virtues; underneath its shade
Outstretch'd, drew from her wounded feet the thorns,
Shed the last tear, breath'd the last sigh, and here
The aged pilgrim rests in trembling hope!

69   *At Beddington, Surrey; 'his name was Greenhill'*

Under thy feate interrd is here
A native born of Oxfordsheere,
First, Life and Learning Oxford gave;
Surry to him his death, his grave.
He once a HILL was, fresh and GREENE;
Now wither'd is not to bee seene.
Earth in Earth shovel'd up is shut,
A HILL into a Hole is put.
But darkesome earth by powre divine
Bright at last as ye Sonne may shine.

70   *In Kew church; for Robert and Anna Plaistow, d. 1728*

At Tyso they were born and bred,
And in the same good lives they led,
Until they came to marriage state,
Which was to them most fortunate.
For sixty years of mortal life,
They were a happy man and wife,
And being so by nature tied,
When one fell sick the other died;
And both together laid in dust,
To wait the rising of the just.
They had six children born and bred,
And five before them being dead,
Their only one surviving son,
Has caused this stone for to be done.

71   *An epitaph formerly in Snodland church, Kent*

> Palmers al our faders were,
> I, a Palmer, lived here;
> And travylled till worne wythe age.
> I ended this world's pylgremage
>
> On the blest Assention daie,
> in the cheerful month of Maie,
> A thousand wyth four hundred seven,
> And took my journey hence to Heaven.

72   *Epitaph for a visitor's dog, on one of the 'High Rocks' at Tunbridge Wells, 1702 (the rock resonates when struck)*

> This scratch I make that you may know
> On this rock lyes ye beauteous Bow;
> Reader, this rock is the Bow's bell,
> Strike't with thy stick, and ring his knell.

73   *Crayford, Kent; epitaph for Peter Snell, the parish clerk, d. 1811*

> The life of this clerk was just threescore and ten,
> Nearly half of which time he had sung out Amen.
> In his youth he had married like other young men,
> But his wife died one day—so he chanted Amen.
> A second he took—she departed—what then?
> He married and buried a third with Amen.
> Thus his joys and his sorrows were treble, but then
> His voice was deep base, as he sung out Amen.
> On the horn he could blow as well as most men,
> So his horn was exalted to blowing Amen.
> But he lost all his wind after threescore and ten,
> And here with three wives he waits till again
> The trumpet shall rouse him to sing out Amen.

74 *Inscription on a stone on the roadside opposite the church at Chart Magna, Kent; for Ann West, 1811*

> The reverend Rector being a hard
> *Austerly rigid* man,
> Within the walls of his church-yard
> He will not let me stand;
> Unless a fee be paid to him,
> Two shillings and two pounds;
> So to the memory of a friend
> I, here am now set down.

75 *Motto on a sundial at Addington, Surrey, 1665*

> Amyddst ye fflowres,
> I tell ye houres.
> Tyme wanes awaye,
> As fflowers decaye.
> Beyond ye tombe
> Freshe fflowrets bloome.
> So man shall ryse
> Above ye skies.

76 *From the Scrap Book of the East India Co. Military College, Addiscombe, Surrey, 1840 (a parody of Gray's* Elegy)

The evening call proclaims the close of day,
The bedroom squads with measured step depart
And to the barracks wend their weary way
To rest the tired limbs and heavy heart.

Now round the beds their martial cloaks they fold
And all in slumber court a brief repose
Save one poor wretch, who troubled with a cold
Performs a solo on his aching nose;

Save that from yonder clumsy-looking bed
Some small cadet doth drowsily complain
Of restless neighbour, who upon him treads
In getting out of bed and in again.

Without the damask curtains' grateful shade
Thro' which the cheerful sun might coyly peep,
Each in a narrow iron bedstead laid,
The gentlemen cadets are forced to sleep.

The loud reveillés of the echoing horn
Reverberating through each aching head
At six precisely, on the morrow's morn,
Shall rouse the victims from their lowly bed.

No cause have they excitement's ills to fear,
In drill and study roll their hours away;
While time speeds on, nought marking his career,
And months take pattern from a single day.

Let not calm reason ask for what intent,
Ideal aims, or fancy pictured gain
They pass their lives in hapless discontent
And two long years at Addiscombe remain.

The toils that made their once blithe tempers sour,
And all the study, all the time they gave
Yield them at length the enviable power
To seek in India an untimely grave.

Not theirs the fault, should future ages find
No record of them in the page of fame,
In one small sphere 'cribb'd, cabin'd, and confin'd'
They sighed for action and a deathless name.

77   *A legend of the rectory at Perivale, Middlesex*

Loud roared the wind at Perivale,
   The rain fell thick and fast,
The Rectory shook in that fierce gale,
   The trees bent to the blast.

*

'Sir Knighte! Sir Knighte,' the pastor said,
   'Go not to that dread room:
The fiend within will strike thee dead;
   Tempt not thy certain doom.'

'I fear no fiend,' the knight replied;
 'But soon I'll crop his ears.
Bring me a light, Sir Priest,' he cried;
 'And have for me no fears.'

'Boast not thy strength,' his reverence said,
 'For know, my son, this nighte
Thou need'st must goe unto thy bedde
 Without a taper's light.'

'Then quickly guide me up the stair,
 And give me the *Door*-key.
I'll make this demon quit his lair,
 And yield the room to me.'

The knight has reached the chamber door,
 And entered it so bold!
When from within a dreadful snore
 Made his heart's blood run cold!

His head he ran against a post
 (The bedpost of the bed),
Which made him think the demon ghost
 Had knocked him on the head.

'Ho! ho,' thought he, 'is this the way
 You treat your company?
Such deadly blows, I needs must say,
 Prove lack of courtesy!'

Then to the bed he groped his way,
 And felt for the bed-clothes,
When from that bed, to his dismay,
 A fiendish snort arose.

The knight cried boldly, 'Who are you?
 Pray, what would you be at?
Speak quickly, fiend, and tell me true,
 Or I'll deal thee a pat!'

A thought occurred to this brave knight—
 A shrewd idea, d'ye see?—
Both fiends and ghosts do all take fright
 At cock-crowing, they say.—

'Cock-a-doodle-doo-o-oo,'
  He crew; then cried, 'My wig!'
As from the bed with much ado
  Up jumpt the Parson's pig.

To the stair-head both pig and knight
  Ran, as if you'd shot 'em,
Over each other in their flight,
  Rolling from top to bottom!

A score of priests since then, we're told,
  The rectory have taken,
To dust has turned that knight so bold,
  The phantom pig to—bacon.

Unearthly sounds do still prevail,
  But from no ghosts—alas!
They come from the Great Western rail,
  When the express trains pass!

78 *Petitions for discharge by the gunner Robert Graham,*
    Woolwich, Kent, 1819

A Petition to the Honourable Board of Ordnance

Ye mun na think me sel'-sufficient,
Nor yet o' common sense deficient,
But, kenning ye are quite efficient
    Me to enlarge—
From durance vile, when thus petitioned,
    Me to discharge.

For years I've served his Majesty,
Who now could weel dispense wi' me,
Gif that ye only could agree
    Yourselves amang
To bless me wi' my liberty,
    And let me gang.

I've served my King in peace an' war,
Both free o' scaith an' free o' scar;
An' now wi'out me I'm awar'
    He weel could ring
O'er his domains, both near an' far,
    In peace a king.

I hae a sister an' a brither,
Beside an auld and widow'd mither,
Whilk, if 'twad please ye to send thither
    Your humble servant,
Our thanks ye'll hae them all togither
    In prayers maist fervent.

They're steept in pourtith to the lip,
Stern poverty it doth them grip;
Affliction's cup they ofttimes sip
    Unto the dregs;
'Tis for to help them han' an' hip
    Your servant begs.

I hae no siller, ye may see,
In lieu o' service for to gie,
Or had I na hae troubled ye
    At a' this time
Wi' this, tho' earnest, wish o' me
    In auld Scotch rhyme.

Sae gin an order ye would gie,
That I might straight discharged be
And sen' it straightway down to me,
    I'll thank ye a',
Ye Honourables honourably,
    Baith great and sma'.

Lang frien's hae I been wi' the muse
This kind then dinna ye refuse,
And I your favour won't abuse,
    But set off hame,
And thank ye lang as e'er ye choose;
    And my name's GRAHAM.

scaith] hurt   ring] reign   pourtith] poverty

The Second Petition

We're told to ask and we'll receive,
But how can I that text believe,
Sin' ye yoursels did me deceive—
    At least forgot
To keep the promise which ye gave
    When lost ye wrot'?

Ye said I should discharged be
At the first opportunity;
But, wae's my heart, I've lived to see
    That you've forgot it,
Although the clerk wrot' word to me,
    My name was notit.

A weary twa months now is past
Sin' I received you first and last;
There's many free who then were fast—
    Still I remain;
Some pity deign on me to cast,
    And loose my chain.

The very company I belang to
Ha' let off chaps baith stout and strang too;
For God's sake there can be no wrang to
    Mention my name.
Send me to that place I belang to,
    Alias hame.

Gin there a godlike gift was given
To us on earth from Him in Heaven,
'Tis that which hales the heart that's riven
    Wi' care and grief;
Just twa, three words to Woolwich driven
    Would send relief.

Then, for the Lord's sake, order ye
That I may soon discharged be;
And let it be peremptory,
    Or they'll na heed it.
Jus' tell them that I maun be free—
    That ye've decreed it!

O, to my cry, then, do ye list;
The like o' me will ne'er be missed;
And may ye a' live lang and blest,
    Wi' ne'er a care;
And aye get that for which ye wist:
    Sae ends my prayer.

79   *A prologue by Francis Newbery of Heathfield Park, Sussex, for
a theatrical performance by his children, at home, 1793*

(Peeping from behind the curtain)

So you're all met! (*coming forward*) and each has got his seat:
With rare keen appetite for this new treat.
I'm glad to see you. What a crowd I view!
So, Tom! Ah, cousin Martha! How do you?
I represent, you see, a footman here,
And now step on to get the tables clear:
And while they dish up, and the feast prepare,
I'll just present you with a bill of fare.
   In times of old, when neighbours met to cheer
With Christmas merriments the closing year,
The sports and pastimes then were rude and rough;
As Hunt the Slipper, Hoop, or Blindman's Buff:
But in these modern and more polished days,
Lo Christmas gambols yeald to real plays,
Actors and actresses we all are grown:—
And here's a Theatre—just come from Town!
Nay, wonder not! for though it may seem droll,
Playhouses now, as well as players, stroll;
And wander round, without committing trespass,
Just as they did of old, in cart of Thespis.
So Drury Lane (but why need I remark it?)
By fire impelled absconded to the Haymarket;
Hop—step—and jump—and by the same remark,
Now Drury Lane is here in Heathfield Park.
Our players too—a comic motley show—
Are all like those in London whom you know.
   First Brother John—a Cambridge maccaroni,

79 maccaroni] fop

49

Swaggers like Palmer—near as stout and bony,
With voice as loud.—If Palmer's rather bigger
Yet John is certainly the better figure.
 Next Bob, a famous fellow at a lunch—
Like Parsons droll, though not so much like Punch.
Parsons, and Quick, by squeaking out, before
They enter, set the galleries in a roar:—
 Robert more easy, natural, and quiet,
Will gain applause, though not with so much riot;
He'll lay no claptraps, practise no finesse:
But with true humour vindicate success.
 Then Brother Frank, who plays a servant's part,
(I wish he may have got it all by heart)
An idle rogue; though smart enough and clever,
To act like Lewis will be his endeavour.
 Next come the Ladies—Well, and what of them?
Of Sister Mary, and her friend Miss M?
The latter plays the Spanish Gouvernante,
An old Duenna, or Tartuffish Aunt;
But though in semblance she's the very part,
And her tongue gives what flows not from the heart;
And though with dowdy dress her figure marring,
In form and air she's Abingdon or Farren.
 Our sister Mary next, brimful of glee;
All life, and spirit, and song, and harmony—
A little tit—scarce higher than your hand—
The true facsimile of Mrs. Bland:—
Nay more (the parallel is no absurd one)
She'll sing Storace, and she'll act the Jordan.
Our Sister Charlotte too (nice girl I 'fegs),
Comes in boy's clothes, and we shall see her legs!
Her legs? And what can tempt them to expose
Their slender ankles, and their pretty toes?
Not the legs merely—Oh! the little witches!
They love to show how well they wear the breeches.
 Then last and least, poor little I appear;
With two huge fellow servants in my rear.
For them I beg your favour to invoke:
Unpractised in these arts, plain country folk,
Who kindly thus contributing their labours,
Perform the real parts of friends and neighbours.

Tartuffish] hypocritically pious, like Tartuffe in Molière's *Tartuffe*
I 'fegs] in faith

But for myself, though vain may be the task, yet
Your minikin performer poor Pinbasket
(Should you allow his pigmy talents scope)
Is anxious to indulge one wish, one hope—
(A Poet's licence—'tis a flight Pindaric)
That little Charles may prove—a little Garrick!
 Thus in rude verse, and doggerel rhime I've shewn ye
Our mimic band—our Dramatis Personæ;
And now they're ready to exert each power
To entertain you with The Midnight Hour;
So I must in, and of my part observant
Will be my Masters', and your—humble servant.

80 *A musical toast, Sussex*

> There was a old woman drawn up in a basket,
> Three or four times as high as the moon,
> And where she was going I never did ask it,
> But in her hand she carried a broom.
> A broom! a broom! a broom! a broom!
> That grows on yonder hill,
> And blows with a yellow blossom,
> Just like a lemon peel.
> Just like a lemon peel, my boys,
> To mix with our English beer,
> And you shall drink it all up,
> While we do say Goliere.
> Goliere! Goliere! Goliere! Goliere!
> While we do say Goliere!
> And you, etc.

81 *'The Farmer's Old Wife'; a Sussex whistling song*

> There was an old farmer in Sussex did dwell,
> (*Chorus of whistlers*)
> There was an old farmer in Sussex did dwell,
> And he had a bad wife, as many knew well.
> (*Chorus of whistlers*)
> The Satan came to the old man at the plough,—
> 'One of your family I must have now.
>
> 'It is not your eldest son that I crave,
> But it is your old wife, and she I will have.'

'O, welcome! good Satan, with all my heart,
I hope you and she will never more part.'

Now Satan has got the old wife on his back,
And he lugged her along, like a pedlar's pack.

He trudged away till they came to his hall-gate,
Says he, 'Here! take in an old Sussex chap's mate!'

O! then she did kick the young imps about,—
Says one to the other, 'Let's try turn her out.'

She spied thirteen imps all dancing in chains,
She up with her pattens, and beat out their brains.

She knocked the old Satan against the wall,—
'Let's try turn her out, or she'll murder us all!'

Now he's bundled her up on his back amain,
And to her old husband he took her again.

'I have been a tormenter the whole of my life,
But I ne'er was tormented till I met with your wife.'

82 *A 'Harvest Home' verse sung in parts of Surrey*

> We have plough'd,
> We have sow'd,
> We have reap'd,
> We have mow'd,
> Ne'er a load
> Overthrow'd—
> Harvest Home!

83 *An 'apple-howling' verse for New Year's Eve; Sussex*

> Stand fast root, bear well top,
> Pray God send us a good howling crop;
> Every twig, apples big;
> Every bough, apples enou;
> Hats full, caps full,
> Full quarter sacks full.

pattens] clogs, or overshoes with an iron base
83 howling] first-rate

84 *Sheep-shearing songs, Sussex*

(i) Come, all my jolly boys, and we'll together go
Abroad with our masters, to shear the lamb and ewe;
All in the merry month of June, of all times in the year,
It always comes in season the ewes and lambs to shear;
And there we must work hard, boys, until our backs do ache,
And our master he will bring us beer whenever we do lack.
Our master he comes round to see our work is doing well,
And he cries, 'Shear them close, men, for there is but little wool.'
'O yes, good master,' we reply, 'we'll do well as we can,'
When our Captain calls, 'Shear close, boys!' to each and every man.
And at some places still we have this story all day long,
'Close them, boys, and shear them well!' and this is all their song.
And then our noble Captain doth unto our master say,
'Come, let us have one bucket of your good ale, I pray.'
He turns unto our Captain and makes him this reply:
'You shall have the best of beer, I promise, presently.'
Then out with the bucket pretty Betsy she doth come,
And master says, 'Maid, mind and see that every man has some.'
This is some of our pastime while we the sheep do shear,
And though we are such merry boys, we work hard, I declare;
And when 'tis night, and we are done, our master is more free,
And stores us well with good strong beer and pipes and tobaccee.
So we do sit and drink, we smoke and sing and roar,
Till we become more merry far than e'er we were before.
When all our work is done, and all our sheep are shorn,
Then home to our Captain, to drink the ale that's strong.
'Tis a barrel, then, of hum cap, which we call the black ram;
And we do sit and swagger, and swear that we are men;
But yet before 'tis night, I'll stand you half a crown,
That if you ha'n't a special care the ram will knock you down.

(ii) Here the rose-buds in June, and the violets are blowing;
The small birds they warble from every green bough;
   Here's the pink and the lily,
   And the daffydowndilly,
To adore and perfume the sweet meadows in June.
'Tis all before the plough the fat oxen go slow;
But the lads and the lasses to the sheep-shearing go.
Our shepherds rejoice in their fine heavy fleece,
And frisky young lambs, with their flocks do increase;
   Each lad takes his lass,
   All on the green grass,

Where the pink and the lily,
And the daffydowndilly, &c.
Here stands our brown jug, and 'tis fill'd with good ale,
Our table, our table shall increase and not fail;
We'll joke and we'll sing,
And dance in a ring;
Where the pink and the lily,
And the daffydowndilly, &c.
When the sheep-shearing's over, and harvest draws nigh,
We'll prepare for the fields, our strength for to try;
We'll reap and we'll mow,
We'll plough and we'll sow;
Oh! the pink and the lily,
And the daffydowndilly, &c.

85 *Two versions of a Brighton fishermen's song at net-casting (the
nets floated between barrels)*

(i)　　　　Watch, barrel, watch! Mackerel for to catch
White may they be, like blossom on a tree.
God send thousands, one, two, and three.
Some by their heads, some by their tails,
God sends thousands, and never fails.

(ii)　　　Watch, barrel, watch! Mackerel for to catch
Watch, barrel, watch,
Mackerel for to catch.
What may they be?
Like blossoms on the tree.
Some by their noses,
Some by their fin,
God send twenty 'last',
And a fair wind in!
Please God we have a good haul!

86 *Verses on the bathing at Brighton, Sussex*

There's plenty of dippers and jokers,
And salt-water rigs for your fun;
The King of them all is 'Old Smoaker,'
The Queen of them 'Old Martha Gunn.'

85 last] loads

54

The ladies walk out in the morn,
   To taste of the salt-water breeze;
They ask if the water is warm,
   Says Martha, 'Yes, Ma'am, if you please.'

Then away to the machines they run,
   'Tis surprising how soon they get stript;
I oft wish myself Martha Gunn,
   Just to see the young ladies get dipt.

87   *'Winter in Brighton'; by Mortimer Collins, 1868*

Will there be snowfall on lofty Soracte
   After a summer so tranquil and torrid?
Whoso detests the east wind, as a fact he
      Thinks 'twill be horrid.
But there are zephyrs more mild by the ocean,
   Every keen touch of the snowdrifts to lighten:
If to be cosy and snug you've a notion
      Winter in Brighton!

Politics nobody cares about. Spurn a
   Topic whereby all our happiness suffers.
Dolts in the back streets of Brighton return a
      Couple of duffers.
Fawcett and White in the Westminster Hades
   Strive the reporters' misfortunes to heighten.
What does it matter? Delicious young ladies
      Winter in Brighton!

Good is the turtle for luncheon at Mutton's,
   Good is the hock that they give you at Bacon's,
Mainwaring's fruit in the bosom of gluttons
      Yearning awakens;
Buckstone comes hither, delighting the million,
   'Mong the theatrical minnows a Triton;
Dickens and Lemon pervade the Pavilion:—
      Winter in Brighton!

If you've a thousand a year, or a minute—
   If you're a D'Orsay, whom every one follows—
If you've a head (it don't matter what's in it)
      Fair as Apollo's—

If you approve of flirtations, good dinners,
   Seascapes divine which the merry winds whiten,
Nice little saints and still nicer young sinners—
   Winter in Brighton!

88   *A poem by G. F. Richardson, a self-educated prodigy in*
languages, born in Brighton c.1820

The Nautilus and the Ammonite

The Nautilus and the Ammonite
   Were launch'd in storm and strife,
Each sent to float, in its tiny boat,
   On the wide wild sea of life.

And each could swim on the Ocean's brim,
   And anon its sails could furl,
And sink to sleep, in the great sea-deep,
   In a palace all of pearl.

And their's was bliss more fair than this
   That we feel in our colder clime,
For they were rife in tropic life,
   In a brighter, happier clime.

They swam mid isles whose summer smiles
   No wintry winds annoy,
Whose groves were palm, whose air was balm,
   Where life was only joy.

They roamed all day, through creek and bay,
   And traversed the ocean deep,
And at night they sank, on a coral bank,
   In its fairy bowers to sleep.

And the monsters vast, of ages past,
   They beheld in their ocean caves,
And saw them ride, in their power and pride,
   And sink in their billowy graves.

Thus hand in hand, from strand to strand,
   They sailed in mirth and glee,
Those fancy shells, with their crystal cells,
   Twin creatures of the sea.

But they came at last to a sea long past,
    And, as they reached its shore,
The Almighty's breath spake out in death,
    And the Ammonite lived no more.

And the Nautilus now, in its shelly prow,
    As o'er the deep it strays,
Still seems to seek, in bay and creek,
    Its companion of former days.

And thus do we, on life's stormy sea,
    As we roam from shore to shore,
While tempest-toss'd, seek the loved—the lost,
    But to find them on earth no more!

89   *Inscription found hanging on a tree in Lover's Walk,
Brighton, where John Holloway buried his wife after
murdering her, 1831*

        Here lay poor Celia,
        Curses be on Holloway,
        He'll wish himself away
        On the great judgement day.

90   *A Sussex cuckoo-rhyme*

        In April, come he will,
        In May, he sings all day,
        In June, he changes his tune,
        In July, he prepares to fly,
        In August, go he must,
        If he stays until September,
        'Tis as much as the oldest man can remember.

91   *An inscription on the pendulum of the tower clock,
St Lawrence's Church, Bidborough, Kent*

When as a child I laughed and wept, ...Time crept.
When as a youth I dreamed and talked, ... Time walked.
When I became a full grown man .... Time ran.

And later as I older grew . . . . Time flew.
Soon I shall find when travelling on . . . . Time gone.
Will Christ have saved my soul by then? . . . . Amen.

92   *A Kent thunderstorm rhyme*

> If it sinks from the north,
> It will double its wrath.
> If it sinks from the south,
> It will open its mouth.
> If it sinks from the west,
> It is never at rest.
> If it sinks from the east,
> It will leave us in peace.

93   *A thunderstorm verse from Sussex*

> Beware of the oak; it draws the stroke.
> Avoid the ash; it courts the flash;
> Creep under a thorn; it can save you from harm.

94   *A children's game song, Middlesex*

> Tripping up the green grass,
>   Dusty, dusty, day,
> Come all ye pretty fair maids,
>   Come and with me play.
>
> You shall have a duck, my dear,
>   And you shall have a swan,
> And you shall have a nice young man
>   A waiting for to come.
>
> Suppose he were to die
>   And leave his wife a widow,
> Come all ye pretty fair maids,
>   Come clap your hands together!
>
>   Will you come?
>   No!

58

Naughty man, he won't come out,
   He won't come out, he won't come out,
Naughty man, he won't come out,
   To help us in our dancing.

      Will you come?
      Yes!

Now we've got our bonny lad,
   Our bonny lad, our bonny lad,
Now we've got our bonny lad,
   To help us in our dancing.

95   *A children's game song from Wrotham, Kent*

       There stands a lady on a mountain,
       Who she is I do not know;
       All she wants is gold and silver,
       All she wants is a nice young man.

       Now she's married I wish her joy,
       First a girl and then a boy;
       Seven years after son and daughter,
       Pray young couple kiss together.

       Kiss her once, kiss her twice,
       Kiss her three times three.

96   *Charm (or prayer) found in the linen purse of the murderer,*
     Jackson, died in Chichester Gaol, 1749

       Ye three holy Kings
       Gaspar, Melchoir, Balthasar,
       Pray for us, now, and the hour of death.

III

SOUTH AND SOUTH-WEST ENGLAND

97 *An inscription on the Palm House doors, Bicton House, East Budleigh, Devon, c.1850*

> The Gardener at a hole looks out
> And holes are plenty hereabout
> A pair of pistols by his lug
> One load with ball the other slug
> A blunderbus of cannon shape
> Just ready to discharge with grape
> Let midnight thief or robber stand
> And pause ere he puts out his hand
> While those who come in open day
> May look but carry nought away.

98 *St Columb, Cornwall; inscription on a silver-coated ball used in an annual hurling match between two villages*

> St Columb Major and Minor
>   Do your best;
> In one of your parishes
>   I must rest.

99 *On a signboard at Kingstag, Dorset, with a picture of a white deer*

> When Julius Caesar landed here
> I was then a little deer.
> When Julius Caesar reigned king
> Round my neck he put this ring.
> Whoever shall me overtake
> Save my life for Caesar's sake.

100 *On a trencher sent by Ben Jonson to the Attorney-General,*
William Noye of Mawgan in Pyder, Cornwall, when the
latter was entertaining King Charles I to dinner; with an
addition inscribed on the trencher when it was returned with
'a good dish of venison'

>   When the world was drowned
>   No deer was found,
>   Because there was noe park;
>   And here I sitt
>   Without a bitt,
>   'Cause Noyah hath all in his Ark.

*

>   When the world was drowned
>   There deer was found
>   Although there was noe park;
>   I send thee a bitt
>   To quicken thy witt
>   Which comes from Noye's Arke.

101 *On a board by a horse-trough, on the road from Salisbury to*
Marlborough

>   A man of kindness to his steed is kind,
>   A brutal action shows a brutal mind.
>   Remember He who made thee, made the brute,
>   He can't complain, but God's all-seeing Eye
>   Beholds thy cruelty and hears his cry.
>   He was designed thy servant, not thy drudge,
>   Remember his creator is thy Judge.

102 *On a notice-board in West Stafford, Dorset*

>   I trust no wise man will condemn
>   A cup of Genuine now and then.
>   When you are faint, your spirits low,
>   Your string relaxed, 'twill bend your bow
>   Brace your drumhead, and make you tight,
>   Wind up your watch, and set you right.

But then again, the too much use
Of all strong liquors is abuse.
'Tis liquid makes the solid loose,
The texture and whole frame destroys.
But health lies in the equipoise.

103   *Verses written on the Oakley Arms, Maidenhead, near Bray
(the reference is to the famous 'Vicar of Bray')*

'Friend Isaac, 'tis strange you that live so near Bray
  Should not set up the sign of the Vicar.
Though it may be an odd one, you cannot but say
  It must needs be a sign of good liquor.'

Answer:

'Indeed, master Poet, your reason's but poor,
  For the Vicar would think it a sin
To stay, like a booby, and lounge at the door,—
  'Twere a sign 'twas bad liquor within.'

104   *Inscription on a picture of 'The Trusty Servant', once in the
entrance to the kitchens, Winchester College*

A Trusty Servant's Portrait would you see,
This emblematic figure well survey.
  The porker's snout, not nice in diet shows;
  The padlock shut, no secrets he'll disclose.
Patient, the ass his master's rage will bear;
Swiftness in errand the stagg's feet declare;
  Loaden, his left hand apt to labour saith;
  The vest, his neatness, open hand, his faith;
Girt with his sword, his shield upon his arm,
Himself & master, he'll protect from harm.

105   *On a window in the Pelican Inn, Newbury; attributed to the
actor James Quin (1693–1766)*

The famous inn at Speenhamland
  That stands below the hill,
May well be called the Pelican
  From its enormous bill.

106   *On a dog's collar, Saltash Fair, Cornwall (nineteenth century)*

> Fools have been peeping and wanting to see!
> I am John Jolliffe's dog! What's that to thee?
> John Jolliffe's my master, Polperro my home,
> So mind your own business and leave me alone.

107   *Inscription on the Basset Cup, St Ives, Cornwall, 1640*

> Iff any discord 'twixt my friends arise
> Wth in the Burrough of Beloved St Ives
> Itt is desyred that this my Cupp of Love
> To everie one a Peace maker may Prove
> Then am I Blest to have given a Legacie
> So like my hartt unto Posteritie.

108   *Inscriptions on two silver cups, referring to the silver mine worked by Sir Bevis Bulmer (Combe Martin, Devon; sixteenth century)*

(i)

> When water workes in Broaken Wharfe
>   At first erected were,
> And Bevis Bulmer, with his art,
>   The waters 'gan to reare,
> Disperced I in earth did lye,
>   Since all beginnings olde
> In place called Combe, where Martin long
>   Had hid me in his molde.
> I dydd no service in the earth,
>   And no manne sate me free,
> Till Bulmer by his skill and charge
>   Did frame mee this to be.

(ii)

> In Martyn's Coombe long lay I hydd,
> Obscured, deprest, with grossest soyle,
> Debasèd much with mixèd lead
> Till Bulmer came, whose skill and toyle,
> Refinèd me so pure and cleare,
> As rycher no where els is seene.

And adding yet a further grace,
    By fashion he did enable
Me worthy for to take a place
    To serve at any Prince's table.
Coombe Martin gave the use alone,
Bulmer the fining and fashion.

109   *On a well, chapel of St Catharine, Melton Abbey,*
      Abbotsbury, Dorset

A husband, Saint Catharine   .
A handsome one, Saint Catharine
A rich one, Saint Catharine   .
A nice one, Saint Catharine   .
And soon, Saint Catharine   .

110   *A Berkshire rhyme*

'Whistle, daughter, whistle, and you shall have a sheep;'
'Mother, I cannot whistle, neither can I sleep.'
'Whistle, daughter, whistle, and you shall have a cow;'
'Mother, I cannot whistle, neither know I how.'
'Whistle, daughter, whistle, and you shall have a man,'
'Mother, I cannot whistle, but I'll do the best I can.'

111   *An old Cornish song; the refrain was 'intended to test the*
      singer's sobriety'

As I trudged on at ten at night
    My way to fair York city,
I saw before a lantern light
    Borne by a damsel pretty.
I her accos't, 'My way I've lost,
    Your lantern let me carry!
Then through the land, both hand in hand,
    We'll travel. Prithee tarry.'
        20, 18, 16, 14, 12, 10, 8, 6, 4, 2,
        19, 17, 15, 13, 11, 9, 7, 5, 3, 1.

She tripp'd along, so nimble she,
  The lantern still a-swinging,
And 'Follow, follow, follow me!'
  Continually was singing.
'Thy footsteps stay!' She answered, 'Nay!'
  'Your name? You take my fancy.'
She laughing said, nor turn'd her head,
  'I'm only Northern Nancy.'
                    20, 18, 16, etc.

She sped along, I in the lurch,
  A lost and panting stranger,
Till, lo! I found me at the Church,
  She'd led me out of danger.
'Ring up the clerk,' she said; 'yet hark!
  Methinks here comes the pass'n;
He'll make us one, then thou art done;
  He'll thee securely fasten.'
                    20, 18, 16, etc.

'Man is a lost and vagrant clown
  That should at once be pounded,'
She said, and laid the matter down
  With arguments well grounded.
For years a score, and even more,
  I've lain in wedlock's fetter,
Faith! she was right; here, tied up tight,
  I could not have fared better.
                    20, 18, 16, etc.

112   *Inscribed on a well, Derry Hill, near Chippenham, Wiltshire*

Here quench your thirst, and mark in me
An emblem of true charity,
Who while my bounty I bestow
Am neither seen nor heard to flow;
Repaid by fresh supplies from Heaven
For every cup of water given.

113 *William Cowper (1731–1800); an inscription for a stone*
 'erected at the sowing of a grove of oaks at Chillington
 [Somerset], the seat of T. Gifford, Esq., 1790'

> Other stones the æra tell,
> When some feeble mortal fell:
> I stand here to date the birth
> Of these hardy sons of earth.
>   Which shall longest brave the sky,
> Storm and frost? these oaks or I?
> Pass an age or two away,
> I must moulder and decay,
> But the years that crumble me
> Shall invigorate the tree,
> Spread the branch, dilate its size,
> Lift its summit to the skies.
>   Cherish honour, virtue, truth!
> So shalt thou prolong thy youth;
> Wanting these, however fast
> Man be fixt, and form'd to last,
> He is lifeless even now,
> Stone at heart, and cannot grow.

114 *Verses written in the sand at Weston-super-Mare, by John*
 Langhorne (1735–79) with his walking-stick, and Hannah
 More (1745–1833) with her riding-crop

> Along this shore
> Walked Hannah More;
>   Waves, let this record last.
> Sooner shall ye,
> Proud earth and sea,
>   Than what she writes, be past.

*

> Some firmer basis, polished Langhorne, choose
> On which to write the dictates of thy Muse;
> Her strains in solid characters rehearse,
> And be thy tablets lasting as thy verse.

115 *A tablet at the Bishop of Chester's retreat at Banwell Cave,
in the Mendip Hills, Somerset*

Here let time's creeping winter shed
His hoary snow around my head,
And while I feel by fast degrees
My sluggish blood wax chill and freeze
Let thought unveil to my fixed eye
The scenes of deep eternity.
Till life dissolving at the view,
I wake, and find the vision true.

116 *Inscription on a stone over the porch door of the vicarage at
Morwenstow, Cornwall; by the vicar, R. S. Hawker
('Hawker of Morwenstow'), 1803–75*

A House, a Glebe a Pound a Day;
A Pleasant Place to Watch and Pray.
Be True to Church—Be Kind to Poor,
O Minister! for Evermore.

117 *Verses by Jewell Doidge written in the parish register at
Saltash, Cornwall, 1753*

When I am full and can't hold more
Pray cast me not quite out of door,
But keep me in the parish chest,
For that's the place I ought to rest.

Although I can't be worked no more,
I am so much use as I was before,
If any strife should chance to spring,
Come to me, I'll decide the thing.

I'll shew you what in me was done
From the first year I was begun,
Which may be of great service too,
To your grand children, after you.

118 *In the parish register, Crediton, Devon, 1565*

> John Warren and Jone Cooke
> But late they undertooke
> Streat corners to sarch
> Now baptised is Margery
> The fruit of hys adultery
> The 20th Daye of March.

119 *Inscription in the belfry of Gulval church, Cornwall*

> Good sirs! our meaning is not small
> That, God to praise, assemblies call;
> And warn the sluggard, when at home,
> That he may with devotion come
> Unto the Church and joyn in prayer;
> Of Absolution take his share.
> Who hears the bells, appears betime,
> And in his seat against we chime.
> Therefore I'd have you not to vapour
> Nor blame ye lads that use ye clapper
> By which are scared the fiends of Hell
> And all by virtue of a Bell.

120 *Inscription on the tenor bell at Lanivet, Cornwall*

> I to the Church the living call,
> And to the Grave do summon all.

121 *Inscriptions on the eight bells at St Austell, Cornwall*

> 1. By music minds an equal temper know
> 2. Nor swell too high nor sink too low
> 3. Music the fiercest grief can charm
> 4. And fate's severest rage disarm
> 5. Music can soften pain to ease
> 6. And make despair and madness please
> 7. Our joys below it can improve
> 8. And antedate the bliss above.

122   *Inscriptions on the peal of eight bells at Alresford,*
       Hampshire, 1811

1. In sweetest sound let each its note reveal
    Mine shall be first to lead the dulcet peal

2. The public raised us with a liberal hand
    We came with harmony to cheer the land

3. May he who England's matchless sceptre sways
    Her sacred honour guard her glory raise

4. May Britons still their ancient freedom boast
    And glittering commerce bless their happy coast

5. Does battle rage, do sanguine foes contend
    We hail the victor if he's Briton's friend

6. When female virtue weds with manly worth
    We catch the rapture and we spread it forth

7. —

8. May all whom I shall summon to the grave
    The blessing of a well spent life receive

123   *Inscriptions on the six bells at Avington, Hampshire, 1771*

1. I mean to make it understood that tho' I'm little yet I'm good.
2. If you have a judicious ear you'll own my voice is sweet and clear.
3. Such woundrous powr to musicks given, it elevates the soul to
    heaven.
4. Ye people all who hear me ring be faithfull to your God and King.
5. While thus we join in chearfull sound may love and loyalty abound.
6. Ye ringers all that prize your health and happiness
    Be sober merry wise and you'll the same possess.

124   *Rules once painted on a board in the ringers' loft,*
       Beaminster, Dorset, 1717

Let awful silence thrice proclaimed bee
Then praises given to ye Trinity
With love and honner pay unto ye King
Thus with a blessing rise ye cheerful ring

*

Hark how the chirping trible sings it clear
And capering Tom comes rolling in ye rear
Hold up on end, or stay! come let us see
What laws are best to keep sobriety
So all consent and to this Law agree;
Who swears or curse, or in an angry mood
Quarils or striks altho' he draws no blood
Who wears his Hat, or spurs, or turns a Bell
Or by unskilful handling mars a peal
Let him pay sixpence for each single crime
'Twill make him causous 'gainst another time
But if the Secston's fault an hindrance bee
We crave from him a double penalty
Who dous our parson disrespect
Our Wardens' orders any time neclegct
Let him be held in foul disgrace
And ever after banished this place
Now round let's go with pleasure to ye ear
And pierce with cheerful sound ye yielding air
And when ye bells is cease, then let us sing
God save ye Church, God Bless ye King.

125   *Bell verses by Thomas Hardy (1840–1928)*

Inscriptions for a Peal of Eight Bells

AFTER A RESTORATION

   I. Thomas Tremble new-made me
     Eighteen hundred and fifty-three:
     Why he did I fail to see.

   II. I was well-toned by William Brine,
     Seventeen hundred and twenty-nine;
     Now, re-cast, I weakly whine!

   III. Fifteen hundred used to be
     My date, but since they melted me
     'Tis only eighteen fifty-three.

   IV. Henry Hopkins got me made,
     And I summon folk as bade;
     Not to much purpose, I'm afraid!

124 causous] cautious

73

V. I likewise; for I bang and bid
In commoner metal than I did,
Some of me being stolen and hid.

VI. I, too, since in a mould they flung me,
Drained my silver, and rehung me,
So that in tin-like tones I tongue me.

VII. In nineteen hundred, so 'tis said,
They cut my canon off my head,
And made me look scalped, scraped, and dead.

VIII. I'm the peal's tenor still, but rue it!
Once it took two to swing me through it:
Now I'm rehung, one dolt can do it.

126   *Verses when the ringers at Bray, near Maidenhead, went on
strike in 1876, and were replaced by a bell-ringing machine*

A 'Striking' Blunder

Too keen after pay,
The Ringers of Bray
Forsook their post of action;
But *Roger* the wise,
To their surprise,
Outwitted the Village faction.

With sinues and thought
So deftly he wrought,
And Fortune so befriended,
It came to pass
That a small wind-*lass*
Does well-nigh what those *men* did.

What *they* could do,
Machinery too
Achieves, to their scant liking;
And since they struck
They find (worse luck)
How *hammers* can be striking.

And now they fret
In a vain regret
That prudence was not stronger.
While memory stands
They may wring their hands,
But they'll ring *those bells* no longer!

127 *A will for Mr Brine's mare, written in the Quarter Sessions*
Rolls, Wiltshire, 1614

Brine had a mare whosoever knew hir,
Som times he rod hir and somtimes he drove her,
She will cary hir Mr through haile winde and raine
So merily to the market, so merily backe againe.

When Brine he perceived yt hir good dayes ware dun,
He turned up hir heeles & pulld of her shun,
Then Brine went trudging & trudging downe the hill
And with his pen and inck horne did write his mares will.

First he bequethed hir eies—that ware so clere and gray
Even to hir Mr Brine to lead him on the way
Next I bequeth my teeth that stand all in a rew
To little John Brunker because he hath so few.

I bequeth my skin, the skin all of my backe
Even to John Chapman to make a woing jack
I bequeth the skin, the skin all of my leggs
To Thomas Tauman to make him bowlting baggs.

I bequeth the tayle that is so faire and rownde
Even to Mary Moore to make a wedding gownd
I bequeth the liver, the liver and the longs
Unto Wm Brunker to maintaine his flatring tounge.

I bequeth the maw, the maw for and the gutts
Unto Mr Shipman to make strings for his bookes
I bequeth the ears that are so faire and right
Unto John Fenill to make feathers for his flight.

127 shun] shoon, shoes   bowlting] sifting

I bequeth the hoofs, the hoofs so faire and rownd
Unto John Self and then to Ma Browne
I bequeth the head for and the robernowke
Unto good wife Brine to make a skimming bowk.

I bequeth the chapps, the chapps that went soe fast
Unto John Spender to eate his neighbors grasse
I bequeth the—gutt, the gutt that is soe fat
Unto old John Branker to grease his squeaking throat.

And I bequeth all other gutts that are soe fat and longe
Even to John Hulber for making of the song.

128   *An epitaph at Speen, (?) Berkshire*

> Here sleeps within this silent grave
> A loyal soldier, just and brave,
> After a short and sudden shock,
> Content he did his life give up.
> Till the last trumpet's awful sound
> He is here in settled quarters bound.

129   *Epitaph for Mary, daughter of Sir Peter Courtney, d. 1655;*
Fowey, Cornwall

> Neer this a rare jewell's set,
> Clos'd uppe in a cabinet.
> Let no sacrilegious hand
> Breake through:—'tis ye Strickt command
> Of the Jeweller: who hath Sayd
> (And 'tis fit he be obey'd)
> I'll require it Safe and Sound
> Both above and under Ground.

130   *An epitaph at Bideford, Devon*

> Here lies the body of Mary Sexton,
> Who pleased many a man, but never vex'd one,
> Not like the woman who lies under the next stone.

127 bowk] pail

131   *On a sampler 'in affectionate remembrance of Charles S....., d. 1881'; Foxham, Wiltshire*

Now no more fatigued no more distressed
No sin no sorrow reach the place
No groans to mingle with the songs
Which warble from immortal tongues
No rude alarms of raging foes
Nor cares to break the long repose
No midnight shaded nor clouded sun
But sacred high eternal noon
What a wonder here appears
He has lost his doubts and fears
Now he sings of sovereign grace
Christ is made his holiness.

132   *Epitaph for Isabell Chiverton, d. 1631; Quethiock, Cornwall*

My birth was in the moneth of May,
And in that month my nuptiall day;
In May a mayde, a wife, a mother,
And now in May nor one nor other.
So flowers floarish, soe they fade;
So things to be undone are made.

My stake heere withers yet there bee
Some lovely branches sproute from me;
On w'ch bestow thine Aprill rayne;
So they the livelier may remayne.
But heere forbeare, for why? 'tis sayd,
Teares fit the living, not the dead.

133   *On two daughters, and a son dying at birth, of Dr Roger Ashton; Rame church, Cornwall, c. 1660*

Here Reader see,
poore Infants three,
Lye like greene fruit pluckt from the Tree;
yet they are blest,
and are att rest,

Though Implum'd birds, forct from their nest.
    one was A Son,
    his Race soone Run,
Hee Liv'd not once to see the Sun.
    I murmur not,
    they were begot,
To the Grave, mankind's Common lot.
    It glads my heart
    their better part
Is now with God, never to part.

134   *On the tomb of the Cole family, Lillington, Dorset*

Reader you have within this grave
    A Cole rak'd up in dust,
His courteous fate saw it was late
    And that to bed he must.
Then do not doubt the Cole's not out
    Tho' it in ashes lies,
The little spark, now in the dark,
    Will like the Phoenix rise.

135   *On a memorial to Mary Ann Ash, at Brockenhurst,*
Hampshire; no date

The trees whose name in life I bore
Now gather round my grave:
They whisper as in days of yore,
Their meaning now I have.
'Tis this I ween they sadly say,
To us so short a span is given,
Then by decay to pass away,
But thou art now God's Ash in heaven.

136   *For Susanna Tesdale; a brass of 1656, later seen in*
Everleigh church, Wiltshire

Susanna signifieth a lillie or a rose

The lillie of vallies by his spirit,
His pure spirit made me a lillie whit;

The rose of Sharon by his bloods merit
My soule advanced to a roses hight,
Susanna a lillie and a rose, though pale,
Here like a whit lillie she fading lyes,
By virtue of the roote of David shall
With orient colours, like a red rose rise.

137   *An inscription in Osmington church, Dorset*

Man's Life

Man is a Glas: Life is
A water that's weakly
walled about: sinne bring
es death: death breakes
the Glas: so runnes
the water out
finis.

138   *Verses under pictures at Pengerswick Castle, Cornwall*

(i)   Perseverance

What thing is harder than the rock?
    What softer is than water cleere?
Yet wyll the same, with often droppe,
    The hard rock perce, as doth a spere
Even so, nothing so hard to attayne,
    But may be hadd with labour and payne.

(ii)   *The one nedith the other ys helpe*

The lame wyche lacketh for to goe
    Is borne upon the blinde ys back;
So mutually betwien them twoo,
    The one supplieth the other's lack:
The blinde to laime doth lend his might,
    The layme to blynde doth yeld his sight.

139 *On the tomb of George King Hipango, a Maori chieftain,*
    d. 1871 aged 19, and buried in Letcombe Regis church,
    Berkshire

> Beneath yon ancient yew tree's shade
> A young New Zealand chief is laid
> From friends and kindred far away
> The Saviour was his strength and stay
> Revealed to him His precious love
> And took him to the realms above.

140 *For Richard Downe, d. 1710; Exbourne, Devon*

> In speechless
> Silence my youthful
> Daye soon sped I
> Left my cradle and
> Come here to bed.

141 *Sampler poems*

(i)   These lines I here present unto the Sight
        Of you, my Friends, to shew how I can work
        My M^{rs} unto me hath shewn her skill
        And here's the Product of my Hand and Needle

        The Needle, an Instrument tho' small
        Is of great Use and benefit to all
        Trust rather to your Fingers ends
        Then to the Promises of Friends.

        Hannah Hockey End this Sampler in The
        13 year of her Age in the Year of our Lord
        1798 Work'd at Mrs Champion's School Shapwick.

141 M^{rs}] mistress

(ii)   Humility

> The bird which soars on highest wing
> Builds on the ground her lowly nest;
> And she that doth most sweetly sing
> Sings in the shade when all things rest.
> In lark and nightingale we see
> What honour hath Humility.

1851.

142 *Robert Herrick (1591–1674); epitaph for Sir Edward Giles
and his wife; Dean Prior church, Devon*

> No trust to Metals nor to Marbles, when
> These have their Fate, and wear away as Men;
> Times, Titles, Trophies, may be lost and Spent;
> But Vertue Rears the eternal Monument.
> What more than these can Tombs or Tomb-stones Say
> But here's the Sun-set of a Tedious day:
> These Two asleep are: I'll but be Vndrest
> And so to Bed: Pray wish us all Good Rest.

143 *Robert Herrick; 'spells' and charms against evil spirits, and
to protect an infant from harm*

> Bring the holy crust of Bread,
> Lay it underneath the head;
> 'Tis a certain Charm to keep
> Hags away, while children sleep.

*

> In the morning when ye rise,
> Wash your hands, and cleanse your eyes.
> Next be sure ye have a care
> To disperse the water farre.
> For as farre as that doth light,
> So farre keeps the evill sprite.

*

143 hags] witch-women

If ye feare to be affrighted
When ye are (by chance) benighted,
In your Pocket for a trust
Carrie nothing but a Crust:
For that holy piece of Bread
Charmes the danger, and the dread.

*

Let the superstitious wife
Neer the childs heart lay a knife:
Point be up and Haft be downe;
(While she gossips in the town)
This 'mongst other mystick charms,
Keeps the sleeping child from harms.

*

Holy Water come and bring;
Cast in Salt, for seasoning:
Set the Brush for sprinkling:
Sacred Spittle bring ye hither;
Meale and it now mix together;
And a little Oyle to either:
Give the Tapers here their light,
Ring the *Saints-Bell*, to affright
Far from hence the evill Sp'rite.

144 *Four prayer-charms*

(i) *to stop bleeding*

Jesus was born in Bethlehem,
Baptised in river Jordan, when
The water was wild in the wood,
The person was just and good,
God spake, and the water stood
And so shall now thy blood—
In the name of the Father, Son, etc.

(ii) and (iii) *for burns or scalds*

Three angels came from the north, east, and west,
One brought fire, another brought ice,

And the third brought the Holy Ghost,
So out fire and in frost,
  In the name, etc.

*

There were three angels came from the East and West,
One brought fire and the other brought frost,
And the third it was the Holy Ghost.
Out fire, in frost, in the Name of the Father, and of the Son, and of
  the Holy Ghost.

(iv) *from Saltash, for burns*

There were two giants came from the East,
One wrought fire and the other wrought frost;
Out fire and in frost;
In the name of Father, Son, and Holy Ghost.

145   *By the rector of Marnhull, Dorset, for his clerk John*
       Warren, d. 1752 aged 94

        Here under this stone
        Lie Ruth and old John,
        Who smoked all his life
        And so did his wife:
        And now there's no doubt
        But their pipes are both out.
        Be it said without joke
        That life is but smoke;
        Though you live to four score,
        'Tis a whiff and no more.

146   *For Thomas Thetcher, d. 1764; in the Cathedral Yard,*
       Winchester

        Here sleeps in peace a Hampshire Grenadier,
        Who caught his death by drinking cold small beer;
        Soldiers, be wise from his untimely fall,
        And when ye're hot drink strong, or none at all.

        An honest soldier never is forgot,
        Whether he die by musket or by pot.

147 *On a tombstone at Bideford, Devon, for Captain Henry*
Clark, d. 1836

Our worthy friend who lies beneath this stone
Was master of a vessel all his own.
House and lands had he, and gold in store;
He spent the whole, and would if ten times more.

For twenty years he scarce slept in a bed;
Linhays and limekilns lull'd his weary head
Because he would not to the poor-house go,
For his proud spirit would not let him to.

The blackbird's whistling notes, at break of day,
Used to awake him from his bed of hay.
Unto the bridge and quay he then repaired
To see what shipping up the river steer'd

Oft in the week he used to view the bay
To see what ships were coming in from sea.
To captains' wives he brought the welcome news,
And to the relatives of all the crews.

At last poor Harry Clark was taken ill,
And carried to the workhouse 'gainst his will;
But being of this mortal life quite tired,
He lived about a month and then expired.

148 *Epitaph for Dolly Pentreath, reputed to have been the last*
native speaker of Cornish; d. 1777 at Mousehole

Old Doll Pentreath, one hundred aged and two,
Deceased, and buried in Paul parish too:—
Not in the church, with people great and high,
But in the church-yard doth old Dolly lie.

147 linhays] open sheds

149 *A Dorset 'lullaby' from Napoleonic times*

The Dorset Nurse and 'Boney'

Baby, baby, naughty baby,
Hush, you squalling thing, I say,
Hush your squalling or it may be,
Boneparte will pass this way.

Baby, baby, he's a giant
Tall and black as Rouen steeple
And he dines and sups, rely on't
Every day on naughty people.

Baby, baby, he will hear you,
As he passes by the house,
And he limb from limb will tear you,
Just as pussy tears a mouse.

150 *Henry Pye (1745–1813; Poet Laureate from 1790), an epigram on the Southampton Canal*

Southampton's wise sons found their river so large,
Though t'would carry a ship, t'would not carry a barge;
So they wisely determined to cut by its side
A stinking canal, where small vessels might glide:
Like a man, who, contriving a hole in his wall,
To admit his two cats,—the one large, t'other small,—
When his great hole was cut for the first to go through,
Would a little one have for the little one too.

151 *Rhymes on Salisbury Cathedral*

(i)   Fair Sarum's Church, besides the stately tower,
           Hath many things in number aptly sorted,
         Answering the year, the month, week, day, and hour,
           But above all (as I have heard reported,
         And to the view doth probably appear)
         A pillar for each hour in the year.

(ii)   As many days as in one year there be,
So many windows in this church you see,
As many marble pillars here appear
As there are hours through the fleeting year,
As many gates as moons one here doth view:
Strange tale to tell, yet not more strange than true.

152   *The 'Legend of Glastonbury', versified in the Somerset dialect*
from oral traditions

Who hath not hir'd of Avalon?
'Twas talk'd of much and long agon:—
The wonders of the *Holy thorn*,
The which, zoon âter Christ was born,
Here a planted war by Arimathé,
Thie *Joseph* that com'd over sea,
And planted Christianity.
Thà zà that whun a landed vust,
(Zich plaʒen war in God's own trust)
A stuck his staff into the groun,
And over his shoulder lookin roun,
Whativer mid his lot bevâll,
He cried aloud now, 'weary all!'
The staff het budded and het grew,
And at Christmas bloom'd the whol dà droo.
And still het blooms at Christmas bright,
But best thà zà at dork midnight.
A pruf o' this, if pruf you will,
Is voun in the name o' *Weary-all Hill!*
Let tell *Pumparles* or lazy *Brue*
That what is told is vor sartain true!

153   *From Saltash, Cornwall*

A Ferry Fable

A bumpkin came to the river's side
    With a sow from his master's store,
And strict command to cross the tide—
    A task which vexed him sore.

152 thà zà] they say   plaʒen] places   mid] might   dà droo] day through

For though the boat was waiting there,
   And the skipper watched the shore—
And the tide was high and the wind was fair,
   For sail or labouring oar—

There still remained a task more stern
   Than ruling wind or tide;
For the sow would neither walk nor turn
   Towards the vessel's side.

The bumpkin screamed—enticed and gored—
   And cursed with might and main;
But still to get the pig on board
   His efforts were in vain.

At length a parson hurried down,
   With chidings oft and long,
Upon the language of the clown,
   Because it was so strong.

'Now cease your oaths,' said Clerico,
   'For naught can they avail;
But slyly give a poke or so,
Till in the way you want to go
You find the lady turning—ho!
   Then pull her by the tail!

The clown obeyed—and, quick as thought,
   The victim was on board.
Though hard to learn, yet quickly taught,
   Are lessons rightly stored.

The bumpkin stared aghast to know
How 'twas that priests so learned grow;
   The skipper stood amazed—
And had it been some years ago,
The parson then and there, I trow,
   'Midst faggots would have blazed.

Now if you wish to reason how
   The parson learnt his plan,
'Tis simply this you have to know—
   He was a married man!

154 *A local song 'well known for many years' at Purton,*
Wiltshire

The Village Baker

Job Jenkins was a baker and
 A very honest elf,
By selling crust and crumbs he made
 A tidy crust himself,
But Job he lived in better days
 When bills were freely paid,
And bakers were thought honest then
 So bread was never weighed.

While walking through the old Churchyard
 He saw some old tombstones,
That long had marked the resting-place
 Of some poor neighbour's bones,
'These bodies long have gone to dust,
 These stones no use,' he said,
'They'll mend my oven and improve
 My very next batch of bread.'

Tom Snooks, the parish mason,
 A very sporting blade,
Who in race horses and the dead
 Had done a tidy trade,
To him Job gave the order,
 Regardless of amount,
And charged it to the Parish
 In his next half-year's account.

The job was done—the bread was baked—
 Job, in his highest glee
Sat up to draw the batch that he
 Might great improvement see,
But soon as drawn he 'slope the pill'
 With horror in his looks,
And rushed out like a madman
 And knocked down Tommy Snooks!

slope the pill] slipped away

'Get up, you wretch, and come and see
  The blunder you have made,
Your tombstone bottom sure will prove
  A deathblow to my trade,
I know that when you're in the whim
  At trifles you don't stick,
And by your trick you've spoilt my batch.
  My cottage, square and brick.'

He took him to the bakehouse,
  Where a curious sight was seen,
The words on every loaf were marked
  That had on tombstone been,
One quartern had 'in memory of'
  Another 'here to pine,'
The third 'departed from this life
  At the age of ninety nine.'

A batch of rolls when they were done
  Had on the bottom plain,
The trusting words distinctly marked
  'In hopes to rise again,'
A batch of penny loaves came next
  Which said 'our time is past,
Thus day by day, we've pined away,
  And come to this at last.'

Tom Snooks now turned his head away
  His laughter to conceal,
He said 'he thought it a nobby way
  In making a bread seal.'
Says Job, 'This seal has sealed my fate
  How can I sell my bread?
To feed the living, when it bears,
  The motto of the dead?'

155 *Windows at Bradfield College, Berkshire*

(i)   The emmet's toil and care,
                        No hour of light to spare.

154 batch] baking

(ii)   The serpent's wisdom, love
                    Of the harmless dove.

(iii)   Divided kingdoms fail,
                    United hosts prevail.

(iv)   Falls the house built on sand,
                    That on rock does stand.

(v)   From smallest seeds we know
                    The mighty tree doth grow.

156   *Verses from the* Royal Military College Magazine,
      Sandhurst, April 1891

The Lay of the Staff College Student

I'm only now a student,
   And not of much account,
But up the ladder of Staff employ
   I very soon mean to mount;
For it most assuredly is a fact,
   Though you may count it chaff,
I am the very man cut out
   For a billet on the Staff.

Chorus
'Tam Marte quam Minerva,'
   Whatever that may be,
I'm not a classical scholar, and so
   It's all high Dutch to me.
'Tam Marte quam Minerva,'
   The motto is not so long,
But that I've made it just fit in
   As the chorus of my song.

Far in the distance looming
   Fresh honours can I see,
When my time for studentship is o'er,
   And a 'graduate' I'll be;
And then the deference and respect
   So justly due to me,
Will be conjured by the magic
   Of the letters *P. S. C.*

156 *P. S. C.*] passed Staff College

An Assistant Adjutant-General
  Is what I'd like to be;
An Assistant Adjutant-General is
  The very post for me.
I'm very adroit at office work,
  And I never do things by half,
And there'll be the deuce and all to pay
  When I am on the Staff.

If you want a man with manners
  The Colonels to cajole,
If you want a pleasant, agreeable man,
  I stand first on the roll;
If you want a man with a cheery laugh
  Or a fascinating leer,
You need not look around the world,
  For I am waiting here.

You're nothing if you cannot take
  A hundred thousand men
To Jericho and feed them there,
  And bring them back again.
The transport is most difficult,
  But are we not aware
Three mules to every army corps
  The extra strain will bear?

But when the foe we have non-plussed
  With strategy galore,
We shall not have expended all
  The weapons we've in store.
We need not risk a battle fierce,
  His armies we'll not meet,
With striking facts from 'syllabi'
  We'll compass his defeat.

We'll tell him of nine army corps
  Which we can quickly send,
And of the perfect transport, too,
  On which they can depend.
We'll tell him of the soldiers brave,
  Who do combine, in truth,
'Maturity of manhood' with
  'Resiliency of youth.'

Meantime, with facts and figures
  My brain I have to cram,
To fit me for that dreadful test,
  The annual exam.
For perfect though my manners be,
  A fact you cannot doubt,
I needs must get my decimal
  Or else I'll be flung out.

157   *In the Visitors' Book, Fowey Cruising School, Cornwall,*
     1975

Let others think about *Hour Angle*,
Of *Declination* let them wrangle,
Azimuth, Zenith, Index Error,
For me, just *Left* and *Right*'s the terror:
Come Muse, assist! Urania, Clio,
Stop *Jibing* at me—HE said *lee-oh*!
Yes, so the skipper, half-despairing
Cried out—yet now, *away* I'm *bearing*.
Man overboard? The base pretender!
It's just a dirty, worn-out fender.
Now jib *aback*, rudder *aweather*,
Helen of Troy rides light as feather,
But in my stomach's such a rumpus
The devil must be in the compass:
To think, to *starboard* and to *port* meant
This bewildering assortment
Of *helm* and *tiller*, *wheel* and *rudder*
The whole conundrum makes me shudder.
The spasms, heebie-jeebies, shivers
(I'll stick to motor boats on rivers).
The *boom* comes over like a cannon,
And there's the rock I nearly ran on;
Yet I perhaps could stop this *yawing*
If *Someone Else* would just stop jawing;
If Skipper'd only give up beefing,
Skip to the Sharp End and do some *reefing*;
It may be, truly, that a double
Scotch would wash away my Trouble,
But mark my words, I want no *Port*—nor
Starboard—and mostly, *no more water*.

158 *Visitors' Book verses, Mullyon, Cornwall, 1872, 'in praise of
the Old Inn and Mrs. Mary Mundy'*

Full many bright things on this earth there be,
Which a pious man may enjoy with glee
    On Saturday or Sunday;
But the brightest thing that chanced to me,
In Cornish land, was when I did see
    The 'Old Inn,' by Mary Mundy.

'Twas on Saturday afternoon
That I was trudging, a weary loon,
    To spend at the Lizard my Sunday,
When thro' the corner of my right eye,
The happy sign I did espy,—
    'OLD INN, by MARY MUNDY.'

So I went in, and out came she,
With a face from which blue devils would flee
    On Saturday or on Sunday;
And I said as soon as I saw her face,
'I could not be housed in a better place,
    So I'll just stay here till Monday.'

Quoth I, 'Could you give me a dinner well spread,—
An old arm chair, and a well-air'd bed,—
    And a good short sermon on Sunday?'
Quoth she, 'Indeed, Sir, that we can,
For I guess no doubt you're a gentleman,
    As sure as my name is Mundy.'

I went upstairs with a bound and a hop,
And I looked around the tight little shop,
    And I said, 'Miss Mary Mundy!
There's not in London a grand hotel
Where, with such comfort, I could dwell,
    As with you, my dear Miss Mundy!'

'You've got the tongue of a gentleman,'
Quoth she, 'I do the best I can
    On Saturday or on Sunday.'

loon] lad

'That's just the thing we all should do;
But they who do it are few, and you
  Are one of the few, Miss Mundy!'

But now to tell the feast she spread,
And with what delicate zest we fed
  On the day before the Sunday,
Would stagger the muse of a Tennyson,
And bring from the devil a benison
  On the head of Mary Mundy.

A London alderman, sleek and fat,
Would sigh for the sight of a duck like that
  Was served to us by Mundy,—
A roasted duck, with fresh green peas,
A gooseberry pie, and a Cheddar cheese,—
  A feast for a god on Sunday.

But the top of her skill I well may deem
Was the dear delight of the Cornish cream,—
  Both Saturday and Sunday,—
That down my throat did gently glide,
Like sweet Bellini's tuneful tide,
  By the liberal grace of Mundy.

And then to crown the banquet rare,
A brandy bottle she did bear,—
  (God bless thee! Mary Mundy!)
And said, 'Full sure a gentleman
Abhors the lean teetotal plan
  On Saturday or Sunday.'

And when my weary frame did glow
With genial warmth from top to toe,
  (Good night! my dear Miss Mundy,)
I slept on bed as clean and sweet
As lass that goes so trim and neat
  With her lover to Church on Sunday.

But why should I go on to sin,
Spinning bad rhymes to the good OLD INN
  While the bell is tolling on Sunday;
I'll go and hear short sermon there,—
Tho' the best of all sermons I declare
  Is the face of Miss Mary Mundy.

And I advise you all to hold
By the well-tried things that are good and old,
    Like this snug house of Mundy,—
The good OLD CHURCH and the good OLD INN;
And the old way to depart from sin,
    By going to Church on Sunday.

And if there be on Cornish cliffs
To swell his lungs with breezy whiffs
    Who can spare but only one day,
Let him spend it here,—and understand
That the brightest thing in the Cornish land
    Is the face of Miss Mary Mundy.

159   *Verses on Mrs Mary Blake, d. 1841, aged 80; Saltash, Cornwall*

A Cockle Woman

Where Tamar's waters roll along,
    O'er muddy banks and rocks,
The ancient Town of Saltash stands,
    Well known for pickle cocks.

It claims the right to shrimp and dredge,
    Within the headlands round,
From Shagstone up to Ogle Tor,
    The Bay and Plymouth Sound.

Throughout the spring and summer months,
    The shrimp net and the rake
Are used to catch a livelihood.—
    T'was so with Mary Blake.

Each morning Mary passed the gate,
    True as the best of clocks,
The Barrack children knew the cry,
    'Will 'e buy any pickle cocks.'

So half a century passed and she
    Cared not for wind or rain,
Blest with the best of health and strength,
    Her trade she did maintain.

Worn out with years no more she'll stir
   Mid kettles, pans, and crocks,
No more on Kinterbury's back
   Rake up the pickle cocks.

160   *'As Tom was a-walking'; Cornwall*

As Tom was a-walking one fine summer's morn,
When the dazies and goldcups the fields did adorn;
He met Cozen Mal, with the tub on her head,
Says Tom, 'Cozen Mal, you might speak if you we'd.'

But Mal stamped along, and appeared to be shy,
And Tom singed out, 'Zounds! I'll knaw of thee why?'
So back he tore a'ter, in a terrible fuss,
And axed cozen Mal, 'What's the reason of thus?'

'Tom Treloar,' cried out Mal, 'I'll nothing do wi' 'ee,
Go to Fanny Trembaa, she do knaw how I'm shy;
Tom, this here t'other daa, down the hill thee didst stap,
And dab'd a great doat fig in Fan Trembaa's lap.'

'As for Fanny Trembaa, I ne'er taalked wi' her twice,
And gived her a doat fig, they are so very nice;
So I'll tell thee, I went to the fear t'other day,
And the doat figs I boft, why I saved them away.'

Says Mal, 'Tom Treloar, ef that be the caase,
May the Lord bless for ever that sweet pretty faace;
Ef thee'st give me thy doat figs thee'st boft in the fear,
I'll swear to thee now, thee shu'st marry me here.'

161   *Verses for an incontinent widow not to lose her tenancy;*
   Berkshire

        Here I am,
        Riding upon a black ram,
        Like a whore as I am;
        And for my Crincum Crancum,

---

160 we'd] would   stap] step   doat fig] ?dried fig   boft] bought
fear] fair

161 Crincum Crancum] tricks

Have lost my Bincum Bancum;
And for my tail's game,
Have done this worldly shame;
Therefore, I pray you, Mr. Steward,
Let me have my land again.

162   *A farmer's and farm-worker's toast, in the apple orchard, on the eve of Twelfth Night, in 'certain parts of Devon'*

Here's to thee, old apple-tree,
Whence thou mayst bud, and whence thou mayst blow!
And whence thou mayst bear apples enow!
Hats full!—caps full!
Bushel—bushel—sacks full,
And my pockets full too! Huzza!

163   *Apple-growing and cider-making; Devon*

An orchard fair, to please,
And pleasure for your mind, sir,
You'd have—then plant of trees
The goodliest you can find, sir;
In bark they must be clean,
And finely grown in root, sir,
Well trimmed in head, I ween,
And sturdy in the shoot, sir.
O the jovial days when the apple trees do bear,
We'll drink and be merry all the gladsome year.

The pretty trees you plant,
Attention now will need, sir,
That nothing they may want,
Which to mention I proceed, sir.
You must not grudge a fence
'Gainst cattle, tho 't be trouble;
They will repay the expense
In measure over double.
O the jovial days, &c.

To give a man great joy,
And see his orchard thrive, sir,
A skilful hand employ

To use the pruning knife, sir.
To lop each wayward limb,
    That seemeth to offend, sir;
Nor fail at Fall, to trim
    Until the tree's life end, sir.
Nor fail at Fall, to trim
    Until the tree's life end, sir.
        O the jovial days, &c.

All in the month of May,
    The trees are clothed in bloom, sir,
As posies bright and gay,
    Both morning, night and noon, sir.
'Tis pleasant to the sight,
    'Tis sweet unto the smell, sir,
And if there be no blight,
    The fruit will set and swell, sir.
        O the jovial days, &c.

The summer oversped,
    October drawing on, sir;
The apples gold and red
    Are glowing in the sun, sir.
As the season doth advance,
    Your apples for to gather,
I bid you catch the chance
    To pick them in fine weather.
        O the jovial days, &c.

When to a pummy ground,
    You squeeze out all the juice, sir,
Then fill a cask well bound,
    And set it by for use, sir.
O bid the cider flow
    In ploughing and in sowing,
The healthiest drink I know
    In reaping and in mowing.
        O the jovial days, &c.

pummy] pomace, apple-pulp

98

164 *A 'Lent Crocking Song'; Okehampton, Devon*

> Lent Crock, give a pancake,
> Or a fritter, for my labour,
> Or a dish of flour, or a piece of bread,
> Or what you please to remember.
> I see by the latch,
> There's something to catch;
> I see, by the string.
> There's a good dame within.
> Trap, trapping throw,
> Give me my mumps and I'll be go.

165 *'Collop Monday'; a song from the boys of Salisbury*

> Shrove-tide is nigh at hand,
> And I am come a shroving;
> Pray, dame, something,
> An apple or a dumpling,
> Or a piece of Truckle cheese
> Of your own making,
> Or a piece of pancake.

166 *A Hampshire April 1st rhyme (used after 12 noon)*

> April fool's gone past
> You're the biggest fool at last;
> When April fool comes again
> You'll be the biggest fool again.

167 *A 'Wallflowers' song; Ogbourne, Wiltshire*

> Water, water, wild flowers,
> Growing up so high,
> We are all maidens,
> And we shall all die,

crock] cake   mumps] ?gifts made to the 'mumpers' who sing the song
165 truckle cheese] a small barrel-shaped cheese

Excepting [Eva Irving],
And she's the youngest of us all,
And she can hop, and she can skip,
And she can turn the candlestick
[or 'She can play the organ'].
Piper shame! Piper shame!
Turn your back to the wall again.
I pick up a pin,
I knock at the door,
I ask for——,
She's neither in,
She's neither out,
She's up the garden skipping about.
Down come——, as white as snow,
Soft in her bosom as soft as glow.
She pulled off her glove,
And showed us her ring,
To-morrow, to-morrow,
The bells shall ring.

168   *Rhyme for a burning cheek; Cornwall*

Right cheek! left cheek! why do you burn?
Cursed be she that doth me any harm.
If it be a maid, let her be staid:
If it be a widow; long let she mourn:
But if it be my own true love,
Burn, cheek, burn!

169   *A charm for a thorn; Cornwall*

Happy man that Christ was born,
He was crowned with a thorn;
He was pierced through the skin,
For to let the poison in.
But His five wounds, so they say,
Closed before He passed away.
In with healing, out with thorn,
Happy man that Christ was born.

170   *A charm against 'Udern ill'; east Cornwall*

      Might come from the Sun,
      Might come from the Moon,
      Might come from the Ground,
      And unto the ground shall it
      return again.
      To Father, Son,
      and Holy Ghost.
      Amen.

171   *A charm for a sprain; Devon*

      Bone to bone, and vein to vein,
      O vein, turn to thy rest again!
        And so shall thine, in the Name of the Father,
                  Son and Holy Ghost.

172   *A dragon-fly ('snake-stanger') song from the Isle of Wight*

      Snakestanger, snakestanger, vlee aal about the brooks;
      Sting aal the bad bwoys that vor the fish looks,
      But let the good bwoys ketch aal the vish they can,
      And car'm away whooam to vry 'em in a pan;
      Bread and butter they shall yeat at zupper wi' their vish,
      While aal the littull bad bwoys shall only lick the dish.

173   *Thomas Deloney (1543–1600); from* Jack of Newbury;
     Berkshire

      Within one roome being large and long,
      There stood two hundred Loomes full strong;
      Two hundred men, the truth is so,
      Wrought in these Loomes all in a rowe,
      By every one a pretty boy,
      Sate making quills with mickle joye,
      And in another place hard by
      An hundred women merrily
      Were carding hard with joyfull cheere
      Who singing sate with voices cleare

And in a chamber close beside,
Two hundred maidens did abide,
In peticoats of stammell red,
And milk-white kerchers on their head.
Their smock sleeves like to winter snow,
That on the Westerne mountains flow,
And each sleeve with a silken band
Was featly tyèd at the hand.

These pretty maids did never lin
But in that place all day did spin:
And spinning so with voices meet
Like nightingales they sung full sweet.
Then to another roome came they,
Where children were in poore aray:
And every one sate picking wooll,
The finest from the course to cull:
The number was seaven score and ten,
The children of poor silly men:
And these their labours to requite
Had everyone a penny at night
Beside their meat and drink all day,
Which was to them a wondrous stay.
Within another place likewise
Full fiftie proper men he spies,
And these were Shearemen everyone,
Whose skill and cunning there was showne:
And hard by them there did remaine
Full foure score Rowers taking paine.
A Dye-house likewise had he then,
Wherein he kept full forty men:
And likewise in his Fulling mill
Full twenty persons kept he still.
Each weeke ten good fat Oxen he
Spent in his house for certaintie,
Beside good butter, cheese and fish,
And many another wholesome dish.
He kept a Butcher all the yeere,
A Brewer eke for Ale and Beere;
A Baker for to bake his Bread,
Which stood his household in good steat.
Five Cookes within his kitchin great

stammell red] the characteristic petticoat-red   lin] cease
shearemen] cloth-workers

Were all the yeare to dress his meat.
Six scullian boyes unto their hands,
To make cleane dishes, pots and pans,
Beside poore children that did stay
To turne the broaches every day.
The olde man that did see this sight,
Was much amaz'd, as well he might:
This was a gallant Cloathier sure,
Whose fame for ever shall endure.

174 *A Dorset rhyme, 'to familiarize a child with the design on the willow-pattern plate'*

Two pigeons flying high,
A little ship sailing by;
A weeping willow drooping o'er,
Three workmen and no more;
Next the warehouse; near at hand
A palace for the lord of land;
An apple tree with fruit o'erhung,
The fencing round will end my song.

175 *A popular rhyme on the cuckoo; Devon*

In the month of April,
He opens his bill;
In the month of May,
He singeth all day;
In the month of June,
He alters his tune;
In the month of July,
Away he doth fly.

176 *A Hampshire bee-keeping rhyme*

A swarm of bees in May
Is worth a load of hay;
A swarm of bees in June
Is worth a silver spoon;
A swarm of bees in July
Is not worth a fly.

173 broaches] spits

177 *South Country weather rhymes*

(i) *from Sussex*

When old hens scratch the ground and clouds have tails,
'Tis time for ships at sea to shorten sails.

(ii) *from Dorset*

Mackerel scales and mare's tails
Make lordly ships to carry low sails.

178 *Cornish weather rhymes*

(i)
        Mist from the hill
            Brings water for the mill;
        Mist from the sea
            Brings fine weather for me.

(ii)
        When the mist comes from the hill,
        Then good weather it doth spill.
        When the mist comes from the sea
        Then good weather it will be.

(iii)
        A rainbow in the morn,
            Put your head in the corn;
        A rainbow in the eve,
            Put your head in the sheave.

179 *A north Wiltshire dialect song, by J. Y. Akerman*

        A Harnet zet in a hollow tree,—
        A proper spiteful twoad was he,—
        And a merrily zung while a did zet
        His stinge as zharp as a baganet,
        'Oh, who's zo bowld and vierce as I?—
        I vears not bee, nor wapse, nor vly!'
                Chorus—Oh, who's zo bowld, etc.

    178 spill] destroy

    179 harnet] hornet   baganet] bayonet

104

A Bittle up thuck tree did clim',
And scarnvully did luk at him.
Zays he, 'Zur Harnet, who giv' thee
A right to zet in thuck there tree?
Although you zengs so nation vine,
I tell'e it's a house o' mine.'
     Chorus—Although you zengs, etc.

The Harnet's conscience velt a twinge,
But growin' bould wi' his long stinge,
Zays he, 'Possession's the best law,
Zo here th' shasn't put a claw.
Be off, and leave the tree to me:
The Mixen's good enough vor thee!'
     Chorus—Be off, and leave, etc.

Just then a Yuccle passin' by
Was axed by them their cause to try.
'Ha! ha! it's very plain,' zays he,
'They'll make a vamous nunch for me!'
His bill was zharp, his stomack lear,
Zo up a snapped the caddlin pair.
     Chorus—His bill was zharp, etc.

MORAL
All you as be to law inclined,
This leetle story bear in mind;
For if to law you ever gwo,
You'll vind they'll allus zarve 'e zo;
You'll meet the vate o' these 'ere two:
They'll take your cwoat and carcass
  too!
     Chorus—You'll meet the vate, etc.

180   *A horse rhyme; Stokeinteignhead, Devon*

If you have a horse with four white legs,
    Keep him not a day;
If you have a horse with three white legs,
    Send him far away;

179 bittle] beetle   nation] 'damnation', extremely   mixen] dunghill
yuccle] yaffle, woodpecker   lear] empty   caddlin] quarrelling

If you have a horse with two white legs,
    Sell him to a friend;
And if you have a horse with one white leg,
    Keep him to the end.

181   *Robert Herrick (1591–1674); an epitaph at Dean Prior, Devon*

Upon *Prew* his Maid

In this little Urne is laid
Prewdence Baldwin (once my maid)
From whose happy spark here let
Spring the purple Violet.

IV

EASTERN ENGLAND

182 *Under a picture of Charles I, formerly in St Lawrence Church, Ipswich*

> Within this Sacred Arch doth lye
> The quintessence of Majesty
> Which being Sett more Glorious Shines
> The best of Kings best of Divines
> Brittain's shame and Brittain's glory
> Mirrour of Princes Compleat Story
> Of royalty One so Exact
> That praise come short and doth detract
> If you would see him to endure
> Behold him in his portraiture
> If such an other you would find
> It must by Angels be designed.

183 *Inscription on a painting of the Spanish Armada as a dragon, hanging in the church tower at Bratoft, Lincolnshire*

> Spain's proud Armado with great strength and power
> Great Britain's state came gapeing to devour,
> This dragon's guts, like Pharoah's scattered hoast
> Lay splitt and drowned upon the Irish coast,
> For of eight score save too ships sent from Spaine
> But twenty-five scarce sound returned again.
>
> non Nobis Domine.

184 *Lines attached to the Duke of Suffolk's horse-trappings at a sixteenth-century tournament*

> Cloth of gold do not despise
> Though thou art matched with cloth of frieze
> Cloth of frieze be not too bold
> Though thou art matched with cloth of gold.

185   *'Rules for a Holy Life', by George Doughty (born 1655), rector of Martlesham, Suffolk*

> Apparel sober, neat, comely,
> Conversation little, honest, heavenly,
> Diet temperate, convenient, frugal,
> Manners grave, courteous, cheerful,
> Prayers short, devout, frequent,
> Recreations lawful, brief, seldom,
> Sleep moderate, quiet, seasonable,
> Thoughts divine, awful, useful,
> Will constant, ready, obedient,
> Works profitable, holy, useful.

186   *On a beam in the ceiling of the parsonage at Meppershall, Bedfordshire*

> If you wish to go into Hertfordshire
> Hitch a little nearer to the fire.

187   *On a fireplace in Coggeshall, Essex*

> The houre runeth
> And time flieth
> As floure fadeth
> So man dieth.

188   *Queen Elizabeth on the notorious spendthrift Sir Andrew Noel, of Brooke, near Oakham (formerly Rutland)*

> The word of denial and letter of fifty
> Is that gentleman's name that will never be thrifty.

189 *Scribbled on the wall beside his bed by George Radcliffe of Hitchin, Hertfordshire, during his last lucid interval (eighteenth century)*

> What use to send for Dr. Lane,
> When you are sick and racked with pain?
> Though you survive his medicine chests
> You'll die of laughter at his jests.

190 *C. S. Calverley (1831–84); the 'Ode to Tobacco', written for Bacon's tobacco shop, Market Hill, Cambridge*

> Thou who, when fears attack,
> Bidst them avaunt, and Black
> Care, at the horseman's back
>   Perching, unseatest;
> Sweet, when the morn is gray;
> Sweet, when they've cleared away
> Lunch; and at close of day
>   Possibly sweetest:
>
> I have a liking old
> For thee, though manifold
> Stories, I know, are told,
>   Not to thy credit;
> How one (or two at most)
> Drops make a cat a ghost—
> Useless, except to roast—
>   Doctors have said it:
>
> How they who use fusees
> All grow by slow degrees
> Brainless as chimpanzees,
>   Meagre as lizards;
> Go mad, and beat their wives;
> Plunge (after shocking lives)
> Razors and carving knives
>   Into their gizzards.

---

190 fusees] large-headed matches for smokers

Confound such knavish tricks!
Yet know I five or six
Smokers who freely mix
  Still with their neighbours;
Jones—(who, I'm glad to say,
Asked leave of Mrs. J.)—
Daily absorbs a clay
  After his labours.

Cats may have had their goose
Cooked by tobacco-juice;
Still why deny its use
  Thoughtfully taken?
We're not as tabbies are:
Smith, take a fresh cigar!
Jones, the tobacco-jar!
  Here's to thee, Bacon!

191   *On the parapet of Joshua Lee's clay pipe works (in 1921),
Sidney Street, Cambridge*

> Little tube of mighty power,
> Charmer of an idle hour,
> Object of my warm desire:
> Lip of wax, and eye of fire.
> And thy snowy taper waist
> With my finger gently braced.
>
> [And thy pretty swelling crest
> With my little stopper presst.]

192   *Verses on a tablet above the door of the disused
pumping-station near Prickwillow, Cambridgeshire (see
Introduction, p. xv)*

Erected A.D. 1842

In fitness for the urgent hour,
  Unlimited, untiring power.
Precision, promptitude, command,
The infant's will, the giant's hand;
Steam, mighty steam, ascends the throne,
And reigns lord paramount alone.

193 *Verses said to have been hung up near the 'Great Bed of Ware', Hertfordshire*

> Take care thou dost thyself no wrong;
> Drink no small beer if thou hast strong,
> And further, do thyself this right,
> Eat no brown bread if thou hast white;
> And if the mistress thou can bed,
> Be sure thou dost not kiss the maid.
> . . . What I have said do thou retain,
> So kiss the horns, and say 'Amen'.

194 *An inscription on the 'Flitch of Bacon' inn at Dunmow, Essex*

> Painted in Gold
> Y^e Flitch behold
> Of famed Dunmow
> Y^e boaste.
> Then here should call
> Fond couples all
> And pledge it
> In a toaste.

195 *Rhymes used for the 'Dunmow Flitch' contest, Dunmow, Essex*

> You shall swear by custom of confession,
> That you ne'er made nuptial transgression;
> Nor since you were married man and wife,
> By household brawls or contentious strife,
> Or otherwise at bed or at board,
> Offended each other in deed or word;
> Or in a twelvemonth and a day,
> Repented not in thought any way;
> Or since the parish clerk said 'Amen,'
> Wished yourselves unmarried again,
> But continued true, and in desire,
> As when you joined hands in holy quire.

*

Since to these conditions without any fear,
Of your own accord do freely swear;
A whole gammon of bacon you shall receive,
And bear it away with love and good leave;
For this is the custom of Dunmow well known,—
Tho' the pleasure be ours, the bacon's your own.

196   *Cooking directions, recorded as attached to swans sold, in*
       Norwich (and as seventeenth-century)

Take three pounds of beef, beat fine in a mortar,
Put it into the swan, that is when you've caught her,
Some pepper, salt, mace, some nutmeg, an onion,
Will heighten the flavour in a gourmand's opinion.
Then tie it up tight with a small piece of tape,
That the gravy and other things may not escape.

197   *Inscription in the George Inn, Wanstead, Essex*

In Memory of
Y^e Cherry Pey
As cost ½ a Guiney
Y^e 17 of July.
That day we had good cheer
I hope to see money a Year.
Da^d Jersey
1752

198   *Pinned up in an inn at Mulbarton, Norfolk*

The Landlord's Kind Caution to his Customers

Right welcome all who visit here,
I'll treat you with good wholesome cheer;
I deal in ale, as chrystal clear,
In porter brown, in good strong beer.
I've rum and gin, and brandy too,
They suit myself and will please you;
My wines would make a Nabob smile;

197 Da^d] ?David

114

My whiskey will your hearts beguile;
My chairs are easy, fires are bright,
So take a seat, yourselves delight;
My tobacco's rich, pipes white as snow,
Alike they're formed to soothe your woe.
I'm ready to attend your call,
But I've no chalk to spoil my wall;
Chalk ever does sweet peace destroy,
Stirs up foul anger, stifles joy.
My liquor's good, my dealing just,
My profit's small—I cannot trust.
I'm sure these lines can cause no sorrow,
So pay to-day, I'll trust to-morrow.
If I refuse to trust a friend,
Or if I trust or money lend,
The one he takes it in disdain,
The other will my house refrain.

199   *Entry in the marriage register, Snelland, Lincolnshire, 1671*

The first day of November
Robert Sherriffe may remember
That he was marryed for all the days of his life
If God be not merciful to him and take his wife.

200   *The Will of a north Essex labourer, 1839*

The Will of James Bigsby of Manningtree

As I feel very queer my will I now make;
Write it down, Joseph Finch, and make no mistake.
I wish to leave all things fair and right, do you see,
And my relatives satisfy. Now, listen to me.
The first in my will is Lydia my wife,
Who to me proved a comfort three years of my life;
The second my poor aged mother I say,
With whom I have quarrelled on many a day,
For which I've been sorry, and also am still;
I wish to give her a place in my will.
The third that I mention is my dear little child;
When I think of her, Joseph, I feel almost wild.
Uncle Sam Bigsby, I must think of him too,

Peradventure he will say that I scarcely can do.
And poor uncle Gregory, I must leave him a part,
If it is nothing else but the back of the cart.
And for you, my executor, I will do what I can,
For acting towards me like an honest young man.
  Now, to my wife I bequeath greater part of my
    store;
First thing is the bedstead before the front door;
The next is the chair standing by the fire side,
The fender and irons she cleaned with much pride.
I also bequeath to Lydia my wife
A box in the cupboard, a sword, gun, and knife,
And the harmless old pistol without any lock,
Which no man can fire off, for 'tis minus a cock.
The cups and the saucers I leave her also,
And a book called *The History of Poor Little Mo*,
With the kettle, the boiler, and old frying-pan,
A shovel, a mud-scoop, a pail, and a pan.
And remember, I firmly declare and protest
That my poor aged mother shall have my oak chest
And the broken whip under it. Do you hear what I
    say?
Write all these things down without any delay.
And my dear little child, I must think of her too.
Friend Joseph, I am dying, what shall I do?
I give her my banyan, my cap, and my hose,
My big monkey jacket, my shirt, and my shoes;
And to Uncle Sam Bigsby I bequeath my high boots,
The pickaxe and mattock with which I stubbed roots.
And poor Uncle Gregory, with the whole of my heart,
I give for a bedstead the back of the cart.
And to you, my executor, last in my will,
I bequeath a few trifles to pay off your bill.
I give you my shot-belt, my dog, and my nets,
And the rest of my goods sell to pay off my debts.
                    JOSEPH FINCH, executor.

201 *On the church font at Barnetby, Lincolnshire*

        Like fruitful vine on thy house side
        So doth thy wife spring out.

200 banyan] ?loose flannel jacket or shirt

Thy children stand like Oliveplantes
Thy table round about.
Thus art thou blest that fearest God,
And he shall let thee see
The promiesed Hierusalem
    and his felicitie.

202   *For the first two wives of Colonel Freeborne; in the*
     churchyard at Prittlewell, Essex, c.1650

Under one stone two precious gems do lie,
Equal in worth, weight, lustre, sanctity:
If yet, perhaps, one of them might excel,
Which most, who knows! ask him who knew them well
By long enjoyment; if he be thus pressed,
He'll pause, then answer, truly both were best;
Were't in my choice that either of the twain
Might be returned to me to enjoy again,
Which should I choose? Well, since I know not whether,
I'll mourn for the loss of both, but wish for neither.
Yet here's my comfort, herein lies my hope,
The time's acoming, cabinets shall ope
Which are locked fast; then, then shall I see,
My jewels to my joy, my jewels me.

203   *Verses cast on a bell for All Saints Church, Maldon, Essex,*
     by Henry Pleasant (c.1700)

When three this steeple long did hold
They were the emblems of a scold,
No music then, but we shall see
What *Pleasant* music six will be.

204   *Inscriptions on three bells at St Ives, Huntingdonshire*

Sometimes joy and sometimes sorrow,
Marriage today and death tomorrow. 1723.

When backward rung we tell of fire,
Think how the world shall thus expire.

When souls are from their bodies torn
'Tis not to dye but to be born.

205　*A ballad upon the monks of Newark Priory near the river*
Wey

The monks of the Wey seldom sung any psalms,
And little they thought of religious qualms;
Ranting, rollicking, frolicksome, gay,
Jolly old boys were the monks of the Wey.
　　　　　　Tralalala! lara la!

To the sweet nuns of Ockham devoting their cares,
They had but short time for their beads and their prayers;
For the love of the maidens, they sighed night and day,
And neglected devotion, those monks of the Wey.　Tralalala . . .

And happy, i' faith, might these monks have been,
If the river had not rolled between
Their abbey dark and their convent grey,
That stood on the opposite side of the Wey.　Tralalala . . .

For daily they sighed and nightly they pined,
Little to anchorite rules inclined;
So smitten with beauty's charms were they,
These rollicking, frolicksome monks of the Wey.　Tralalala . . .

But the scandal was great in the county near –
They dared not row across for fear;
And they could not swim, so fat were they,
These oily, amorous monks of the Wey.　Tralalala . . .

Loudly they groaned for their fate so hard,
From the smiles of these beautiful maids debarred,
Till a brother hit on a plan to stay
The love of these heart-broken monks of the Wey.　Tralalala . . .

'Nothing', quoth he, 'should true love sunder;
Since we canot go over, let us go under;
Boats and bridges shall yield to-day—
We'll dig a tunnel beneath the Wey.'　Tralalala . . .

To it they went with right good will,
With spade and shovel, pike and bill;
And from evening's close to the dawn of day
They worked like miners all under the Wey.   Tralalala ...

And every night as this work begun,
Each sang of the charms of their favourite nun;
'How surprised they will be, and how happy', said they,
'When we pop in upon them from under the Wey.'   Tralalala ...

And for months they kept grubbing and making no sound,
Like other black moles, darkly under the ground;
And no one suspected such going astray,
So sly were these amorous monks of the Wey.   Tralalala ...

At last, this fine work was brought near to a close,
And early one morn from their pallets they rose,
And met in their tunnel with lights to survey,
If they'd scooped a free passage right under the Wey.   Tralalala ...

But, alas for their fate! as they smirked and they smiled,
To think how completely the world was beguiled,
The river broke in, and it grieves me to say,
It drowned all the frolicksome monks of the Wey.   Tralalala ...

O, Churchmen, beware of the lures of the flesh,
The net of the devil hath many a mesh;
And remember, whenever you're tempted to stray,
The fate that befel the poor monks of the Wey.   Tralalala ...

206   *Once in the east window of St Mary, Luton (preserved in
the Heralds' Visitation Book, 1566)*

> Jesus Christ, most of myght,
> Have mercy on John le Wenlock, Knight,
> And of his wiffe Elizabeth,
> Which owt of this world is past by death.
> Which ffounded this chapell here.
> Help them with your hearty prair
> That they may com to that place
> Where ever is joy and solace.

207   *In Boston church, Lincolnshire*

My Corps with Kings and Monarchs sleeps in bedd,
My soul with sight of Christ in heaven is fedd,
This lumpe that lampe shall meet, and shine more bright
Than Pheobus when he streams his clearest light.

> Omnes sic ibant sic imus ibitis ibunt.

208   *Dryden (1631–1700), epitaph on Mrs Margaret Paston of*
       Barningham, Suffolk

So fair, so young, so innocent, so sweet;
So ripe a Judgment, and so rare a Wit,
Require at least an Age, in One to meet.
In her they met; but long they cou'd not stay,
'Twas Gold too fine to fix without Allay:
Heav'ns Image was in her so well exprest,
Her very Sight upbraided all the rest.
Too justly ravish'd from an Age like this;
Now *she* is gone, the World is of a Piece.

209   *Epitaph for Mary Girling, d. 1771; Little Welnetham,*
       Suffolk

It can hardly be said she died;
But having steer'd through every course of life,
The girl, the maid, the woman and the wife,
She softly landed on that silent shore,
Where billows never break or tempests roar,
Where peacefull scepters for the Patient grow,
And crowns repay our long fatigues below.

210   *In St Andrew's Church, Chesterton, Cambridge*

Near this Place lies Interred
ANNA MARIA VASSA,
Daughter of GUSTAVUS VASSA the AFRICAN
She died July 21 1797,
Aged 4 Years.

Should simple village rhymes attract thine eye,
Stranger, as thoughtfully thou passest by,
Know that there lies beside this humble stone
A child of colour haply not thine own.
Her father born of Afric's sun-burnt race,
Torn from his native fields, ah foul disgrace;
Through various toils at length to Britain came
Espous'd, so Heaven ordain'd, an English dame,
And follow'd Christ; their hope two infants dear.
But one, a hapless Orphan, slumbers here.
To bury her the village children came,
And dropp'd choice flowers, and lisp'd her early fame;
And some that lov'd her most as if unblest,
Bedew'd with tears the white wreath on their breast:
But she is gone and dwells in that abode
Where some of every clime shall joy in God.

211 *A monument in Isleham church, Cambridgeshire, to Barbary*
Thimblethorpe, d. 1619, aged seven years

Whoso ear chance for to behould this tombe
Shal see a flower blasted in hir bloom
For all are like to flowers grasse or hay
That this houre springs next dies & fades awaye
Even so this maid whos tender youth might have
Lived longer heare & not possesst hir grave
So soone but God that knoweth best
What is for us did take hir soul to rest
And whilst hir corps intierd awhile doth sleep
This marble tomb obsequious tears shal weepe
Then let this tombe to all be as a merror
To tel us life is but breath to trust it error.

212 *In the church at St Ives, Huntingdonshire*

In memory of Elizabeth, Joseph, Phœbe and
Mary Townsend, who died in their infancy.

Bold infidelity, turn pale and die!
Beneath this stone three infant ashes lie,
Say—are they lost or saved?
If death's by sin they sinned because they're here,

If heaven's by works, in heaven they can't appear,
Reason—ah! how depraved!
Review the Bible's sacred page, the knot's untied
They died, for Adam sinned—they live, for Jesus died.

213 (i) *Hadleigh, Suffolk; for Roland Taylor, the rector, burnt on*
Aldham Common in 1555; (ii) is recorded as an inscription
on the common; compare (iii) on other East Anglian Marian
martyrs

(i)   Gloria in altissimis Deo.

Of Rowland Taillor's fame I shewe
    An excellent devyne
And Doctor of the civill lawe
    A preacher rare and fyne.

Kinge Henry and Kinge Edward's dayes
    Preacher and Parson here
That gave to God contynuall prayse
    And kept his flocke in feare.

And for the truthe condempned to die
    He was in fierye flame
Where he received pacyentlie
    The torment of the same.

And strongely suffred to thende
    Whiche made the standers by
Reioice in God to see their frende
    And pastor so to Dye.

Oh, Taillor were this myghtie fame
    Uprightly here inrolde
Thie deedes deserve that thie good name
    Were siphered here in gold.

(ii)   1555
            D. TAYLER · IN DE
        FENDING · THAT WASGOOD
            AT THIS PLAS LEFT
                HIS BLODE.

(iii)   When William Allen at Walsingham
         For trueth was tried in fiery flame;
         When Roger Cooe, that good olde man,
         Did lose his lyfe for Christe's name;
         When these *with other* were put to death,
         We wishte for our Elizabeth.

214   *Epitaph for John Warren, builder, who died during the*
      rebuilding of the tower of Great St Mary's Church,
      Cambridge, in 1608

                A speaking stone
             Reason may chaunce to blame;
                  But did it knowe
             Those ashes here do lie
                  Which brought the Stones
             That hid the Steeple's shame,
                  It would affirm
             There were no Reason why
                  Stones should not speake
             Before theyr Builder die.
                  For here John Warren
             Sleeps among the dead
                  Who with the Church
             His own Life finished.

215   *Verses inscribed on a ringers' pitcher (it held sixteen quarts);*
      Hinderclay, Suffolk

             From London I was sent,
             As plainly doth appear;
             It was with this intent,
             To be filled with strong beer.

           Pray remember the pitcher when empty.

216   *Ely Cathedral; a monument in the south porch*

                In memory of
             WILLIAM PICKERING,
           who died Decr 24. 1845
              aged 30 years

also Richard Edger
who died Decr 24. 1845
aged 24 years.

The Spiritual Railway

The Line to heaven by Christ was made
With heavenly truth the Rails are laid,
From Earth to Heaven the Line extends.
To Life Eternal where it ends

Repentance is the Station then
Where Passengers are taken in,
No Fee for them is there to pay
For Jesus is himself the way

God's Word is the first Engineer
It points the way to Heaven so dear,
Through tunnels dark and dreary here
It does the way to Glory steer.

God's Love the Fire, his Truth the Steam,
Which drives the Engine and the Train,
All you who would to Glory ride,
Must come to Christ, in him abide

In First and Second, and Third Class,
Repentance, Faith and Holiness,
You must the way to Glory gain
Or you with Christ will not remain

Come then poor Sinners, now's the time
At any Station on the Line.
If you'll repent and turn from sin
The Train will stop and take you in.

217 *In Hessle cemetery, Hull; for William Harrison, mariner*

Long time I ploughed the ocean wide,
   A life of toil I spent;
But now in harbour safe arrived
   From care and discontent.
My anchor's cast, my sails are furled,
   And now I am at rest;

Of all the ports throughout the world,
Sailors, this is the best.

218   *William Cowper (1731–1800); at Weston Underwood*
church, Buckinghamshire

Here lies one who never drew
Blood himself, yet many slew.
Gave the gun its aim, and figure
Made in field, yet ne'er pulled trigger.
Armed men have gladly made
Him their guide, and him obeyed.
At his signified desire
Would advance, present, and fire.
Stout he was and large of limb,
Scores have fled at sight of him.
And to all this fame he rose,
By only following his nose.
Neptune was he called, not he
Who controls the boist'rous sea,
But of happier command
Neptune of the furrowed land.
And your wonder, vain, to shorten,
Pointer to Sir John Throckmorton.

219   *In the village church at Colkirk, Norfolk (formerly in the*
now ruined church in the nearby hamlet of Oxwick); for
Samuel Smithe, d. 1663

Samuel Smithe
Anagr.

SEE HIM: All must;
SEE HIM in Dust,
Then think: All must.

SEE HIM, A man, A son of Adam's Race,
Compos'd of Earth, & of a Soule Divine,
But now that Soule flown to a higher place,
Has left its dust enclosed in this Shrine.
Then Reader; read thy selfe & say All must.
Thine Hower glasse is measur'd by his Dust.
SEE HIM, A strong man, who so healthfull was,

As if Dame Nature purposely contriv'd
A peece for lasting, but we see, Alas,
No constitution proves a man long liv'd:
For to Death's might Jawes 'tis all but one
The softest Gristle, or the hardest bone.
SEE HIM, A Rich man, who in wealth did flow
As if Pactolus flow'd into his Chest;
But when Death comes to strike the fatall blow
No golden bribes can buy off the Arrest.
Heav'ns Lawes forbid; for to Attempt to buy
The gift of breathing is flat Simony.
SEE HIM, A learned man, in whom the Arts
Erected had an University:
His industry well matched with strong parts
Had deeply div'd i' th' muses treasury.
Now nought remaines, unles perchance a Verse
Hang, as a feeble relique, on his herse.
SEE HIM, a great Logician, who the knotts,
And fallacyes so throughly understood,
Perplexing questions, & ensnaring Plotts,
With Syllogismes in figure and in Mood:
But Death defeats all Logick Subtilty;
For none must the Conclusion deny.
SEE HIM, a Lawyer whose both Tongue & Head
Deep Judgement had, and pleasing fluency;
But when Death comes it is in vain to plead,
For still the issue is that all must dye.
Nor wonder if that Lawyers mortall are;
Death's Office is to call men to the Barr.
SEE HIM an able Statesman who the Art
And Rules of Policy exactly knew,
But when the fatall Archer throws his dart,
Then man & all his thoughts must perish too.
Ransack the Tombes, & see if thou canst tell,
'Mongst many Skulls, which was Achitophel?
SEE HIM, a Saint, 'mongst whose bright Ornaments
Religion was still the Crown and flowre,
No wonder then that he is flown from hence,
For Sparkes fly upwards. Reader, say no more:
For no man to the life the fire can paint,
No more the picture of a glorious Saint.

Pactolus (long o)] river in Asia Minor supposed to carry gold in its sands
logick] logical   issue] outcome

220 *A village girls' May-Day song, Hertfordshire*

> The first of May has come again,
>   The best time of the year,
> And we have all come round once more
>   To taste of your strong beer;
>
> If you have not got any strong
>   We'll be content with small;
> We'll take the cup and drink it up,
>   And thank the Lord for all!
>
> O a garland, a garland, a very pretty garland,
>   As ever you wish to see
> It's fit for the Queen Victoria,
>   So please remember me.
>
> Awake, awake, good people all,
>   Awake and you shall hear
> How Christ the Saviour died for us,
>   Who lovéd us so dear.
>
> So dear, so dear, has Christ lovéd us,
>   And for our sins was slain,
> We had better leave off our wickedness
>   And turn to the Lord again.
>
> Goodbye, goodbye, I must be gone,
>   I can no longer stay;
> God bless you all, both great and small,
>   And send you a joyful May.

221 *A Suffolk children's game song*

> Golden apple, lemon and a pear,
> Bunch of roses she shall wear,
> Golden and silver by her side,
> I know who shall be her bride.
> Take her by the lily white hand,
> Lead her cross the water,
> Give her kisses one, two, three,
> Mrs. Gilburn's daughter.

Now you're married, I wish you joy,
Father and mother you must obey,
Love one another like sister and brother,
And now's the time to kiss away.

222 *Children's lace-making songs or 'tells' (counting-rhymes); (i)*
from Renhold, Bedfordshire; (ii) from Yardley Hastings,
Northamptonshire; (iii) on the Mr Fox legend, from
Bedfordshire (see the notes)

(i)   Needle pin, needle pin, stitch upon stitch,
Work the old lady out of the ditch.
If she is not out as soon as I,
A rap on the knuckles shall come by and by.
A horse to carry my lady about—
Must not look off till twenty are out.

*

Hang her up for half an hour,
Cut her down just like a flower.

(ii)   Twenty pins have I to do,
Let ways be ever so dirty.
Never a penny in my purse,
But farthings five and thirty.

Betsy Bays and Polly Mays,
They are two bonny lasses;
They built a bower upon the tower,
And covered it with rushes.

(iii)   The Fox

Nineteen miles as I sat high
Looking for one, and two passed by,
I saw them that never saw me—
I saw the lantern tied to a tree.

The boughs did bend and the leaves did shake
I saw the hole the Fox did make.
The Fox did look, the Fox did see
I saw the hole to bury me.

223 *An account of Harwich (said to have been printed in the* Essex Review, *but 'they exist only in Ms., and have been attributed to Theodor Hook', 1788–1841)*

> Old Harwich stands
> Upon two strands
>   Between the sea and Stour:
> Its round redoubt
> Might keep rogues out
>   If it had but a better door.
>
> The harbour's view
> Is fine, 'tis true,
>   If you knew but where it lay.
> For the houses are placed
> With such excellent taste
>   That they all look the other way.
>
> From filthy slips
> You may see the ships,
>   We counted just thirteen:
> Two in the flood,
> Five in the mud,
>   And six in quarantine.
>
> From Mistley Hall
> 'Tis what they call
>   About ten miles in a Carriage.
> But as long as I may
> At Mistley stay
>   Be hang'd if I go to Harwich.

224 *A 'Musick Speech' composed by Dr Roger Long, and delivered by him to the University assembled in Great St Mary's Church, Cambridge, in 1714*

The *humble Petition* of the Ladies, who are all ready to be eaten up
  with the Spleen,
To think they are to be lock'd up in the Chancel, where they can
  neither see nor be seen;
But must sit i' the Dumps by themselves all stew'd and pent up,
And can only peep through the Lattice like so many Chickens in a
  Coop;

Whereas last Commencement the Ladies had a Gallery provided
   near enough
To see the Heads sleep, and the Fellow-Commoners take Snuff.
'Tis true for every Particular how 'twas order'd then we can't so
   certainly know,
Because none of us can remember so long as Sixteen Years ago;
Yet we believe they were more civil to the Ladies then, and good
   Reason why,
For if we all stay'd at home your Commencement wou'dn't be
   worth a Fly:
For at *Oxford* last Year this is certainly Matter of Fact,
That the Sight of the Ladies and the Music made the best Part of
   their Act.
Now you should consider some of us have been at a very great
   Expence
To rig our selves out, in order to see the Doctors commence:
We've been forc'd with our Manteau-makers to hold many a
   Consultation,
To know whether Mourning or Colours wou'd be most like to be in
   Fashion:
We've sent to Town to know what Kind of Heads and Ruffles the
   Ladies wore,
And have rais'd the Price of Whalebone higher than 'twas before;
We've got Intelligence from Church, the Park, the Front-box and
   the Ring,
And to grace *St Mary's* now wou'dn't make our Cloaths up in the
   Spring.
In Flounces and Furbelows many Experiments have been try'd,
And many an old Gown and Petticoat new scour'd and dy'd.
Some of us for these three Months have scarce been able to rest,
For studying what sort of Complexion wou'd become us best;
And several of us have almost pinch'd our selves to Death with
   going straight lac'd,
That we might look fuller in the Chest, and more slender in the
   Waste.
And isn't it now intolerable after all this Pains and Cost
To be coop'd up out of Sight, and have all our Finery lost?

225   *Epigrams on George I's gift of books to the University of*
       Cambridge; he also sent cavalry troops to Oxford

(i)   King George observing, with judicious eyes,
        The state of both his Universities,
        To Oxford sent a troop of horse; and why?

That learned body wanted loyalty.
To Cambridge books he sent, as well discerning
How much that loyal body wanted learning.

(ii)   The King to Oxford sent a troop of horse,
For Tories own no argument but force;
With equal skill to Cambridge books he sent,
For Whigs admit no force but argument.

226 *An epigram on Hinchcliff, master of Trinity, who put a bad
singer into the College choir, because he had a vote for
Peterborough (where Hinchcliff was also bishop); by Lort
Mansel, later master of Trinity College*

'A singing-man and yet not sing!
   How justify your patron's bounty?'
'Forgive me; you mistake the thing:
   My voice is in another county!'

227 *An epigram on the marriage of the master of Corpus Christi
College, Cambridge (bride and bridegroom were both very
thin); by Lort Mansel*

Saint Paul has declared, that persons though twain
In marriage united one flesh shall remain;
But had he been by when, like Pharaoh's kine pairing,
Dr. Douglas of Benet espoused Miss Mainwaring,
The Apostle, methinks, would have altered his tone,
And cried, These two splinters shall make but one bone!

228 *A Suffolk song*

There wus a man lived in the West,
   Limbo clashmo!
There wus a man lived in the West,
He married the wuman that he liked best,
With a ricararo, ricararo, milk in the morn
   O' dary mingo.

He married this wuman and browt her hom,
    Limbo clashmo!
He married this wuman and browt her hom,
  And set her in his best parlour rom,
With a ricararo, ricararo, milk in the morn
    O' dary mingo.

My man and I went to the fowd,
    Limbo clashmo!
My man and I went to the fowd,
  And ketcht the finest wuther that we could howd,
With a ricararo, ricararo, milk in the morn
    O' dary mingo.

We fleed this wuther and browt him hom,
    Limbo, clashmo!
We fleed this wuther and browt him hom,
  Sez I, Wife, now youar begun yar doon,
With a ricararo, ricararo, milk in the morn
    O' dary mingo.

I laid this skin on my wife's back,
    Limbo clashmo!
I laid this skin on my wife's back,
  And on to it I then did swack,
With a ricararo, ricararo, milk in the morn
    O' dary mingo.

I 'inted har with ashen ile,
    Limbo clashmo!
I 'inted har with ashen ile,
  Till she could both brew, bake, wash and bile,
With a ricararo, ricararo, milk in the morn
    O' dary mingo—mingo.

229   *A ballad against the early evictions to clear land for*
       sheep-ranching, known in East Anglia

    The blacke shepe is a perylous beast
    Cuius contrarium falsum est.

---

228 fowd] fold   fleed] flayed   'inted] anointed

The leon of lyme ys large and long.
The beare to fyght is stowte and strong,
But off all beastes that go or crepe
The myghtiest ys the horned shepe.

The shepe ys off a monstrous myght
What thyng soever his hornes on lyght
He bearyth down bothe castell and towre;
None is him licke in marciall powre.

Syx hundred horseys with cart and plough
I have earst knowen where nowght ys now
But grene moll-hilles, they are layde playne,
This cruell beast over all dothe raygne.

This shepe he is a wycked wight
Man, woman and childe he deuowreth quite,
No hold, no howse can him wythstande
He swaloweth up both sea and lande.

Men were wont ones off shepe to fede
Shepe now eate men on dowtfull dede;
This woolwysshe shepe, this rampyng beast
Consumeth all thorow west and est.

Halfe Englande ys nowght now but shepe
In every corner they playe boe-pepe;
Lorde, them confounde by twentye and ten
And fyll their places with cristen men.

230 *A harvest song from north Lincolnshire*

Ohd woman, ohd woman,
  Thoo mun goä shearin';
Noä, maister, noä,
  For I'm dull o' hearin'.

Ohd woman, ohd woman,
  Thoo mun shear or thoo mun bind;
Noä, maister, noä,
  For, you see, I'm stoän blind.

dowtfull] dreadful   woolwysshe] wolvish

230 shearin'] reaping with a sickle

Ohd woman, ohd woman,
   Then thoo mun goä beg;
Noä, maister, noä,
   For I'm laame o' my leg.

231   *A Suffolk dairy song*

He.   If you with me will go, my love,
            You shall see a pretty show, my love,
              Let dame say what she will;
            And if you will have me, my love,
            I will have thee, my love,
              So let the milk pail stand still.

She.   Since you have said so, my love,
            Longer I will go, my love,
              Let dame say what she will;
            If you will have me, my love,
            I will have thee, my love,
              So let the milk pail stand still.

232   *Verses on the 'low Fen-man' by 'Fen Bill Hall', d. at Lynn,*
     1825

Born in a coy, and bred in a mill,
Taught water to grind, and Ducks for to kill;
Seeing coots clapper claw, lying flat on their backs
Standing upright to row, and crowning of jacks;
Laying spring nets for to catch ruff and reeve,
Stretched out in a boat with a shade to deceive.

Taking geese, ducks, and coots, with nets upon stakes,
Riding in a calm day for to catch moulted drakes;
Gathering eggs to the top of one's wish,
Cutting tracks in the flags for decoying of fish.
Seeing rudds run in shoals 'bout the side of Gill sike,
Being dreadfully venom'd by rolling in slake;
Looking hingles and sprinks, trammels, hoop-nets and teamings,
Few persons I think can explain all their meanings.

---

232 coy] a decoy, a hide   clapper claw] fight   crowning of jacks] ?killing
pike   slake] ?slike, mud

233   *A ballad by Alfred Hutchinson ('Hurricane Hutch'), a Grimsby skipper, about the wreck of the Grimsby trawler* Howe, *on 19 November 1931*

The Wreck of the *Howe*

One night on the rocks off Bear Island
   A trawler named the *Howe* ran ashore,
Right on those cursed hidden 'blinders',
   To remain there a wreck evermore.
No tugs in the world could have saved her
   But one went his luck there to try
And found her a wreck that was hopeless,
   To leave her laid there, high and dry.

Her Skipper was a man named McGregor,
   As brave as the brave known to be,
He said: 'Now she's a wreck, boys, for ever,
   But you'll still take your orders from me.
Your Lives all depend on good discipline,
   So be cheerful and keep a big heart.
For the sake of your wives and your families
   Each of you must play your part.'

But out in that dark Arctic region
   Just imagine the dire plight of the crew,
With their ship on the rocks of Bear Island
   There was nothing on earth they could do.
Their 'Sparks' was a brave lad of twenty,
   His message for help he had sent.
Thank God it was answered by plenty,
   And bravely to her aid they went.

They found her a wreck at the mercy
   Of a sea that no pen can describe.
They couldn't get anywhere near her
   Yet times out of number they tried.
On the deck they could see the poor fellows standing,
   And who would deny they were brave,
Facing their deaths, calm and steadfast,
   On the brink of a sailor's grave.

blinders] submerged rocks   Bear Island] island *c.*200 miles south of Spitz-bergen   Sparks] radio operator

So round to the lee of the Island,
    Each vessel sent picked men ashore
To battle across Land that was barren
    And untrodden by human foot before.
And God only knows what hardships,
    They faced on that bleak winter night,
Hands, faces, feet were frost-bitten
    But they struggled on without sup or bite.

On the *Howe*, to that brave seaman, Harper,
    A rope round his body they tied,
To swim to a point that meant rescue.
    He failed, but I praise him, he tried.
He was pulled back on board by his comrades,
    And there on that wreck he Lay 'beat',
But a hero, if ever there was one,
    The whitest of men you could meet.

Still high on those rocks up above them,
    With courage, those men struggled on,
Till they found them, and brought off the rescue,
    They saved the whole crew, everyone.
Those Lads were brought back to Grimsby,
    And to see them again—it was grand!
We know not one half what they suffered,
    But we kid them that we understand.

We thank you, brave men, for that rescue,
    Your deed was truly gallant—well done!
It may not have gone down to history,
    It is even forgotten by some.
But I myself, a fisherman—
    Will remember to my dying day,
And no gold in the world could repay you,
    Had they called it a job for pay.

And a word for you that were rescued,
    For some of you are well known to me.
No words could I write that could praise you enough,
    For your conduct, so gallant at sea.
You held up that fine British tradition,
    You sent up its prestige, sky high,
Those grim nights on the rocks at Bear Island,
    Where in silence you were prepared to die.

Well, that is the life of the fisher
   As told in this tale of the sea,
Lives are so often the price
   Of that fish you have eaten for tea.
But seldom you'll hear these men grumble,
   It's come day, or go day with them.
Just trusting to God in his mercy,
   And thank Him for that—Amen!

234   *'A Ballad in Memory of the Fishermen from Hull and*
      Grimsby who lost their lives in the Gale of 8 and 9
      February 1889'; by W. Delf, a Grimsby fisherman

Methinks I see some little crafts spreading their sails a-lee
As down the Humber they did glide bound in the Northern sea,
Methinks I see on each small craft a crew with hearts so brave,
Going to earn their daily bread upon the restless wave.

Methinks I see them as they left the land all far behind,
Casting the lead into the deep their fishing grounds to find;
Methinks I see them on the deck working with a will,
To shoot their net into the deep either for good or ill.

Methinks I see them shoot their trawl upon the Thursday night,
And saw the watch upon the deck, and everything was right;
Methinks I see them yet again when daylight did appear,
All hands working with a will getting off their gear.

Methinks I see the net on board and fish so fresh and gay,
And all were busily engaged clearing them away;
Methinks I see them put away into the ice below,
And then the sea began to rise, and the wind did stronger blow.

Methinks I heard the skipper say, 'My lads, we'll shorten sail,
As the sky to all appearance looks like an approaching gale';
Methinks I see them yet again, and all on board was right,
With sails close reef'd, the deck cleared up, and sidelights burning
   bright.

Methinks I see them yet again, the midnight hour was passed,
Their little craft was battling there with the fiery blast;
Methinks I heard the skipper say, 'Cheer up, my lads, be brave,
We'll trust in Him who rules the deep, in Him who alone can save.'

Methinks I read the thoughts of them who now are called away,
They were thinking of their loved ones dear many miles away;
Thinking of wife and children dear, and aged parents too
Who no more will see them here again in this world below.

Great God, Thou sees each sorrowing heart, the widow in distress,
Thou knows the little children dear, who now are fatherless;
Comfort and cheer them here below, and lead them by Thy hand,
And at last may they meet with their loved ones dear in the
   promised land.

235   *A fishermen's song; Mundesley, Norfolk*

> Pray God lead us;
> Pray God speed us;
> From all evil defend us.
> Fish for our pains God send us.
> Well to fish and well to haul,
> And what He pleases to pay us all.
> A fine night to land our nets,
> And safe in with the land.
> Pray God, hear my prayer.

236   *A poem to the Grimsby Town football team, for the Cup*
      Competition, 1936

> Here's wishing luck to Grimsby Town
>   In their effort to attain
> The greatest honour and renown
>   In England's national game.
>
> Hartlepool, Port Vale and then
>   Manchester they had beat,
> Middlesbrough came to stem
>   Their tide, but met defeat.
>
> No fancy price has Grimsby paid
>   For any of their players,
> But classic teams have been dismayed
>   By our ninety-minute stayers.

So, when these Arsenal cracks, you play,
    Just give the crowd a treat,
Show 'em you're as good as they—
    You simply can't be beat.

There's thousands saving up with zest
    To swell that great assembly
And add their voices to the rest
    The day you play at Wembley!

Then all the critics you'll confound—
    Of this they dare not dream—
That in the Final would be found
    An 'unfashionable' team.

To Bestall and his gallant men
    The very best we'll sup,
For, as certain as these words I pen,
    You're going to win the Cup.

237   *Agricultural customs, (i) in 1800, (ii) in 1900; Lincolnshire*

(i)
        Farmer at the plough,
        Wife milking cow
        Daughter spinning yarn,
        Son threshing in the barn,
        All happy to a charm.

(ii)
        Father gone to see the show,
        Daughter at the pian-o
        Madame gaily dressed in satin,
        All the boys learning Latin,
        With a mortgage on the farm.

238   *A charm against illnesses in general; Cambridgeshire*
       Fenlands

        Make a black cat spit on mutton fat
        Then rub it inside a horse's hat.
        Scrape it off within a week
        Then go outside a toad to seek
        And make it sweat into a pot.

With wooden spoon mix the lot,
And you will have a healing balm
To keep the body free from harm.

239   *A charm for cutting an elder tree; Lincolnshire*

Owd gal, gi' me of thi wood,
An' I will gi' thee some of mine
When I grow into a tree.

240   *A verse for sowing wheat; (?) Norfolk*

When the weirling shrieks at night,
Sow the seed with the morning light;
But 'ware when the cuckoo swells its throat,
Harvest flies from the mooncall's throat.

241   *A verse from Essex*

The robin and the redbreast,
   The robin and the wren,
If ye take out of their nests,
   Ye'll never thrive again;
The robin and the redbreast,
   The martin and the swallow,
If ye touch one of their eggs,
   Bad luck will sure to follow.

242   *A Suffolk shoe-rhyme*

Trip at the toe,
Live to see woe;
Wear at the side,
Live to be a bride;
Wear at the ball,
Live to spend all;
Wear at the heel,
Live to spend a deal.

---

240 weirling] shrike   mooncall] ?cuckoo, or nightingale

243   *A Suffolk harvest-home song*

Here's a health unto our master,
   The founder of the feast!
I wish, with all my heart and soul,
   In heaven he may find rest.
I hope all things may prosper,
   That ever he takes in hand;
For we are all his servants,
   And all at his command.
Drink, boys, drink, and see you do not spill,
For if you do, you must drink two,—it is your master's will.

Now our harvest is ended,
   And supper is past;
Here's our mistress' good health,
   In a full flowing glass!
She is a good woman,—
   She prepared us good cheer;
Come, all my brave boys,
   And drink off your beer.
Drink, my boys, drink till you come unto me,
The longer we sit, my boys, the merrier shall we be!

In yon green wood there lies an old fox,
Close by his den you may catch him, or no;
Ten thousand to one you catch him, or no.
His beard and his brush are all of one colour,—
                    (Takes the glass and empties it off.)
I am sorry, kind sir, that your glass is no fuller.
'Tis down the red lane! 'tis down the red lane!
So merrily hunt the fox down the red lane.

244   *A nineteenth-century 'village rhyme' on the weather;*
      Bedfordshire

'Well, Duncombe, how will be the weather?'
'Sir, it looks cloudy altogether;
And coming across our Houghton Green,
I stopped and talked with old Frank Beane
While we stood there, sir, old Jan Swain
Went by, and said he knowed 'twould rain;

The next that came was Master Hunt,
And he declared he knew it wouldn't;
And then I met with Farmer Blow—
He plainly said he didn't know.
So, sir, when doctors disagree,
Who's to decide it—you or me?'

245   *A local rhyme, once known around Boston, Lincolnshire*

Boston Boston Boston!
Thou hast nought to boast on
But a grand sluice, and a high steeple,
And a proud conceited ignorant people,
And a coast which souls get lost on.

246   *A rhyme from Lincolnshire*

Sad is the burying in the sunshine,
But bless'd is the corpse that goeth home in rain.

V

THE MIDLANDS

247 *On a chimney-piece in the 'Giant's Room', Chatsworth, Derbyshire*

> A founting Stagge the water brooke desireth,
> Even so my soule the lyvinge Lorde requireth.

248 *Verses said to have been written by Princess (later Queen) Elizabeth, on a shutter in the room where she was confined, in the old manor at Woodstock*

> Oh Fortune! How thy restless wavering state
> Hath fraught with cares my troubled witt,
> Witness this present prison; whither fate
> Could beare me, and the joys I quit.
> Thou causedst the guiltie to be losed
> From bands wherein are innocents inclosed;
> Causing the guiltles to be straite[s] reserved,
> And freeing those that death well deserved:
> But by her envie can be nothing wroughte;
> So God send to my foes all they have thoughte.

> Anno Dom; 1555.   Elizabeth Prisoner

249 *Epitaph for Thomas Mannaley, stabbed, near the Town Hall at Bromsgrove, Worcestershire, 3 May 1819*

> Beneath this stone lie the remains,
> Who in Bromsgrove street was slain,
> A currier with his knife did the deed,
> And left me in the street to bleed;
> But when archangel's trump shall sound,
> And souls to bodies join—that murderer
> I hope will see my soul in heaven shine.

250 *Verses affixed to the inn at Collins Green, Oxfordshire*

> Stop, traveller—stop: within this peaceful shade
> His favourite game the Royal Martyr play'd;

247 founting] ?fainting

145

Deprived of honours, fortune, friends and rank,
Drank from the bowl, and bowl'd for what he drank;
Sought in a cheerful glass his cares to drown,
And chang'd a guinea, ere he lost a crown.

251   *In the Visitors' Book, Stratford-upon-Avon, Warwickshire,*
1810 (in 1793, at the suggestion of Edmond Malone, the
bust of Shakespeare had been whitewashed)

Stranger to whom this monument is shewn,
Invoke the Poet's curse upon Malone
Whose meddling zeal his barbarous taste betrays
And smears his tombstone as he marr'd his plays.

252   *A verse recipe for Christmas pudding, in the parish records,*
Longstone, Derbyshire (before 1871)

T'Crismas Puddin

If you wish ta ma'e a puddin e which ivvery won delights,
Ov a duzzen new leyd eggs, yo mun ta'e th' yokes an whites;
Beat em well up in a bason till thay throrly comboine,
An shred an chop sum suit up partickelarly foine.

Ta'e a paand a well stoaned reasins, an a paand a currans
   dried,
A paand a paanded sugar, an a paand a peel beside;
Stir em aw well up together, wi a paand a wheaten flaar,
An let em stond ta sattle fur a quarter ov an haar.

Then tee t'puddin in a cloth, an put it intu't 'pot—
Sum foaks loike t'watter cowd, an sum prefer it hot—
Bur tho ah dunno which a theese tow methods a shud preise,
Ah know it owt to boil an haar fur ivvery paand it weighs.

Wen t'puddins ta'en aat at pot, an put on ter a dish, caw t'childer, an
let em march befoar it az its carried intu't sittin rowm, wi little flags e ther
honds, to stick intow it wen its placed on't table. Yo might larn em ta
shaat aat t'loines, or to sing em.

253   *Samuel Butler (1612–80); lines from his poem 'Hudibras'*
      on a Staffordshire figure of Hudibras drawing his sword

> The trenchant blade, Toledo trusty,
> For want of fighting was grown rusty,
> And ate into itself, for lack
> Of some body to hew and hack.

254   *Tablet over the main entrance, Jesus' Hospital, Rothwell,*
      Northamptonshire

> God Bless our Governors prolong their days
> who plac'd us here to render Heaven our prayers
> To live contented, private and resigned
> Free from life's toils and humours of Mankind
> Pleased with wise Agurs Mediocrity
> Too low for envy for Contempt too high
> What we now have we thankfully possess
> Till we exchange for greater happiness

> > Henry Dormer Principal
> > 1721.

255   *On the gable of the inn at Ford, Oxfordshire*

> Ye weary travellers that pass by,
> With dust and scorching sunbeams dry
> Or be-numbed with snow and frost
> With having these bleak Cotswolds crosst,
> Step in and quaff my nut-brown ale
> Bright as rubys mild and stale,
> Twill make your laging trotters dance
> As nimble as the suns of France,
> Then ye will own ye men of sense
> That neare was better spent six pence.

> > **254** prayers] ?praise   Agurs] ?Age's
> > **255** stale] old, well-matured

256 *Verses worked on a tapestry map made near Barcheston,*
      Warwickshire, and showing the Thames Valley

This worke thus wrought with curious hand and rare invented arte
In stately vewe Glocestersheire describes in every parte
When Saxons heare posseste the raigne Gleavecester they it name
And Britons it Kaer Glowye call and yf you liste the same
In native tonge to knowe arighte thus muche it is to saye
A citie fayer soe cald of eld whos bewtie to this day
Right wel commendes the britishe name this sheire whos fertill soyle
Of corn and grayne greate plentie yelds by labors gaynfull toyle
In threefold partes devided is on easte doth Cotteswold stand
Moste fertill hilles for sheep and w . . . yre not in this land.

257 *Verses worked on a tapestry map of Warwickshire,*
      Gloucestershire, and Herefordshire

On this side which the Sonne doth warme, With his declininge
      beames,
Severn and Teme in channels deepe, Doo run too ancient stremes,
Thes make the neibors pasture riche, Thes veld of fruit great store,
And do convay thro'out the shire, Commoditis many more.

*

Heare hills doo lift their heads aloft, From whence sweet springs
      doo flow,
Whose moistur good doth firtil make, The valleis couch belowe.
Hear goodly orchards planted are, In fruite which doo abounde,
Thine ey wold make thin harte rejoyce, To see so pleasant grounde.

258 *On a weathercock; Olney, Buckinghamshire*

> I never crow, but stand to show
> Whence winds do blow.   1829.

259 *On the clock-tower at Emberton, Buckinghamshire*

> Time's on the wing, how swiftly he speeds his way,
> Hast'ning to sink in one continuous day—
> Pause, passing trav'ler—what thy destiny

257 veld] ?'yeld', yield

When death unveils a vast eternity?
Live then in Christ—in Christ eternal gain,
No Christ—no hope but everlasting pain!

260   *On a house in Solihull, Warwickshire*

> Luke Bull lives here,
> He'll sweep your chimney very clear.
> With his brush, sweeper, and machine
> He'll make your chimney very clean.
> And if it ever should take fire,
> He'll put it out, at your desire.

261   *A verse at the entrance to the old manor house, Grafton,*
near Bromsgrove, Worcestershire

> Plenti and grase
> Bi in this place.

> While every man is pleased in his degree,
> There is both peace and uniti.
> Solomon saith there is none accord,
> When every man would be a lord.

262   *A verse on the toll-gate keeper near Hartlebury,*
Worcestershire (d. 1825), who insisted on taking the usual
toll on an occasion when the king passed through

> On Wednesday last old Robert Sleath,
> Passed through the turnpike gate of Death;
> To him Death would no toll abate,
> Who stopped the King at Worcester gate.

263   *(i) in the parish registers at Everton, Nottinghamshire;*
compare (ii) in the parish register at St Mary's Church,
Hornsea, Yorkshire

(i)

> Advent marriage doth deny,
> But Hilary gives thee liberty;
> Septuagesima says thee Nay,

Eight days from Easter says you may;
Rogation bids thee to contain,
But Trinity sets thee free again.

(ii) When Advent comes do thou refraine
till Hillary set ye free againe
next Septuagesima saith thee nay
but when Lowe Sunday comes thou may
yet at Rogation thou must tarrie
till Trinitie shall bid thee marry.

264 *Inscriptions on the bells at Bakewell, Derbyshire*

1. When I begin our merry Din
This Band I lead from discord free;
And for the fame of human name,
May every Leader copy Me.

2. Mankind, like us, too oft are found
Possess'd of nought but empty sound.

3. When of departed Hours we toll the knell,
Instruction take and spend the future well.

4. When men in Hymen's Bands unite,
Our merry peals produce delight;
But when Death goes his dreary Rounds,
We send forth sad and solemn sounds.

5. Thro' grandsires and Tripples with pleasure men range,
Till Death calls the Bob and brings on the Last Change.

6. When Vict'ry crowns the Public Weeal
With Glee we give the merry Peal.

7. Would men like us join and agree
They'd live in tuneful Harmony.

8. Possess'd of deep sonorous Tone
This Belfry King sits on his throne;
And when the merry Bells go round,
Adds to and mellows ev'ry Sound;

So in a just and well pois'd State,
Where all Degrees possess due Weight,
One greater Pow'r one greater Tone
Is ceded to improve their own.

265   *Bell inscriptions at St Helen's Church, Worcester (all dated 1706 except 7, dated 1712)*

1. *Blenheim.*   First is my note, and Blenheim is my name;
For Blenheim's story will be first in fame.

2. *Barcelona.*   Let me relate how Louis did bemoan
His grandson Philip's flight from Barcelon.

3. *Ramilies.*   Deluged in blood, I, Ramilies, advance
Britannia's glory on the fall of France.

4. *Menin.*   Let Menin on my sides engraven be;
And Flanders freed from Gallic slavery.

5. *Turin.*   When in harmonious peal I roundly go,
Think on Turin, and triumphs on the Po.

6. *Eugene.*   With joy I hear illustrious Eugene's name;
Fav'rite of fortune and the boast of fame.

7. *Marlborough.*   But I for pride, the greater Marlborough bear;
Terror of tyrants, and the soul of war.

8. *Queen Anne.*   The immortal praises of queen Anne I sound,
With union blest, and all these glories crowned.

266   *'A Song on the Famous Peal of 7308 Grandsire Cators Rung by the Society of All Saints Ringers, in Worcester, On the 28th of November, 1774'*

Ye lovers of ringing now give your attention
Unto these few words which my song it will mention:
It is of Seven Thousand Three Hundred and Eight,
By the Youths of All Saints that was rung quite compleat:
In the year Seventy-four, now remark what I say,

In the month of November, the twenty-eighth day,
This peal was compleated, which was to the fame
Of the Youths of All Saints, who shall still bear the name.

RICHARD PAINE to the treble, I speak in his praise,
That I ne'er heard a bell better rang in my days;
For over the large bells he struck her quite clear,
And his compass at lead kept as true as a hair:
THOMAS HILL he the Second did steadily ring,
And in the Tittoms she sweetly did sing;
Though some seem to sneer at his prophetic dream,
Yet the Youths of All Saints they shall still bear the name.

JOSEPH STONE to the Third, he kept her stiff in hand,
And just at his own pleasure did her command;
He cut her in compass, and tuck'd her so tight,
Through the whole Seven Thousand Three Hundred and Eight:
THOMAS SPINNER the Fourth, for a solid hand's he,
And in ringing a length he rings quite steadily;
He marks his course bell, and sticks close to the same,
And the Youths of All Saints they shall still bear the name.

GEORGE ROE to the Fifth he did cheerfully stand,
And he struck her right well, both at back stroke and hand;
'There's beauty!' he cry'd, and so smooth did he pull,
And smiled when the large bells at home they did roll:
At the Sixth RICHARD HERBERT, he looked quite sharp,
And ne'er was observ'd in his course once to warp;
For to finish the peal, Sir, it was his whole aim,
And the Youths of All Saints they shall still bear the name.

WILLIAM KENDAL the Seventh, so smart a young lad,
Did call the peal true, and he made each heart glad;
The Changes he plac'd in the Tittoms so tight,
And he told out just Fifty Times Nine, Seven, Eight:
JOHN BRISTOW, the Eighth, rang so solid and clear,
That no fault was discern'd by the most curious ear;
All his thoughts at that time he to ringing did frame,
And the Youths of All Saints they shall still bear the name.

To the Ninth THOMAS BARKER stood sturdy and stout,
And with hearty good-will he did swing her about;
Right boldly and bravely he stuck to her tough,
And he ne'er once faulter'd, or said he had enough:

Tittoms] a kind of peal

To the Tenor GEORGE WAINWRIGHT stood like heart of oak,
And to this famous peal gave the finishing stroke;
When the clapper came out, which just answer'd the dream!
And the Youths of All Saints they shall still bear the name.

Four Hours and a Half and Six Minutes they were,
The people with watches in hands did declare;
And said the performers were worthy of praise,
For they ne'er heard a peal better rang in their days:
So here's a good health to those that wish us well,
And those that do envy us they cannot excell;
Those that wish us well, boys, we wish them the same,
And the Youths of All Saints they shall still bear the name.

Thomas Hill dreamed three times, in one night, that he was ringing at All-Saints and each time awaked with the thought of the Tenor's Clapper falling out at the end of the peal; which was verified this day, for as soon as George Wainwright gave the finishing stroke, the clapper broke through the middle [original footnote].

267 *A 'bell rhyme'; Derbyshire*

> Crich two roller-boulders,
> Winfield ting-tangs,
> Alfreton kettles,
> And Pentrich pans,
> Kirk-Hallam candlesticks,
> Cossall cow-bells,
> Denby cracked puncheons,
> And Horsley merry bells.

268 *Verses about the bells of some churches, (i) in Northamptonshire, (ii) in Northampton city*

(i)

> 'Pancakes and fritters,'
>   says the bells of Saint Peter's.
> 'Where must we fry 'em?'
>   says the bells of Cold Higham.
> 'In yonder land-thurrow'
>   says the bells of Wellingborough.
> 'You owe me a shilling,'
>   says the bells of Great Billing.

268 thurrow] furrow

'When will you pay?'
   says the bells at Middleton Cheney.
'When I am able,'
   says the bells at Dunstable.
'That will never be,'
   says the bells at Coventry.
'Oh, yes it will,'
   says Northampton Great Bell.
'White bread and sop,'
   says the bells at Kingsthrop.
'Trundle a lantern,'
   says the bells at Northampton.

(ii)   'Roast-beef and marsh-mallows,'
   say the bells at All Hallows.
'Pancake and fritters,'
   say the bells of Saint Peter's.
'Roast beef and boil'd,'
   say the bells of Saint Giles.
'Poker and tongs,'
   say the bells of Saint John's.
'Shovel, tongs, and poker,'
   say the bells of Saint Pulchre's.

269   *In the cathedral, Peterborough, Northamptonshire; these nine*
couplets, one to each window, narrated the conversion of
King Wulfhere; before 1603

The hart brought Wulfade to a well,
That was besyde Seynt Chaddy's cell.

Wulfade askyd of Seynt Chad,
'Where is the hart that me hath lad?'

'The hart that hither thee hath brought,
Is sent by Christ that thee hath bought.'

Wulfade prayed Chad, that ghostly leech,
The faith of Christ him for to teach.

Saint John's] a hospital
269 leech] healer

154

Seynt Chad teacheth Wulfade the feyth,
And words of baptism over him seyth.

Seynt Chad devoutly to mass him dight,
And hoseled Wulfade Christ his Knight.

Wulfhere contrite hyed him to Chad,
As Ermenyld him counselled had.

Chad bade Wulfhere, for his sin,
Abbeys to build his realm within.

Wulfhere endued, with high devotion,
The Abbey of Brough with great possession.

270   *By James Granger, vicar of Shiplake, Oxfordshire, on Tom
Pidgeon his gardener*

These blooming flowers which lately sprung
From sun and rain, from earth and dung,
By Tom with conscious pride are shown
As a creation of his own.
To them he daily would repair,
And thought no nymph was half so fair;
Gazed on their charms with ravished eyes,
And sheltered from the inclement skies.
Though old, he bows at beauty's shrine,
And owns its energy divine;
The roseate bloom, the dimple sleek,
Which once he saw in Bridget's cheek,
Continue to exert their power,
And captivate him in a flower.

271   *Epitaph for John Holden, d.1844 aged 5; St Leonard's,
Frankley, Worcestershire*

So soon I though thou would'st not fade
   So soon thy bloom be gone;
So very soon thy form be laid
   Beneath the churchyard stone.
But life is like a taper's ray,
Which slightest breeze may waft away.

269 him dight] prepared himself   hoseled] administered the Sacrament to

272 *Epitaphs in Holy Trinity Church, Belbroughton,*
Worcestershire

(i) *for Richard Phillpots, landlord of the Bell Inn, d. 1766*

> To tell a merry or a wond'rous tale
> Over a chearful glass of nappy ale
> In harmless mirth was his supreme delight,
> To please his guests or friends by day or night.
> But no fine tale, how well soever told
> Could make the tyrant Death, his stroke with-hold;
> That fatal stroke has laid him here in dust
> To rise again once more with joy we trust.

(ii) *for Richard Hughes, d. 1892 aged 83*

> When the ripe corn demands the reaper's hand
> Why should we murmur, if it leaves the land;
> Or why regret, when full of faith and years,
> The pious Christian quits this vale of tears?
> And such was he whose name inscribes this stone
> Who lived unblam'd and died without a groan.

273 *For James Simmonds, d. 1867; Holy Trinity Church,*
Lickey End, Worcestershire

> He is gone a little before,
> His loss I am left to deplore;
> In heaven I know I shall meet him
> Never to part any more.

274 *Epitaph for the Son of the fourth Lord Wharton, d. 1642*
aged nine months; Wooburn church, Buckinghamshire

> Nine months wrought me in ye wombe:
> Nine more brought me to this tomb.
> Let an infant teach thee (man)
> Since this life is but a span,
> Use it so that thou maist be
> Happy in ye next with me.

272 nappy] foaming

275　*For Ione Fowke, d. 1572; Brewood, Staffordshire*

> This vertuous dame whyle that she lyved heer,
> A godly matron was but Christ her ancre hold
> Who will her corpes restore in Heaven's clere
> Where now her soule her Saviour dothe behold
> Lo here of lyfe the course and fatall race
> That mortall fleshe uppon the earth must ronne
> The which bothe yonge and old must trace
> When as the Lord cuttes of the thred well sponne.

276　*Thomas Carew (1595–1639?), epitaph for Maria*
Wentworth, d. 1632; Toddington, Bedfordshire

> And here the precious dust is layd;
> Whose purely-tempered Clay was made
> So fine, that it the guest betray'd.
>
> Else the soule grew so fast within,
> It broke the outward shell of sinne,
> And so was hatch'd a Cherubin.
>
> In heighth, it soar'd to God above;
> In depth, it did to knowledge move,
> And spread in breadth to generall love.
>
> Before, a pious duty shind
> To Parents, courtesie behind,
> On either side an equall mind,
>
> Good to the Poore, to kindred deare,
> To servants kind, to friendship cleare,
> To nothing but her selfe, severe.
>
> So though a Virgin, yet a Bride
> To every Grace, she justifi'd
> A chaste Poligamie, and dy'd.
>
> [Learne from hence (Reader) what small trust
> We owe this world, where vertue must
> Fraile as our flesh, crumble to dust.]

275　cuttes of] cuts off

277   *Epitaph for Mrs Pakington, d. 1667; Chaddesley Corbett,*
Worcestershire

> 'Twas Providence preserved this marble here
> By white to speake her candor and now beare
> Inscribed this epitaph to usher forth
> Her many vertues, prudence, goodness, worth;
> And oh, I am confined to straights and must
> Smother the rest; conclude here lies the dust
> Of Mris. Pakington, who was a wife
> And widow—rare exemplar in each life
> A derelict of six and twenty yeares.
> The sun may be obscured, and spangled spheres,
> Yet (maugre death) her fame continewes bright.
> Vertue's a glow-worm, and will shine by night.

278   *Closing lines of the epitaph for Nicholas Greenhill, rector,*
d. 1650; Whitnash, Warwickshire

> This Greenhill periwig'd with Snow
>   Was levil'd in the Spring,
> This Hill ye nine and three did know,
>   Was sacred to his King.
> But he must down, although so much divine,
> Before he rise, never to set, but shine.

279   *Epitaph for Thomas Oldfield ('Old Dummy'), d. 1872*
aged 86; Brewood, Staffordshire

> Bereft alike of hearing and of speech,
> He yet fulfilled the task within his reach;
> A life of honest useful service led,
> And laboured to the last for daily bread.
>
> Reader! whoe'er thou art, as faithful be
> In using better gifts vouchsafed to thee.

candor] probity

278 nine and three] ?the Muses and the Graces

280 *Matthew Prior (1664–1721); verses under a portrait of
Thomas Britton (d. 1714), a coal merchant of Higham
Ferrars, Northamptonshire*

> Tho' doomed to small-coal, yet to arts allied,
> Rich without wealth, and famous without pride,
> Music's best patron, judge of books and men,
> Beloved and honoured by Apollo's train.
> In Greece, in Rome, sure never did appear
> So bright a genius in so dark a sphere;
> More of the man had probably been saved
> Had Kneller painted and Virtu grav'd.

281 *For the landlord of the White Lion, Upton-on-Severn,
Worcestershire*

> Beneath this stone in hope of Zion
> Doth lie the landlord of 'The Lion';
> Resigned unto the heavenly will,
> His son keeps up the business still.

282 *On the monument to Robert Crews, d. 1731, in Thame
church, Oxfordshire; removed by special direction of
Dr Samuel Wilberforce, bishop of Oxford*

> In the morning when sober, in the evening when mellow,
> You scarce ever met such a jolly good fellow.

283 *Epitaph for Richard Colsborne, 1715; Woodstock,
Oxfordshire*

> It was decreed that I should die
> By a sky rocket in my eye
> The first of August 'tis well known
> That brought me to my dismall doom
> Rejoicing the King George was come
> Which sent me forth to my long home.

280 Virtu] George Vertue (1684–1756), famous English engraver who worked for
Kneller

284   *For John Dale, barber-surgeon; Bakewell church, Derbyshire*

Know posterity, that on the 8th of April, in the year of grace 1737, the
rambling remains of the above said John Dale were, in the 86th yeare of
his pilgrimage, laid upon his two wives.

> This thing in life might raise some jealousy,
> Here all three lie together lovingly,
> But from embraces here no pleasure flows,
> Alike are here all human joys and woes;
> Here Sarah's chiding John no longer hears,
> And old John's rambling Sarah no more fears;
> A period's come to all their toilsome lives,
> The good man's quiet; still are both his wives.

285   *Verses under Sir Henry Lee's picture at Ditchley Park,*
Oxfordshire (1718); his right hand is lying under his dog's
head

> Reason in Man can not effect such love,
> As nature doth in them that reason want;
> Ulisses true and kinde his dog did prove,
> When Faith in better frendes was very scante.
> My travailes for my frendes have beene as true,
> Though not as far as fortune did him beare;
> No frend my love and faith devided knew,
> Though neither this nor that once equal'd were.
> Only my Dog, wherof I made no store,
> I find more love, then them I trusted more.

286   *Epitaph for Philip Roe, parish clerk, d. 1815; on a tablet*
in the church at Bakewell, Derbyshire

> The vocal Powers, here let us mark,
> Of PHILIP, our late Parish Clerk
> In church, none ever heard a Layman
> With a clearer Voice say Amen!
> Oh! none with Hallelujah's Sound,

Like Him can make the Roofs resound.
The Choir lament his Choral Tones,
The Town—so soon here lie his Bones.
Sleep undisturbed, within thy peaceful shrine,
Till angels wake thee with such tones as thine.

287 *Epitaph in Dinton churchyard, Buckinghamshire, for Samuel*
Payne, d. 1809 aged 80

I've plodded thro' life's weary way,
In various callings of the day,
A ploughboy first, in Suffolk born,
I turned straight furrows for the corn,
In days when farmers lodged their men,
And held their conduct under ken.
The squires chariot next I drove;
By industry to rise I strove.
I then, alas! engaged an inn,
Temptation strong to vice and sin.
Ere long I left the revel scene,
For purer ways and more serene,
And village children next did train
And aimed subjection to maintain,
To God, to Parents, Pastors, Masters
And guide them thus through life's disasters.
Now my works in death are ended;
Worthless all with error blended.
In penitence and faith, O Lord!
I lean on Christ, the incarnate Word.
At the Archangel's thrilling blast,
Oh! take me to Thyself at last.

288 *Epitaph for Captain Gervase Scrope (d. 1705), written by*
himself (he died soon after composing these verses); Coventry

Here lyes an Old Tossed TENNIS BALL,
Was Racketted from Spring to Fall
With so much heat and so much hast,
Time's arm for shame grew tyr'd at last.
Four kings in CAMPS he truly serv'd
And from his Loyalty ne'er swerv'd.
FATHER ruin'd, the SON slighted,

And from the CROWN ne'er requited,
Loss of ESTATE, RELATIONS, BLOOD,
Was too well known but did no good.
With long CAMPAIGNS and paines o' th' GOUT
He cou'd no longer hold it out.
Always a restless life he led,
Never at quiet till quite dead.
He marry'd in his latter dayes
ONE who exceeds the common praise;
But wanting breath still to make known
Her true AFFECTION and his OWN,
Death kindly came, all wants supply'd,
By giving REST which life deny'd.

289 *An inscription at Bridgford on the Hill, Nottinghamshire*

Sacred to the memory of John Walker, the only son of Benjamin and Ann Walker, Engineer and Palisade Maker; died September 22nd, 1832, aged 36 years.

Farewell, my wife and father dear;
My glass is run, my work is done,
And now my head lies quiet here.
That many an engine I've set up,
And got great praise from men;
I made them work on British ground,
And on the roaring seas;
My engine stopp'd, my valves are bad,
And lies so deep within;
No engineer could there be found
To put me new ones in.
But Jesus Christ converted me,
And took me up above,
I hope once more to meet once more,
And sing redeeming love.

290 *Epitaph for Thomas Scaife, a railway engineer who lost his
life in 1840 through the explosion of an engine boiler;
St John's, Bromsgrove, Worcestershire*

My *engine* now is cold and still,
No water does my *boiler* fill;

My *coke* affords its flame no more,
My days of usefulness are o'er.
My *wheels* deny their wonted speed,
No more my guiding hands they heed;
My *whistle*, too, has lost its tune,
Its shrill and thrilling sounds are gone;
My *valves* are now thrown open wide,
My *flanges* all refuse to guide,
My *clacks*, also, tho' once so strong,
Refuse to aid the busy throng.
No more I feel each urging breath,
My *steam* is now condensed in death.
Life's *railway* o'er, each station past,
In death I'm stopped and rest at last.
Farewell, dear friends, and cease to weep,
In Christ I'm safe, in Him I sleep.

291   *For Captain Andrew Wambey, in the chancel at Naunton
Beauchamp, Worcestershire*

Here lies, retired from worldly deeds,
An old officer of the Invalids,
Who in the army was born and bred,
But now lies quarter'd with the dead.
Stripp'd of all his warlike show,
And laid in box of oak below,
Confin'd in earth, in narrow borders,
He rises not till further orders!

292   *Epitaph for Joseph Slater, clock and watch maker, d. 1822;
Uttoxeter, Staffordshire*

Here lies one who strove to equal time,
A task too hard, each power too sublime;
Time stopped his motion, o'erthrew his balance wheel,
Wore off his pivots tho' made of hardened steel;
Broke all his springs, the verge of life decayed,
And now he is as though he'd ne'er been made.
Not for the want of oiling; that he tried;
If that had done, why then he'd ne'er have died.

---

290 clacks] valves of steam-engine boiler feed-pipes

Such frail machine till time's no more shall rust,
And the archangel wakes our sleeping dust;
Then with assembled worlds in glory join,
And sing—'the hand that made us is divine.'

293   *Three Worcestershire versions of a blacksmith epitaph:*
(i) for Mark Tyzack, d. 1795, Norton; (ii) for Richard
Turner, d. 1803, St Peter's Church, Powick; (iii) for
Richard Stephens, d. 1831, St John's Church, Claines

(i)   My Scythe and hammer lies reclin'd
My Bellows too has lost their winde
My Iron is spent my steel is gone
My Scythes are set my work is done
My fires extinct my forge decay'd
My body in the dust is laid.

(ii)   My sledge and hammer lie reclin'd,
My bellows too have lost its wind;
My fire's extinguished, forge decayed,
And in the dust my vice is laid;
My coal is spent, my iron's gone,
My last nail drove, my work is done.

(iii)   His sledge and hammer he has declin'd,
His bellows it has lost its wind;
His fire's extinct, his forge is decay'd,
And in the dust his vice is laid;
His coal is spent, his iron's gone,
His nails are drove, his work is done.

294   *Lord Byron (1788–1824); epitaph for John Adams of*
Southwell, Nottinghamshire, a carrier, who died of
drunkenness, 1807

John Adams lies here, of the parish of Southwell,
A *Carrier* who *carried* his can to his mouth well;
He *carried* so much, and he *carried* so fast,
He could *carry* no more—so was *carried* at last;
For, the liquor he drank, being too much for one,
He could not *carry off*,—so he's now *carri-on*.

295 *Byron; an inscription on the burial monument of his*
Newfoundland dog 'Boatswain', buried at Newstead Abbey,
Nottinghamshire, 1808

When some proud son of man returns to earth,
Unknown to glory, but upheld by birth,
The sculptor's art exhausts the pomp of woe,
And storied urns record who rests below;
When all is done, upon the tomb is seen,
Not what he was, but what he should have been:
But the poor dog, in life the firmest friend,
The first to welcome, foremost to defend,
Whose honest heart is still his master's own,
Who labours, fights, lives, breathes for him alone,
Unhonoured falls, unnoticed all his worth,
Denied in heaven the soul he held on earth:
While man, vain insect! hopes to be forgiven,
And claims himself a sole exclusive heaven.
Oh man! thou feeble tenant of an hour,
Debased by slavery, or corrupt by power,
Who knows thee well must quit thee with disgust,
Degraded mass of animated dust!
Thy love is lust, thy friendship all a cheat,
Thy smiles hypocrisy, thy words deceit!
By nature vile, ennobled but by name,
Each kindred brute might bid thee blush for shame.
Ye! who perchance behold this simple urn,
Pass on—it honours none you wish to mourn:
To mark a friend's remains these stones arise;
I never knew but one, and here he lies.

296 *Verses hung by the mantelshelf at the Isaac Walton Inn,*
Dovedale, Derbyshire

Lord give me grace that even I
May catch so fine and fat a fish
That there will be no need to lie
To gratify my wildest wish.

*

Hullo, what's this, what's this;
No wish to lie about a fish?
Why man 'twould spoil 'bout half the sport
To give no more than true report!

297 *A 'Mr Fox' song from near Derby (see note to no. 222)*

Oh read me this riddle and read it aright,
Where was I last Saturday night?
The wind blew, the cock crew,
I waited for one, and there came two,
The woods did tremble, the boughs did shake,
To see the hole the fox did make;
Too little for a horse, too big for a bee,
I saw it was a hole just a fit for me.

298 *Part of a lace 'tell', Northamptonshire*

The Wedding Day

Nineteen long lines hanging over my door,
The faster I work it'll shorten my score.
But if I do play it'll stick to a stay;
So ho! little fingers, and twink it away,
For after to-morrow comes my wedding day.

My shoes are to borrow, my husband to seek,
So I cannot get married till after next week.
And after next week it will be all my care
To prink and to curl and to do up my hair.

Six pretty maidens, so neat and so clean,
Shall dance at my wedding next Monday morning.
Down in the kitchen the cook she will run,
And tell Mr. Bellman to ring the ting-tang.

299 *A Worcestershire charm for a girl to dream of her future husband*

On this blessed Friday night
I put my left shoe o'er my right,
In hopes this night that I may see

The man that shall my husband be,
In his apparel and in his array,
And in the clothes he wears every day;
What he does and what he wears,
And what he'll do all days and years;
Whether I sleep or whether I wake,
I hope to hear my true love speak.

300   *From Ashbourne, Derbyshire; a charm for St Valentine's Eve*

I sow hempseed, hempseed I sow,
He that loves me best,
Come and after me mow.

301   *The 'Green Grass' song; Frodlingham, Lincolnshire, and
also in Nottinghamshire*

Stepping on the green grass
    Thus, and thus, and thus;
Please may we have a pretty lass
    To come and play with us?
We will give you pots and pans,
    We will give you brass,

        No!

We will give you anything
    For a bonny lass.

        No!

We will give you gold and silver,
    We will give you pearl,
We will give you anything
    For a pretty girl.

        Yes!

You shall have a goose for dinner,
    You shall have a darling,
You shall have a nice young man
    To take you up the garden.

But suppose this young man was to die
  And leave this girl a widow?
The bells would ring, the cats would sing,
  So we'll all clap together.

302   *An Oxfordshire weather-almanac verse*

Janiver
Freeze the pot by the fire;
If the grass grow in Janiveer
It grows the worse for't all the year;
The Welshman 'ud rather see his dam on the beir
Than to see a fair Februeer;
March wind and May sun
Makes clothes white and maids dun;
When April blows his horn,
It's good both for hay and corn;
An April flood
Carries away the frog and her brood;
A cold May and a windy
Make a full barn and a findy;
A May flood never did good;
A swarm of bees in May
Is worth a loady of hay;
But a swarm in July
Is not worth a fly.

303   *A May-Day song; probably Nottinghamshire*

Remember us poor mayers all,
  And thus do we begin,
To lead our lives in righteousness,
  Or else we die in sin.

We have been rambling all this night,
  And almost all this day,
And now returned back again,
  We have brought you a bunch of May.

302 dam] wife   findy] substantial, solid

A bunch of May we have brought you,
   And at your door it stands,
It is but a sprout, but it's well budded out
   By the work of our Lord's hands.

The hedges and trees they are so green,
   As green as any leek,
Our Heavenly Father, He watered them
   With his Heavenly dew so sweet.

The heavenly gates are open wide,
   Our paths are beaten plain,
And if a man be not too far gone,
   He may return again.

The life of man is but a span,
   It flourishes like a flower;
We are here to-day, and gone to-morrow,
   And are dead in an hour.

The moon shines bright, and the stars give a light,
   A little before it is day,
So God bless you all, both great and small,
   And send you a joyful May.

304   *A 'Cattin and Clementing' song; the villages in the song all*
      lie between Stourport and Worcester

Catherine and Clement come year by year,
Some of your apples and some of your beer,
Some for Peter, some for Paul,
Some for the merry boys under your wall.
   Peter was a good old man,
   For his sake then give us some;
None of the worst, but some of the best,
And pray God send your souls to rest.
Butler! Butler! fill the bowl,
Dash it up against the wall;
Up the ladder, and down with the can,
Give us a red apple and we'll be gone.

A plum, a plum!
A cherry, a cherry!
A good cup of perry,
Will make us all merry.

We go a Cattin, a Cattin go we,
From Hitton to Titton, as soon as you shall see;
From Mitton to Pitton, Hartlebury all three,
Round by old Kiddy, and good Hillintree;
Then down to old Arley, Astley and Shrawley go nimbly,
And finish we up at Holt, Hallow, and Grimley.

305   *Another version; also from Worcestershire*

St. Clement's! St. Clement's! a cat by the ear!
A good red apple—a pint o' beer!
Some o' your mutton, some o' your vale!
If it's good gie us a dale,
If its naught gie us some saut!

Butler, butler, fill the bowl—
If you fill it of the best,
God will send your soul to rest:
But if you fill it of the small,
The Devil take butler, bowl, and all.

306   *A Derbyshire rhyme on local places*

When Chesterfield was heath and broom,
Leech Fend was a market town.
Now Leech Fend is all heath and broom
And Chesterfield a market town.

307   *Oxfordshire 'weather-wise advice to anglers'*

When the wind is in the east,
Then the fishes do bite least;
When the wind is in the west,
Then the fishes do bite best;

perry] pear cider

305 vale] veal   dale] deal   saut] salt

306 Leech Fend] once a piece of boggy ground between Chesterfield and Sheffield

When the wind is in the north,
Then the fishes do come forth;
When the wind is in the south,
It blows the bait in the fishes' mouth.

308   *A Worcestershire rhyme*

Cut thistles in May,
They grow in a day;
Cut them in June,
That is too soon;
Cut them in July,
Then they will die.

309   *A charm against bleeding, Worcestershire version*

Jesus was born in Bethlem,
Baptised in the river Jordan;
The water was wild and wood,
But he was just and good;
God spake, and the water stood,
And so shall now thy blood.

310   *A Northamptonshire charm against festering from a thorn*

Our Saviour was of virgin born,
His head was crowned with a crown of thorn;
It never cankered nor festered at all;
And I hope in Jesus Christ this never shall.

311   *'A metrical adage . . . common in Cheshire'*

The Robin and the Wren
Are God's cock and hen,
The Martin and the Swallow,
Are God's mate and marrow.

311 marrow] match, partner

312 *A lacemakers' song from Weston Underwood,*
    Buckinghamshire

    A lad down at Olney looked over a wall,
    And saw nineteen little golden girls playing at ball.
    Golden girls, golden girls, will you be mine?
    You shall neither wash dishes nor wait on the swine.
    But sit on a cushion and sew a fine seam,
    Eat white bread and butter and strawberries and cream.

313 *A sampler worked by 'Mary Ogden Aged 10 years February*
    15 1810'; showing a picture of 'Bilsdon Cross' (?Billesdon,
    Leicestershire)

        Children like tender Oziers Bend the Bow,
        And as they first are fashioned always grow
        For what we learn in youth to that alone
        In Age we are by second nature prone.

314 *A rhyme from the 'Eton College Chronicle', 1897*

        The Slacker

        I well remember, since the day
        I put my sailor suit away,
            And donned an Eton jacket,
        I felt it was no use to try
        To fight against my destiny:—
            And that was just to 'slack it.'

        Let others toil at oar or bat,
        Or strive a little ball to pat,
            With fingers or with racket;
        Let others face the rain and storm
        In a tight-fitting uniform:—
            I'll stay at home and slack it.

        For aught I care, the hare may run
        From dawn of day to set of sun:
            I do not wish to track it:

    314 slack] also 'tuck', food (Eton slang)

I very much prefer to stop
Indoors, or else in——'s shop,
   In sock forget to slack it.

A couch, a cushion for one's head,
At night two candles shaded red,
   Above one on a bracket:
A tin of biscuits, and a book
At which, with intervals, to look:—
   That is the way to slack it.

If in an author, prose or verse,
A somewhat tougher nut occurs,
   I do not try to crack it;
Other Etonians, I believe,
Come here instruction to receive:—
   I only came to slack it.

My Tutor says, if I don't mend
My lazy habits, in the end
   He'll take my head and smack it;
Though what he says he mostly does,
I'm sure that no amount of blows
   Would make me cease to slack it.

So, Mr. Editor, I send
To you, a sympathetic friend,
   This unassuming packet:
Let other poets change their rhymes:
I make one serve a dozen times,
   And that's the way to slack it.

315   *Oxford; 'A Parent's Prayer to the Proctors'*

O Proctors, shut the Gates at Ten
   Or, better still, at Nine!
The blacked-out City will be flushed
   With Insolence and Wine.

My little boy is straight from School
    His morals quite untarnished;
Satan indeed could find no house
    More truly swept and garnished.

He has been shielded eighteen years
    From Evil's lightest breath,
And can you now expose him to
    Fates that are worse than Death?

Black are the streets as mines of coal
    Where Satan's miners delve,
And it is known *the Worst Occurs*
    Between Eleven and Twelve.

Oxford is full of soldiers now,
    Singing their nasty songs,
For Satan bares his fork at night
    And these are Satan's prongs!

We know too well that soldiers are
    Lewd, vulgar and contentious,
Foul-mouthed, obscene, undisciplined
    And brutally licentious.

They might affront my little lad
    In some Cimmerian street,
Grin like a dog and vent an oath,
    Or knock him off his feet.

And then there is a thing to which
    I scarcely dare allude
But fear compels me to be frank,
    (I hope I am no Prude).

I hear that since the soldiers came
    A *Female Influx* rages
Now added to the 'last enchant-
    Ments of the Middle Ages'.

Cimmerian] dark

174

Suppose, (I mean), my little boy,
  While wearing Cap and Gown,
Succumbed to a Stipendia-
  Ry Venus of the Town!

My little boy would go to Hell,
  Though clearly meant for Heaven;
O *please*, dear Proctors, shut the Gates
  Not later than Eleven!

The Female Colleges combine,
  (Though none of their affair),
To beg an early closing-time;
  O hearken to their prayer!

Then, too, dear Proctors, (though I'm sure
  No *selfish* thought could guide you),
It's one hour less for you to walk
  With Bull-dogs brave beside you.

Kind Proctors! For my little boy,
  And for yourselves as well,
O close the College Gates at Ten
  To close the Gates of Hell!

316 *A dramatic prologue for Oxford University players, c.1900,*
    by George (?Lord) Curzon

  O, gentle audience, Don and Undergraduate—
  Less gentle might be if o'er long I bade you wait
  The Curtain's rising—at this shrine of Science
  We meet to join in nuptial alliance
  Oxford, a bachelor *praeclaro nomine*,
  And the famed Grecian maiden called Melpomene.
  For her hath he vows of allegiance taken,
  For him hath she all other lovers forsaken;
  Her Virtue's self as pledge for her suffices,
  To him a sponsor generous *our* VICE is.
  Not singly comes the Bride, nor by a small staff
  Attended, but a goodly train. Jack Falstaff,
  Old England's Dionysus, God whose votaries
  'Tis said still linger in Collegiate Coteries.
  For still men love the '*Sack*'—until they've got it!
  To others are more tragic parts allotted,
  Three Henries, one of them the Fourth—enigma

More hard to crack than head of OSMAN DIGMA—
Next Hotspur, while the third (or fifth) is Prince Hal;
These for the Bride all suffrages convince shall,
Till each voice, bidden to pass judgment on her,
Giving them 'honours' shall so give her honour.
Nor less the Bridegroom's following, for Doctors,
Learned Professors, Heads of Houses, Proctors,
Players with whose fierce strife but late resounded
A neighb'ring Theatre, have in this compounded
For anæsthetic loss by gain æsthetical.
And now join hands in union most poetical.
'Tis *feigned* that then the gallery swelled the Babel—
This time at least, Sirs, let it be no fable!
But bid the Bride as now the curtain rises
Loud welcome to a home beside the Isis.

317   *An Oxford song for an amateur dramatic banquet (see the note)*

The Boare is dead!
Loe heare is his head;
    What man could have done more
Than his head of to strike,
Meleager like,
    And bring it as I doe before.

He livinge spoyled
Where good men toyled,
    Which made kind Ceres sorrye;
But now dead and drawne
Is very good brawne,
    And we have brought it for ye.

Then sett down ye Swineyard,
The foe to ye Vineyard;
    Let Bacchus crowne his fall.
Lett this Boares-head and mustard
Stand for Pigg, Goose, and Custard,
    And so ye are welcome all.

Osman Digma] Osman Digna, a leader of the Mahdi's troops in the Sudan in the 1880s,
not finally captured until 1900

317 swineyard] swineherd, i.e. the boar as master of the herd

318   *The 'Boar's Head Song', The Queen's College, Oxford*

> The Boares head in hand bear I,
> Bedeck'd with bays and rose-mary
> And I pray you, Masters, merry be
>   *Quotquot est in convivio.*
>
> Chorus: *Caput Apri defero*
>   *Reddens laudes Domino.*
>
> The Boar head, as I understand,
> Is the bravest dish in all the land,
> Being thus bedeck'd with a gay garland
>   Let us *servire cantico.*
>
> (Chorus)
>
> Our steward hath provided this
> In honour of the King of bliss,
> Which on this day to be served is
>   *In Reginensi Atrio.*
>
> (Chorus)

319   *The 'Mallard Song' for All Souls' Night; All Souls College, Oxford*

> The griffine, bustard, turkey and capon,
>   Lett other hungry mortalls gape on
> And on their bones with stomacks fall hard
>   but lett All Souls men have the mallard.
>
> The Romans once admir'd a gander
>   more then they did their best commander
> because hee saved, if some don't fooll us
>   The place named from the scull of Tolus.
>
> The poets fam'd Jove turn'd a swan
>   But lett them prove it if they can
> So mak't appeare it's not at all hard
>   Hee was a swapping swopping mallard.

319 scull of Tolus] the Roman Capitol, facetiously taken as Latin *caput Toli*, 'head of Tolus'   swapping, swopping] outsize

Some storys strange are told I trow
  By Bales, Holinghead and Stow
Of Cocks and bulls and other queir things
  That happ'd in the reign of theire kings.

He was swapping all from bill to eye
  He was swapping all from wing to thigh
His swapping toole of generation
  Out swappèd all the winggèd nation.

Then let us drink and dance a galliard
  In the remembrance of the mallard,
And as the mallard doth in poole
  Let's dabble, dive and duck in bowle.

(Hough the bloud of King Edward, by the bloud of King
  Edward,
It was a swapping swapping mallard.)

320   *A children's Christmas Eve carol from Eckington, Derbyshire*

I saw three ships come sailing by,
Come sailing by, come sailing by,
I saw three ships come sailing by,
At Christmas Day in the morning.

I asked them what they had got there,
They had got there, they had got there,
I asked them what they had got there,
At Christmas Day in the morning.

They said they had a Saviour there,
A Saviour there, a Saviour there,
They said they had a Saviour there,
At Christmas Day in the morning.

They washed his head in a golden bowl,
In a golden bowl, in a golden bowl,
They washed his head in a golden bowl
At Christmas day in the morning.

319 Bales, Holinghead, Stow] John Bale, Raphael Holinshed, John Stow, Tudor
historians   hough] ho!

They wiped his head with a diaper towel,
With a diaper towel, with a diaper towel,
They wiped his head with a diaper towel
At Christmas day in the morning.

They combed his hair with an ivory comb,
With an ivory comb, with an ivory comb,
They combed his hair with an ivory comb
At Christmas day in the morning.

And all the bells in heaven did ring,
Heaven did ring, heaven did ring,
To think that Christ was born a king
At Christmas day in the morning.

321   *Verses on the trades in Bromsgrove, 1851; by a native, John
Harris Scroxton*

We have makers of buttons and makers of nails,
Builders of coaches for roads and for rails;
Artists in leather, in mortar, in wood,
Artists in paint—both indifferent and good;
Makers of candles, soap, soda, and salt,
Concoctors of drinks, both from crabs and from malt;
Constructors and menders of watches and clocks,
Repairers, and vendors, and—pickers of locks;
We have sowers, and reapers, and grinders of grain,
And dispensers of food, both for stomach and brain;
Manufact'rers of bread, pastry, butter, and cheese,
And makers of verses—far better than these;
We have some who teach music, and some who can draw,
Expounders of gospel, exponents of law;
We have men who write sermons, and men who write books;
For ailing, we've doctors, for healthy, we've cooks;
We have some who can lecture, and some who can speak,
And some who can gabble both Hebrew and Greek;
We have schools for the lofty and schools for the low,
Both nurs'ries of virtue and nurs'ries of woe;
We have drunkards and sober, both good men and bad,
Some wise and some foolish, some sane and some mad;
We have dealers in gossip, detraction, and lies,
Who feast upon carrion, like maggots and flies;
We have those who are honest, and upright, and true,
And those who in gaol ought long penance to do.

322　*A north Midlands 'miners' law' verse; seventeenth century*

> For stealing oar twice from the minery,
> The thief that's taken twice fined shall be,
> But the third time that he commits such theft,
> Shall have a knife stuck through his hand to th' haft,
> Into the stow, and there to death shall stand,
> Or loose himself by cutting loose his hand,
> And shall forswear the franchise of the mine,
> And always lose his freedom from that time.

323　*Contemporary verses by Crane, the 'Bird of Bromsgrove',*
　　Worcestershire, on the flood of Friday, 13 April 1792

> My native place, how strong thou art,
> An arméd force to take thy part;
> Afar from thee I never roam,
> But once have seen thee overcome;
> In fancy now I view the fight,
> O'er yonder hills,—a gloomy sight.
> Both in a thundering, roaring pet,
> Two mighty clouds in contact met:
> They fell together by the ears,
> And burst into a flood of tears;
> The ploughing torrent's course I traced,—
> Walls, bridges vanish'd, land laid waste.
> The thievish stream, quite unawares
> Broke in, and stood to no repairs;
> Seven feet in depth came foaming down
> In open day, to take the town:
> Bore things away with swift despatch,
> With every one 'twas watch and snatch,
> Bawling and screaming out, stop! stop
> My timber! catch my pail and mop;
> My table, with the tea-things on,
> My heart is broke, my china's gone!
> My pigs, my malt will all be spoil'd,
> Shut my malt-house! oh, save my child!

322 stow] kind of windlass used in mining in Derbyshire

To see the vessels setting sail,
Loaded with spirits, wines, and ale,
Even mighty men were turning pale;
In every vein their blood ran chill,
And women's tongues, for once, stood still.

324 *A Midlands gypsy song by Henry Sherriff, nineteenth century (see the note)*

True Love

My mother's gone awandering
Away to yonder town.
My father in the alehouse
Is safely settled down.
There's not a girl to gossip,
There's not a lad at home.
I'm all alone and waiting.
So come, my darling, come.
Tell me what I'm doing,
By the firelight here,
All for you love, all for true love
All for luck, my dear!

I told the lady's fortune
In that big house nearby,
No Gypsy could have done it
More cleverly than I.
I promised her she'd marry
A Lord with heaps of gold,
She filled my hand with silver
As much as I could hold.
I can chatter, I can flatter
Gorgios far and near,
All for you love, all for true love
All for luck my dear.

Oh, Romanies are cunning,
I know what I'm about.
I hid away the money
Where no one found it out.

324 Gorgios] non-Gypsies (a Romany word)

I bought some flour last evening
I bought it secretly.
Come now, the cake is ready
And no one here to see
Meal so white, money bright
Baked together here,
All for you love, all for true love
All for luck my dear.

325 *A ballad on a Lincolnshire champion; found in*
Nottinghamshire (see the note)

You gentlemen Draw near
And the truth I will Declare;
I will tell you of a Russeller so bold
And he Lives in Lincolnshire.

Bill Scrimshaw is his name,
In Claypool Town Does dwell;
He is the Don both far and near,
And he is known very well.

On the 21st of November last
This Rustling Match was made
Between Bill Scrimshaw and the Derbyshire Don
Which never was afraid.

When these Champions did meet
This Russelling for to try,
'Here's 5 to 1 again Bill Scrimshaw'
The Derbyshire Dons Did cry.

John Scrimshaw standing by
And hearing what was said,
Saying 'I comd here my brother to back
And your 5 to one I take.'

---

325 russeller] wrestler   rustling, russelling] wrestling   don] expert; person
of distinction

Then Haley up and then arose
And he flew into a rage,
Saying 'I am come here this Wager to win
Or Die upon the stage.'

Bill Scrimshaw gave a smile
But nothing he did say;
He soon tripped up the Derbyshire Don
All on the stage he lay.

'So now I flung your Don
You Gentlemen you see,
And if you have got a better Don,
Pray bring him unto me.

'Bill Scrimshaw is my name
In Claypool town do Dwell;
I am the Don both far and near,
And I am known very well.'

These Lincolnshire Lads shall wear cockades,
And their Ribbons shall be blue;
Bill Scrimshaw was a tight young lad,
And he was always staunch and true.

326   *Verses on a holiday at St Anne's Well, Nottingham, 1864*

Old 'Sentan's Well'—that is, the Well
Of Ann the Saint (I try to spell
   The name by which it goes)—
Is down a pleasant lane, I trow,—
At least it was, some years ago,
   As many a lover knows;
But then improvement comes—and may
Have swept the Well and all away.

Now, if you please, we will suppose,
And do our utmost to disclose
   A pleasant recreation,—
The lads and lasses of the town,
In Sunday suit and Sunday gown
   And—happy expectation,
And full of glee, and on their way
To spend some special holiday.

Suppose the maidens prim and spruce;
The boys, a pack of hounds let loose,—
   With such they're fairly classed!
And last, suppose them at the Well;
Which being done, I'll try to tell
   You how the time was passed;
And, aided by Remembrance, trace
The merry pastimes of the place.

To scamper over all, and look
In every corner, every nook,
   Is very quickly done
By all the boys; ah me! the girls
At present anxious for their curls,
   Though quite as full of fun,
Each other's arms have interlaced
And for a time are sober-paced.

The door is found, that cutler's friend—
So crammed with names, and still the end
   Of many a treasured blade—
And soon is duly cut and hack'd
To record other names;—in fact,
   That door at last was made
To bear so much, old jokers say
'Twas altogether cut away.

But soon collected all are seen
Upon the level bowling-green;—
   At last, the fiddler's come!
A dance the order of the day,
And merrily they trip away,
   And loud the joyant hum:
There's nothing like a merry dance
The charms of beauty to enhance!

And rural games spring up around:
The little boys are 'stag and hound'
   Each other capturing;
Some play at 'Tag,' and 'Tick,' or 'Hit,'
And 'Duck come under the water-kit,'
   And 'Kissing in the ring'—
All sorts of olden games are seen
Upon that level bowling green.

       water-kit] large bucket

And then the swing! 'tis hung between
A pair of trees whose heads of green
　　Throw such a pleasant shade,
That many gladly there resort,
Fatigued and heated with the sport
　　Their boisterous games had made,
And seated on the rope, or chair,
Are swung with laughter in the air.

Some run the 'Shepherd's Race'—a rut
Within a grass-plot deeply cut
　　And wide enough to tread—
A maze of path, of old designed
To tire the feet, perplex the mind,
　　Yet pleasure heart and head;
'Tis not unlike this life we spend;
And where you start from, there you end.

At length within the arbour laid
By many a tidy willing maid—
　　For all are willing now—
The tea, and best of all—the buns!
And even tired nature runs
　　Before such gods to bow;
Oh, tea and buns! ye have a part
I think, in every human heart!

And when the night has fairly stayed
The out-door games, why then are played
　　As many games within;
But these, with song and recitation
I'll leave to your imagination—
　　And all the noisy din.
Delighted, when the day is done,
The fiddler is the only one!

VI

THE WELSH BORDERS

The propyrté of every shire
I shal you telle and ye will here.
Herefordshire, sheeld and spere;
Worsetershire, wryng pere.
Gloucestershire, sho and nayle;
Brystowe, shippe and sayle.
Oxenfordshire, gyrde the mare;
Warwykshire, bynd bere.
London, resortere;
Sowtherey, gret bragere.
Esex, ful of good hoswyfes:
Middlesex, ful of stryves.
Kentshire, hoot as fire;
Sowseks, ful of dyrt and myre.
Hertfordshire, ful of wode;
Huntyngdonshire, corne ful goode
Bedfordshire is nought to lakke;
Bokynghamshire is his maakke.
Northamptonshire, full of love
Benethe the gyrdyll and noth above.
Lancastreshire, fayre archere;
Chestreshire, thwakkere.
Northumbreland, hasty and hoot;
Westmerland, tprut Scotte.
Yorkshire, ful of knyghtys;
Cambrygeshire, ful of pykes;
Holond, ful of grete dykes.
Northfolk ful of wyles;
Southfolk ful of styles.
I am of Shropshire, my shines be sharpe;
Ley wode to the fyre, and dresse me my harpe.
Notynghamshire, ful of hogges;
Derbyshire, ful of dogges.
Leycetershire, ful of benys;
Staffordshire, ful of quenys.
Wilkshire, fayre and playne;

wryng pere] probably a pear pressed ('wrung') for cider   bynd bere]
?(bitter) beer from hops   resortere] visitor, ?'hanger-on'   maakke] match,
equal   noth] ?naught   tprut] ?the proud   shines] ?possibly 'eyes'
quenys] (?loose) women

Barkshyre, fyll the wayne.
Hampshire, drye and wete;
Somersetshire, good for whete.
Devenshire, myghty and stronge;
Dorseteshire wil have no wronge.
Pynnokshire is not to prayse;
A man may go it in to dayes.
Cornewayle, ful of tynne;
Walys, full of goote and kene.
That Lord that for us all dyde dye,
Save all these shires! Amen, say we.

328 *A verse scratched on a window of the Yacht Inn at Chester;*
      attributed to Jonathan Swift

Rotten without and mouldering within,
This place and its clergy are all near akin!

329 *A broadside posted in a country inn in Gloucestershire,*
      c.1655 (read down the two columns, the verses are Roman
      Catholic in sentiment, read straight across they are Anglican)

I hold as faith	What *England's church* alows
What *Rome's* church saith	My conscience disavows
Where the *King's* head	That *church* can have no shame
The flocks misled	That holds the *Pope* supreame.
Where the *altars* drest	There's service scarce divine
The peoples blest	With table, bread, and wine.
He's but an asse	Who the *communion* flies
Who shuns the *masse*	Is *catholick* and wise.

330 *On an inn window at Ledbury, Herefordshire*

Yes, virgin window, I presume
  The first to scribble here;
But with a wish to save thee from
  Each brother sonneteer.

327 Pynnokshire] the parish of Pinnock, Glos., often so called in early sources
go it in to dayes] go all over it in two days   goote and knee] ?goats and kine

Oh, never here may word obscene
   Offend the virtuous eye;
Nor vicious passion crimson o'er
   The blush of modesty.

Sure the abandon'd wretch was born
   Of Erebus and night,
Who writes but with design to shock
   Those eyes that seek the light!

331   *George Herbert (1593–1633); a stanza from his poem 'The Windows', in a vestry window at West Kirby, Wirral, Cheshire*

Lord, how can man preach thy eternall word?
   He is a brittle crazie glasse:
Yet in thy temple thou dost him afford
   This glorious and transcendent place,
   To be a window, through thy grace.

332   *A panel at the Merchant Seamen's Almshouses, Bristol*

Freed from all storms, the tempest and the rage
Of billows, here we spend our age;
Our weather-beaten vessels here repair,
And from the merchants' kind and generous care
Find harbour here. No more we put to sea
Until we launch into eternity,
Unless our widows whom we leave behind
Should want relief, they too a shelter find.
Thus all our anxious cares and sorrow cease,
While our kind Guardians turn our toils to ease.
May they be with an endless Sabbath blest
Who have afforded unto us this rest.

333   *Lines attached to a door in St Mary's Church (?Chester), after Lord Duncan's naval victory (1797)*

Ye wicked people, are these your pranks,
To murther men and give God thanks?
O pray leave off, and go no further,
For God requires no thanks for murther.

334 *Inscription on almshouses at Bargate, Leominster,*
Herefordshire, beside a carving of a nearly naked man, with
a hatchet by his side

He who gives away all before he's dead,
Let 'em take this Hatchet, and knock him on ye Head.

335 *Verses on a sampler; worked by M. A. Tipper, New Orphan*
House, Bristol, 1868

Jesus, permit thy gracious name to stand,
    As the first efforts of an infant's hand,
And, while her fingers on the canvas move,
    Engage her tender thoughts to seek thy love,
With thy dear children let her have a part,
    And write thy name, thyself, upon her heart.

336 *Verses on an old etching of nailshops, at Cradley,*
Worcestershire; by Sir Frank Short (1857–1945)

By the sweat of their brow they—exist.
Sunrise to them is over-late, and sun-down but a lighting of their
    work lamps.
As little sleep to them as maybe, and not much but smoke to
    swallow.
Simple and sturdy hearts, men and women that work and make a
    nation,
Where is your reward?
Great God! that there be nailshops down in hell for others to try!

337 *Verse for a grant of land to the Hopton family; Shropshire*

Hopton, County of Salop.
To the heyrs male of the Hopton, lawfully begotten.

To me and to myne, to thee and to thine,
While the water runs, and the sun doth shine;
For lack of heyrs to the king againe,
I William, king, the third year of my reign,
Give to the Norman Hunter,

To me that art both leive and deare,
The hoppe and hoptoune,
And all the bounds up and downe,
Under the earth to hell,
Above the earth to heaven,
From me and from mine,
To thee and to thine,
As good and as faire
As ever they myne were,
To witness that this is sooth,
I bite the white wax with my tooth,
Before Jugg, Marode, and Margery,
And my third son Henry,
For one bow and one broad arrow,
When I come to hunt upon Yarrow.

338 *In the Parish Register at Melverley, Shropshire, 17
December 1760*

This morning I have put a Tye
No man could put it faster
Tween Matthew Dodd, the man of God
And modest Nellie Foster.

John Lewis Clk.

339 *'Milton's Well', near the Ey Brook, Gloucestershire; verses by
W. H. C. Plowden, c.1866*

'Tis said beside these lovely glades,
These crystal streams, these sylvan shades,
Where feathered songsters on their wing
In heavenly chorus join and sing,
That Milton penned immortal lays
On Paradise and Heaven's praise,
Each object there that greets the eye
Raises the poet's thoughts on high,
No earthly things can there intrude
On lovely eyford's solitude,
But beauteous nature reigns supreme
And Paradise is all his theme.

337 leive] lief, beloved   hoptoune] ?hop-enclosure

340   *On a pillar in the churchyard, Areley Kings, Worcestershire*

> Three things there be in very deede,
> Which make my heart in grief to bleede:
> The first doth vex my very heart,
> In that from hence I must departe;
> The second grieves me now and then,
> That I must die, but know not when;
> The third with tears bedews my face,
> That I must die, nor know the place.

I. W.
fecit, Anno Dm̄i.
1687.

341   *On one of the bells at Evesham Abbey, Worcestershire*

> I sound the sound that doleful is,
>   To them that live amiss;
> But sweet my sound is unto such
>   As live in joy and bliss.
> I sweetly tolling, men do call
> To taste on food that feeds the soul.

342   *Inscriptions on the bells at Bromborough, Cheshire; 1880*

1. When the full ring its tuneful voice shall raise,
    Let me be first to lead the call of praise.

2. Gladsome we peal, from out the Church's tower,
    To God's great glory, and his love and power.

3. To worship duly Heaven's Almighty Lord,
    Our sweetest chimes unite with one accord.

4. When wedded love makes two as one abide,
    Their joys we share, and spread it far and wide.

5. From Mersey's bank sounds forth our sacred glee,
    And courts responsive echoes from the Dee.

6. Aloft are we, but loftier points the spire,
That heavenward man should raise his heart's desire.

7. May every strain melodious we outpour,
Stir all who hear God's goodness to adore.

8.   Gloria in Excelsis Deo.

343 *A ringers' inscription formerly at Tong church, Shropshire;
1694*

If that to Ring you doe come here,
You must ring well with hand and eare.
  keep stroak of time and goe not out;
  or else you forfeit out of doubt.
Our law is so concluded here;
For every fault a jugg of beer,
  if that you Ring with Spurr or Hat;
  a jugg of beer must pay for that.
If that you take a Rope in hand;
These forfeits you must not withstand.
  or if that you a Bell ov'r-throw;
  It must cost Sixpence e're you goe.
If in this place you sweare or curse;
Sixpence to pay, pull out your purse.
  come pay the Clerk it is his fee;
  for one (that swears) shall not goe free.
These laws are old, and are not new;
therefore the Clerk must have his due.

344 *Shropshire bell-jingles*

'A nut and a kernell,'
say the bells of Acton Burnell.
'A pudding in the pot,'
say the bells of Acton Scott.

Pitch 'em and patch 'em,
say the bells of Old Atcham.
Hold up your shield,'
say the bells of Battlefield.

'Wristle, wrastle,'
say the bells of Bishop's Castle.
'Up, Severn, and down, Morfe,'
say the bells of Bridgnorth.
'Roast beef and mutton,'
say the bells of Church Stretton.
'Hop, skip, and run,'
say the bells of Clun.
'Axes and brummocks,'
say the bells of Clungunnus.
'Under and over,'
say the bells of Condover.
'A stick and a stone,'
say the bells of Edgton.
'You're too fond of beer,'
say the bells of Ellesmere.
'Why don't you ring louder?'
say the bells of Hope Bowdler.
'Because we are beaten,'
say the big bells of Eaton.
'Buttermilk and whey,'
say the bells of Hopesay.
'An old lump of wood,'
say the bells of Leebotwood.
(or 'Lay a bottle in the wood,'
say the bells of Leebotwood.)
'Roas' goose an' gonder,'
say the bells of Longnor.
'How dare you do so?'
say the bells of Ludlow.
'Because I've a mind,'
say the bells of Leintwardine.
(or 'White bread and red wine,'
say the bells of Leintwardine.)
'We must all die,'
say the bells of Lydbury.
'An owl in the tree,'
say the bells of Norbury.
'Three crows on a tree,'
say the bells of Oswestry.
'Roast beef and be merry,'
say the bells of Shrewsbury.

Morfe] a nearby hill   brummocks] broom-hooks, billhooks   Clungunnus]
Clungunford

'Itchy and scabby,'
say the bells of the Abbey.
'Three naked lads,'
(or 'Three golden spades,')
say the bells of St. Chad's.
'Three silver pikels,' (or 'golden pikels')
say the bells of St. Michael's.
'Three golden canaries,'
(or 'Buttercups and daisies,'
or 'A new-born baby,')
say the bells of St. Mary's.
'A boiling pot and stewing pan,'
say the bells of Julian.
'You're a rogue for sartin,'
say the bells of St. Martin.
'Up the ridge and down the butt,'
say the bells of Smethycote.
'Roast beef and mutton,'
say the bells of Old Upton.
'Jack, and Jim the tailor,'
hang the rogue the ringer.
'Ivy, holly, and mistletoe,'
say the bells of Wistanstow.

345   *In St Julian's Church, Shrewsbury, for Henry and Anne*
      Corser, who died in 1692 within a day of each other

We man and wife
Conjoyned for life,
Fetched our last breath
So near, that Death
Who part us would
Yet hardly could
Wedded againe
  In Bed of Dust
Here wee remain
  Till rise we must
A double prize this Grave doth finde,
If you are wise, keep it in minde.

344 pikels] pitchforks   butt] ?mound

346   *Epitaph for Elizabeth Barklam (d. 1797), her husband, and his brother; High Ercall, Shropshire*

When terrestrial all in chaos shall Exhibit effervescence,
Then Celestial virtu's in their most Refulgent Brilliant essence,
Shall with beaming Beauteous Radiance thro' the Ebullition shine,
Transcending to Glorious Regions Beatifical Sublime:
Human power absorb'd deficient to delineate such Effulgent Lasting
   Sparks,
Where honest plebeians ever shall have presidence o'er ambiguous
   great monarchs.

347   *St Mary's, Shrewsbury; on the west wall of the tower, outside*

> Let this small monument record the name
> Of Cadman, and to future times proclaim
> How by'n attempt to fly from this high spire
> Across the Sarbrine stream he did acquire
> His fatal end. 'Twas not from want of skill
> Or courage to perform the task he fell:
> No, No, a faulty cord being drawn too tight
> Hurried his soul on high to take her flight
> Which hid the body here below, good-night.
>
> Feb. 2nd, 1739; aged 28.

348   *On a clock; Shrewsbury, c.1745*

> I labour here with all my might,
> To tell the hour by day and night,
> Therefore example take by me,
> And serve thy God as I serve thee.

presidence] ?precedence   ambiguous] untrustworthy
347   Sarbrine] Sabrina, Severn

349 *An epitaph in Abenhall (or Abinghall) churchyard,*
Gloucestershire

> As I was riding on the road
>   Not knowing what was coming,
> A bull that was loggered and pressed
>   After me came running.
>
> He with his logger did me strike
>   He being sore offended
> I from my horse was forced to fall
>   And thus my days were ended.

350 *Epitaph for Bridget Granville, d. 1627; in Bristol Cathedral*

> By birth a Grenvill, and that name
> Was enough epitaph and fame
> To make her lasting, but the stone
> Would have this little more be known;
> She was, while she did live, a wife
> The glorie of her husband's life,
> Her sex's credit and the sphere
> Wherein the virtues all move here;
> And 'tis no doubt but grief had made
> The husband, as the wife, a shade,
> But that his death Heaven doth defer
> Awhile to stay and weep for her.

351 *Part of an epitaph for Sir Thomas Stanley in Tong church,*
Shropshire; 'said to have been written by Shakespeare, not
ten years old when Sir Thomas died'

> Not Monumental Stone preserves our fame,
> Nor Skye-aspiring Pyramids our name,
> The memory of him for whom this stands
> Shall outlive Marble and Defacer's Hands;
> When all to Tyme's Consumption shall be given,
> Stanley for whom this stands shall stand in Heaven.

349 loggered] tethered to a 'logger' or block of wood, to hinder straying

352   *For Thomas Lee, d. September 1859 aged 84, in the parish of Pipe and Lyde, Herefordshire*

> Mourner who sittest in the churchyard alone,
> Scanning the lines on this marble tomb,
> Plucking the weeds from thy loved one's bed,
> Planting the myrtle and the rose instead,
>   Look up with tearful eye,—
>   Jesus of Nazareth passeth by.

353   *Epitaph for the Revd Edward Skepton, d. 1630; Alderley, Cheshire*

Here lies below an aged sheepheard, clad in heavy clay,
Those stubborne weedes which come not off unto the judgment
  day,
Whilom he led and fed with welcome paine his careful sheepe,
He did not feare the mountaines highest top, nor vallies deepe,
That he might save from hurte his faithful flock which was his care,
To make them strong he lost his strength, and fasted for their fare;
How they might feed, and grow, and prosper, he did daily tel,
Then having shewed them how to feede, hee bade them all farewell.

354   *On the tomb of John Abel, a leading 'black-and-white' architect of the time of Charles I; Sarnesfield, Herefordshire*

> This craggy stone a covering is for an architect's bed,
> That lofty buildings raised high yet now lies low his head;
> His line and rule so death concludes are locked up in stone,
> Build they who list or they who wist, for he can more build none.

355   *In the churchyard at Berkeley, Gloucestershire*

> Here lyeth Thomas Peirce, whom no man taught,
>   Yet he in Iron, Brasse, and Silver wrought;
> He Jacks, and Clocks, and Watches (with art) made,
>   And mended too when others' worke did fade.
> Of Berkeley five tymes Mayor, this Artist was,

354 wist] ?know (how)

And yet this Mayor, this Artist, was but grasse.
When his owne Watch was downe on the last day,
   He that made Watches, had not made a key
To winde it up, but uselesse it must lie,
   Until he rise againe no more to die.

     He deceased the 25 of Feb., 1665, Ætatis 77.

356   *David Garrick (1717–79), an epitaph on James Quin,*
      d. 1766; in Bath Abbey

   That tongue which set the table in a roar
   And charmed the public ear is heard no more;
   Closed are those eyes, the harbingers of wit,
   Which spake before the tongue what Shakespeare writ;
   Cold is that hand which living was stretched forth
   At friendship's call to succour modest worth.
   Here lies James Quin: deign reader to be taught
   Whate'er thy strength of body, force of thought,
   In nature's happiest mould however cast,
   To this complexion thou must come at last.

357   *'An Anatomical Epitaph on a Invalid, written by himself'*
      (William Goldwin of Bristol, c.1900)

   Here lies an head that often ach'd,
   Here lie two hands that always shak'd;
   Here lies a brain of odd conceit,
   Here lies an heart that often beat;
   Here lie two eyes that daily wept,
   And in the night but seldom slept;
   Here lies a tongue that whining talk'd,
   Here lie two feet that feebly walk'd;
   Here lie the midriff and the breast,
   With loads of indigestion prest;
   Here lies the liver full of bile,
   That ne'er secreted proper chyle;
   Here lie the bowels, human tripes,
   Tortur'd with wind and twisting gripes.
   Here lies that livid dab the spleen,
   The source of Life's sad tragick scene,
   That left side weight that clogs the blood,

And stagnates nature's circling flood;
Here lie the nerves so often twitch'd
With painful cramps and poignant stitch;
Here lies the back oft' rack'd with pains,
Corroding kidneys, loins and reins;
Here lies the skin *per* scurvy fed,
With pimples and eruptions red.

Here lies the man from top to toe,
That fabrick fram'd for pain and woe;
He catch'd a cold, but colder Death
Compress'd his lungs, and stopt his breath;
The organs could no longer go,
Because the bellows ceas'd to blow.
Thus I dissect this honest friend,
Who ne'er till death, was at wit's end;
For want of spirits here he fell,
With higher spirits let him dwell,
In future state of peace and love,
Where just men's perfect spirits move.

358 *Verses for the 'Wap' celebrations; Randwick, Gloucestershire*

When Archelus began to spin
And 'Pollo wrought upon a loom;
Our trade to flourish did begin,
Though conscience went to selling broom.

The Lady Helen's wanton son
Did eat his food with sweet content,
He had not then disturbed the peace,
But he to Greece a wooing went.

As Helen then sat carding wool,
Whose beauteous face did cause such strife,
He had not then broke through these rules,
Which caused so many to lose their lives.

When cedar trees grew stout and strong,
And pretty birds did sing on high,
The weavers lived more void of strife
Than princes of great dignity.

358 Archelus] Hercules

When princes' sons kept sheep in fields
And queens made cakes with oaten flour,
And men to lucre did not yield,
Which brought good cheer in ev'ry bow'r.

Though the giants so hughant high
Did fight with spears like weavers' beams,
And men in iron beds did lie
Who brought the poor to hard extremes.

But David with a sling and stone,
Not fearing great Goliath's strength,
He pared his brains and broke his bones,
Though he's nine feet and a span in length.
Let love and friendship still agree
To hold the Banns of Amity.

359   *Two 'Soulers' Songs' from Cheshire; 'souling' was collecting on All Souls' Day, or on All Hallows' Eve*

(i) You gentlemen of England, I would have you to draw near,
To these few lines which we have wrote, and you soon shall
    hear
Sweet melody of music all on this evening clear,
For we are come a-souling for apples and strong beer.
Step down into your cellar, and see what you can find,
If your barrels are not empty, I hope you will prove kind,
We'll come no more a-souling, until another year.
Cold winter it is coming on, dark, dirty, wet and cold,
To try your good nature this night we do make bold,
This night we do make bold, with your apples and strong beer;
We will come no more a-souling until another year.

All houses that we've been at, we have had both meat and
    drink,
So now we're dry with travelling, and hope you'll on us think;
I hope you'll on us think, with your apples and strong beer.
God bless the master of this house, and the mistress also,
And all the little children that round the table go,
Likewise young men and maidens, your cattle and your store,
And all that lies within your gates, I wish you ten times more;
I wish you ten times more with your apples and strong beer,
For we'll come no more a-souling until another year.

358 hughant] ?huge and

(ii)   Soul Day, Soul Day, Saul,
One for Peter, two for Paul,
Three for Him who made us all.
An apple or pear, a plum or a cherry,
Any good thing that will make us merry.
And put your hand into your pocket and pull out your keys,
Go down into the cellar, bring up what you please,
A glass of your wine, or a cup of your beer,
And we'll never come souling till this time next year.
We are a pack of merry boys all in a mind,
We have come a-souling for what we can find.
   Soul, Soul, sole my shoe,
If you have no apples, money will do.
Up with your kettle, and down with your pan,
Give us an answer, and let us be gone.

360 *A 'Pace-Egging' (i.e. Easter egg) song; Cheshire*

Here come four or five hearty lads all of one mind;
We have come a' paste-egging if you will prove kind;
If you will prove kind, and never will fail,
We'll treat our young lasses to the best of X ale.
     Fol di-diddle dol-di-day.

The next that steps in is Lord Nelson, you see
With a bunch of blue ribands tied on to his knee,
With a star on his breast like silver do shew,
And he comes a' paste-egging with his jolly crew.
     Fol di-diddle dol-di-day.

The next that steps in is a lady so gay,
Who from her own country has run far away,
With the red cap and feathers that look very fine,
And all her delight is in drinking red wine.
     Fol di-diddle dol-di-day.

The Master and Mistress that sit by the fire,
Put your hand in your pocket, that's all we desire;
Put your hand in your pocket, and pull out your purse,
And give us a trifle—you'll ne'er be any worse.
     Fol di-diddle dol-di-day.

Some eggs and strong bacon we'll never deny,
For the eggs we can suck while the bacon doth fry.
Now all ye young lasses, just mind what ye are about,
If you give nought, we'll take nought, so we'll bid you good
    night.
        Fol di-diddle dol-di-day.

361   *Part of a Cheshire Maying song*

All on this pleasant evening together come are we,
   For the summer springs so fresh, green, and gay,
To tell you of a blossom that buds on every tree,
   Drawing near to the merry month of May.

Rise up, the master of this house, all in your chain of gold,
   For the summer springs so fresh, green, and gay;
We hope you're not offended, this night we make so bold,
   Drawing near the pleasant month of May.

Oh! rise, the mistress of this house, with gold upon your breast,
   For the summer springs so fresh, green, and gay;
And if your body be asleep, we hope your soul's at rest,
   Drawing near to the merry month of May.

362   *The 'Green Gravel' song; Forest of Dean, Gloucestershire*

Round the green gravel the grass is so green,
And all the fine ladies that ever were seen;
Washed in milk and dressed in silk,
The last that stoops down shall be married.

[Johnnie Smith] is a nice young man,
And so is [Bessie Jones] as nice as he;
He came to the door with his hat in his hand,
Inquiring for [Miss Jones].

She is neither within, she is neither without,
She is up in the garret a-walking about.
Down she came, as white as milk,
With a rose in her bosom as soft as silk.

Silks and satins be ever so dear,
You shall have a kiss my dear,
So off with the glove and on with the ring—
To-morrow, to-morrow, the wedding begins.

363 *'T' Bull's i' t' Barn' song; Shropshire and elsewhere*

As I was going o'er misty moor
I spied three cats at a mill-door;
One was white and one was black,
And one was like my granny's cat.
I hopped o'er t' style and broke my heel,
I flew to Ireland very weel,
Spied an old woman sat by t' fire,
Sowing silk, jinking keys;
Cat's i' t' cream-pot up to t' knees,
Hen's i' t' hurdle crowing for day,
Cock's i' t' barn threshing corn,
I ne'er saw the like sin' I was born.

364 *The 'Green Grass' song and another children's game song;*
both known at Berrington, Shropshire

(i)   Walking up the green grass,
           A dust, a dust, a dust!
        We want a pretty maiden
           To walk along with us.

We'll take this pretty maiden,
    We'll take her by the hand,
She shall go to Derby,
    And Derby is the land!

She shall have a duck, my dear,
    She shall have a drake,
She shall have a nice young man
    A-fighting for her sake!

363 hurdle] enclosure

Suppose this young man was to die,
   And leave the poor girl a widow;
The bells would ring and we should sing,
   And all clap hands together!

(ii)   Here stands a lady on a mountain,
Who she is I do not know;
All she wants is gold and silver,
All she wants is a nice young man.

Choose from you east, and choose you west,
Choose you the one as you love best.

Now Sally's got married we wish her good joy,
First a girl, and then a boy;
Twelve months a'ter a son and daughter,
Pray young couple, kiss together.

365   *A New Year's Eve wassailing song; Gloucestershire*

Wassail! Wassail! all over the town,
Our toast it is white, our ale it is brown:
Our bowl it is made of a maplin tree,
We be good fellows all; I drink to thee.

Here's to ——, and to his right ear,
God send our maister a happy New Year;
A happy New Year as e'er he did see—
With my Wassailing Bowl I drink to thee.

Here's to ——, and to his right eye,
God send our mistress a good Christmas pye:
A good Christmas pye as e'er I did see—
With my Wassailing Bowl I drink to thee.

Here's to Filpail, and to her long tail,
God send our measter us never may fail
Of a cup of good beer, I pray you draw near,
And then you shall hear our jolly Wassail.

Be here any maids, I suppose here be some;
Sure they will not let young men stand on the cold stone;
Sing hey O maids, come trole back the pin,
And the fairest maid in the house, let us all in.

    365 maplin] maple   trole] turn   pin] door-peg

Come, butler, come bring us a bowl of the best:
I hope your soul in Heaven will rest:
But if you do bring us a bowl of the small,
Then down fall butler, bowl, and all.

366 *Verses on the springs at Bath, by a clergyman named Groves,*
     of Claverton, Gloucestershire

When Bladud once espied some Hogs
Lie wallowing in the steaming bogs,
Where issue forth those sulphurous springs,
Since honor'd by more potent Kings,
Vex'd at the brutes alone possessing
What ought t' have been a common blessing,
He drove them thence in mighty wrath,
And built the mighty Town of Bath.
The hogs thus banished by their Prince,
Have liv'd in Bristol ever since.

367 *A 'popular rhyme', 'the letter H's petition to the inhabitants*
     of Shrewsbury', and their reply

Whereas I have by you been driven,
From house, from home, from hope, from heaven,
And plac'd by your most learn'd society
In exile, anguish, and anxiety,
And used, without one just pretence,
With arrogance and insolence;
I here demand full restitution,
And beg you'll mend your elocution.

*

Whereas we've rescued you, Ingrate,
From handcuff, horror, and from hate,
From hell, from horse-pond, and from halter,
And consecrated you in altar;
And placed you, where you ne'er should be,
In honour and in honesty;
We deem your pray'r a rude intrusion,
And will not mend our elocution.

368　*A 'popular rhyme' from south Cheshire*

> There was a lad,
> An' he had noo dad,
> An' hey jumped into a *peaswad*;
> *Peaswad* was sŏ full,
> Hey jumped into a roarin' bull;
> Roarin' bull was sŏ fat,
> Hey jumped into a gentleman's hat;
> Gentleman's hat was sŏ fine,
> Hey jumped into a bottle o' wine;
> Bottle o' wine was sŏ narrow,
> Hey jumped into a wheilbarrow;
> Wheilbarrow did sŏ wheil,
> Hey jumped into a hoss's heil;
> Hoss's heil did sŏ crack,
> Hey jumped into a mare's back;
> Mare's back did sŏ bend,
> Hey jumped into a tatchin'-end;
> Tatchin'-end set a-fire,
> Blowed him up to Jeremiah;
> Puff, puff, puff.

369　*Herefordshire riddles*

(i)
> There was a thing was three days old
> 　When Adam was no more;
> The same thing was but three weeks old
> 　When Adam was four score.

(ii)
> I have a cock on yonder hill
> I keep him there for a wonder
> And every time the cock doth crow
> It lightens, hails and thunders.

370　*Shropshire riddles*

(i)
> Behind the bush, behind the thorn,
> I heard a stout man blow his horn.

368 peaswad] pea-pod　　　　tatchin'-end] cobbler's thread

He was booted and spurred, and stood with pride,
With golden feathers by his side;

His beard was flesh, and his mouth was horn,
I am sure such a man never could have been born.

(ii)   As I was going over London bridge I saw a steel house,
It had four-and-twenty windows and wouldn't hold a mouse.

371   *A Herefordshire charm for a girl to see her future husband*

I put this under my head
To dream of the living and not of the dead;
To dream of the young man that I am to wed;
Not in his apparel or in his array,
But in the clothes he will wear every day.

372   *A Shropshire charm for a girl to see her future husband*

This is the blessed Friday night;
I draw my left stocking into my right,
To dream of the living, not of the dead,
To dream of the young man I am to wed.

373   *Verses published in 1831, adapted from Welsh fairy songs*

From flow'ry meads, and form so green,
   Companions hasten here,
The silv'ry moon in splendor's seen,
   No mortals now are near;
And gently sweeps the southern breeze
   The foliage among,
And sweetly heard from yonder trees
   The nightbird chants her song.

The well-swept hearth, the clean-kept floor,
   And blazing fire we love,
With water near, we ask no more,
   And for such far we'll rove.

Come tune your pipes, and close the ring,
  In concert join as one,
Till twilight's seen we'll dance and sing,
  Then disappear from man.

I'll go just now where Gwenwi sleeps,
  Who keeps her floor so clean,
I'll tell her where her sweetheart keeps,
  I'll do the same to Jane:
I'll tell them when they'll come again,
  Array'd in Sunday dress,
To give the long-wished kiss, and then
  Enjoy the fond caress.

Chorus

Bring, bring, the trefoil bring,
  With acorns grace the feast,
Whilst in yon grove we form a ring,
  Bring, bring of nuts the best;
Their juice, more sweet than mead e'er made,
  We'll suck, and keep the shell;
To drink the milk of Moll, the jade,
  Whose house is not clean'd well.

374 *A Herefordshire place-rhyme*

> When Ladie Lift puts on her shift
>   she fears a downright rain,
> but when she doffs it you will find
>   the rain is o'er, and still the wind,
>   and Phoebus shines again.

375 *A speech delivered in 1608 on Widemarsh Moor, near Hereford, before a Morris dance; the dancers were all between 96 and 106 years old*

> Ye servants of our mighty King,
> That come from Court one hundred mile
> To see our race and sport this spring,

374 Ladie Lift] a clump of trees on a high hill near Weobley, Herefordshire

Ye are welcome—that is our country stile—
And much good doe you. We are sorie
That Hereford hath no better for yee,
A Horse, a Cock, Trainsents, a Bull,
Primero, Gleeke, Hazard, Mumchance—
These sports through time are grown so dull,
As good to see a morris dance.
Which sport was promised in jest,
But payd as truly as the rest.
A race? quoth you. Behold a race,
No race of horses, but of men,
Men borne not ten miles from this place,
Whose courses outrun hundreds ten,
A thousand years on ten men's backs,
And one supplies what other lacks.

376   *The story of the 'Loppi'ton Bar', communally composed in
Loppington, Shropshire, in 1822*

In Loppington town there now doth dwell,
A cobbler who is known full well;
Going out to milk one morning fa'r,
In Elkes's fallow he spied a bar.

Then down he throws his milking-can,
And off he runs to his wife Ann;
He says, 'My dear, I do declar',
In Elkes's fallow I've see'd a bar!'

'My dear, what do you tell me now?
For sure the bar he'll bite our cow!
Sure they are most dreadful things
For they can bite as well as grin.'

Then off to Freeman's he did run,
To fetch the big dog and the gun,
Cart-ropes and pikels, likewise stakes
To bait the bar at Loppi'ton Wakes.

---

trainsents] train-scents, drag-hound chases   primero, gleeke] card games
hazard, mumchance] dice games

376 bar] bear   pikels] pitchforks

The village it did quickly rise
To hear the cobbler's mournful cries;
They surely thought he had been bitten,
But they were very much mistaken.

Bold Alexander run with speed,
He vow'd he'd kill the monstrous jeed;
Likewise the blacksmith with his shovel,
Aud vowed he'd kill the monstrous devil.

The Milner gazing in his room,
'You fools, it's only the full o' the moon!
But if it really should be so
The whole o' the town will have to go'.

Says Todd, 'This is a curious thing,
For bears are apt to bite and grin;
But if she proves their overthrow
The Milner and I shall be forced to go.'

[*Verse wanting?*]

Now munna this cobbler ha' bin bould
To ha' walked twice round him while he growled?
And munna-d his hearing ha' bin good
To ha' heard the growls of a chump o' wood?

377 *The 'Ellesmere Pool legend', as versified by the Revd Oswald
Fielden, vicar of Frankton, near Ellesmere, Shropshire*

I've heard it said, where now so clear
The water of that silver mere,
   It once was all dry ground;
And on a gentle eminence,
A cottage with a garden fence,
   Which hedged it all around.

And there resided all alone,
So runs the tale, an aged crone,
   A witch, as some folks thought.
And to her home a well was near,
Whose waters were so bright and clear,
   By many it was sought.

376 jeed] ?jade   milner] miller   chump] lump

But greatly it displeased the dame
To see how all her neighbours came
 Her clear cool spring to use,
And often was she heard to say,
That if they came another day,
 She would the well refuse.

'Upon this little hill,' said she,
'My house I built for privacy,
 Which now I seek in vain:
For day by day your people come
Thronging in crowds around my home,
 This water to obtain.'

But when folks laughed at what she said,
Her countenance with passion red,
 She uttered this dread curse:
'Ye neighbours one and all beware!
If here to come again you dare
 For you 'twill be the worse!'

Of these her words they took no heed,
And when of water they had need
 Next day, they came again.
The dame, they found, was not at home,
The well was locked: so they had come
 Their journey all in vain.

The well was safely locked. But though
You might with bolts and bars, you know,
 Prevent the water going,
One thing, forsooth, could not be done,
I mean forbid the spring to run,
 And stop it overflowing.

And all that day, as none could draw,
The water rose full two feet more
 Than ever had been known.
And when the evening shadows fell,
Beneath the cover of the well
 A stream was running down.

It flowed on gently all next day,
And soon around the well there lay
   A pond of water clear;
And as it ever gathered strength,
It deeper grew, until at length
   The pond became a mere.

To some, alas! the flood brought death;
Full many a cottage lies beneath
   The waters of the lake;
And those who dwelt on either side
Were driven by the running tide
   Their homesteads to forsake.

And as they fled, that parting word
Which they so heedlessly had heard,
   They now recalled, I ween!
The dame was gone; but where once stood
Her cottage, still above the flood
   An island may be seen.

378   *The 'Bagbury Ghost'; verses by Susan Jones, 'one of the
many verse-makers in humble life in Shropshire'*

I have heard a curious story, but I don't believe it's true,
About the Ghost of Bagbury and the things it used to do.
So draw your chair up closer and make a cheerful light,
And I'll tell you all about it as we're sitting here to-night.
There was once a wicked Squire who lived at Bagbury Hall,
So rich that half the country round, his own he used to call;
But so dreadfully fierce-tempered and so free of kicks and knocks,
That people said he would not die, but change into an ox.
As time passed on their prophecies were partly verified—
He certainly became an ox, although at first he died.
And if we may believe the tales the country-people told,
There never was a ghost before so vicious or so bold.
He used to haunt the roads by night with flaming eyes and horns,
And drive poor travellers into brooks, or over stones and thorns.
He'd shake the cottage walls and roofs from night till morning clear,
Till people trembled in their beds, and could not sleep for fear.
Or else he'd enter quietly when all were fast asleep,
And fling the plates and dishes down in one great broken heap.

The things the house-wives valued most, or oftenest did require,
They'd find them broken on the ground or burning in the fire.
Such things as these could not be borne in country or in town,
And so they begged the parson's help to come and read him down.
'O yes,' the good man said; 'if you will bring him to the Church,
I'll read him down into a shoe, and lay him in the porch.'
I do not know what means they used, the creature to ensnare,
But it's a fact they went to Church and somehow got him there.
And then the parson read and read till night began to fall,
And then the ghost, to their delight, looked very weak and small;
But can't you fancy their alarm when all the lights burnt out!
They had no more; the reader stopped; he could not see without.
Straightway the ghost began to grow, until 'twas very plain
He'd soon be larger than before, and all their labour vain.
It must have grieved them as the form increased before their eyes
Until the very walls were cracked with his enormous size.
When oh! there passed a traveller, his lantern in his hand:
They were not long before they all gave him to understand.
He brought his light, the parson read, the ghost shrunk all away,
Till they could squeeze him in the shoe, and there he lies this day.

379   *By the Revd Mr Booker, at Tedstone Delamere,*
      Herefordshire

Lines

To a beautiful and romantic brook, destitute of any appropriate
name, which amidst rocks and woods traverses the parish of
Tedston Delamere, and then falls into the Teme.

Thou lovely brook, without a name,
Unchronicled, unknown to fame,
Would Maro's or the Sabine muse,
Thy poet's warm wish not refuse,
Thou shouldst become as proud a stream,
As ere was made a poet's theme.
    The alders on thy banks which grow,
The zephyrs which around thee blow,
The woods which o'er thee tow'r sublime;
These in my verse to latest time
Should live. Thy gurgling waters clear
Which now are seen, now disappear,
Where finny tribes delighted play
Through summers' bright and cheerful day,
Should boast renown; and ev'ry flower

That sips the dew or drinks the shower,
On thy romantic margin green,
In fadeless beauty should be seen.
  Thy meadows smooth where fountains spring,
The various birds which near thee sing,
Not absent her whose warbling throat,
Charms the still night's ear with her note;
Thy rocks and dark embow'ring dells,
Where pensive meditation dwells—
All, all, immortal honours claim,
Thou lovely brook without a name!
  Yet tho' no verse of mine may live,
A name to thee thy bard will give,
Through Tedstone *Delamere*'s rich plains,
Where crown'd with hops, Pomona reigns,
Thou musically flow'st along,
In concord with the woodman's song;
Still flowing, grace those plains so fair,
And hence be called, THE DELAMERE.
  Then shall some wight, in after-time,
Immortalize thee in his rhyme;
And thus, though in far sweeter lay,
Reclining on thy margin say,
On thy rude banks, O stream! once rov'd
A shepherd swain who truly lov'd:
But ah! his fair-one and her charms
Were sever'd from his faithful arms.
—Of treasures such as these bereft,
The scenes of former bliss he left,
His wonted fold too, and his sheep,
And oft near thee would walk and weep;
Or seated in some shady nook,
Would note thy beauties in his book,
And as the peasants near him came,
Would wipe his tears and ask thy name:
'It has no proper name,' they cri'd,
''Tis pity,' he rejoin'd, and sigh'd.
Then pond'ring on thy banks would go,
And let thy murmurs sooth his woe—
No proper name! and yet these fields,
Where various plenty Nature yields,
Afford to thee a native sway,
Thro' scenes where thou must wish to stay—
Fields, from the *Virgin Mother* fair,

Entitled Tedstone *Delamere*!
What tho' thy source be not divine,
Hence lovely stream, that name be thine!

380 *Verses on the ancient traditional fair at Chester*

Beggars and vagabonds, blind, lame, and sturdy,
Minstrels and singers with their various airs,
The pipe, the tabor, and the hurdy-gurdy,
Jugglers and mountebanks with apes and bears,
Continued from the first until the fourteenth day
An uproar like ten thousand Smithfield fairs.
There were wild beasts and foreign birds and creatures,
And Jews and foreigners with foreign features.
All sorts of people there were seen together,
All sorts of characters, all sorts of dresses;
The fool with fox's tail and peacock's feather,
Pilgrims and penitents, and grave burgesses;
The country people with their coats of leather,
Vintners and victuallers with cans and messes;
Grooms, archers, varlets, falconers, and yeomen;
Damsels and waiting maids and waiting women—
The vulgar, unenlightened conversation
Of minstrels, menials, and courtesans and boors
(Although appropriate to their meaner station)
Would certainly revolt a taste like yours;
Therefore, I shall omit the calculation
Of all the curses, oaths, and cuts and stabs
Occasioned by their dice and drink and drabs.

381 *The rhyme for 'Willow pattern' ware; written in
Staffordshire before 1813*

Two pigeons flying high,
Chinese vessel sailing by,
Weeping willow hanging o'er,
Bridge with three men, if not four,
Chinese temple, there it stands,
Seems to cover all the land,
Apple tree with apples on,
A pretty fence to end my song.

VII

NORTH-EAST ENGLAND

382 *Verses by 'Mr Ford, the village poet', on a tree split in a
storm; Silkstone, Yorkshire, 1863*

When didst thou first behold the blush of morn?
When wast thou once a tender sapling born?
A seed by the wind far o'er the land,
Or wast thou planted by a human hand,
In memory of some long-forgot event?
How many ages, say, hast thou here spent?
Speak, if thy knotted trunk has got a tongue,
And tell us how things looked when thou wast young.

383 *On the lintel of a tower door at Byland Abbey, Yorkshire*

Here hills and waving groves a scene display,
And part admit and part exclude the day:
See rich industry smiling on the plains,
And peace and plenty tell VICTORIA reigns!
Happy the MAN, who to these shades retires,
Whom NATURE charms, and whom the muse inspires.
Who wandering thoughtful in this silent wood,
Attends the duties of the wise and good:
To observe a mean, be to himself a friend,
To follow NATURE, and regard his end.

384 *On Stones House, Todmorden, near Rochdale, Lancashire*

Friend I dwell here
And have in store
A little worldly pelf
Which on my friend
I keep to spend
As well as on myself
Whatever fare
Thou findest here
Take welcome for the best
That having got
Disdain thou not
For wanting of the rest.

385   *Inscription over the doorway of the post office at*
Lastingham, Yorkshire (the missing word is perhaps 'strife'
in its archaic sense of 'striving' or 'strong effort')

> The Hap of a Life
> Good or Ill . . .
> The Choyce of a Wife.

386   *On the sign of the Angel Inn, Silkstone, Yorkshire*

> Faith and Grace this house doth keep,
>   An Angel guards the door.
> Faith is dead, the Angel fled,
>   And Grace is now no more.

387   *Sign on a wayside inn near Ripon, Yorkshire*

> The maltster doth crave
> His money to have,
>   The exciseman says, 'Have it I must.'
> By that you may see
> How the case stands with me,
>   So I pray you, don't ask me to trust.

388   *Verses inscribed, in the early nineteenth century, by a parson,*
on the window of an inn between Northallerton and
Boroughbridge, Yorkshire

> Here in my wicker chair I sitt,
> From folly far, and far from witt,
> Content to live, devoid of care,
> With country folks and country fare;
> To listen to my landlord's tale,
> And drink his health in Yorkshire ale;
> Then smoak and read the *York Courant*;
> I'm happy and 'tis all I want.
> Though few my tythes, and light my purse,
> I thank my God it is no worse.

389 *A 'Barber's forfeits' verse, collected in Yorkshire in the eighteenth century*

Rules for Seemly Behaviour

First come, first serve—then come not late;
And when arrived, keep your state;
For he who from these rules shall swerve,
Must pay the *forfeits*—so observe.

Who enters here with boots and spurs,
Must keep his nook, for if he stirs,
And give with armed heel a kick,
A pint he pays for ev'ry prick.

Who rudely takes another's turn,
A forfeit mug may manners learn.

Who reverentless shall swear or curse,
Must lug seven farthings from his purse.

Who checks the barber in his tale,
Must pay for each a pot of ale.

Who will or cannot miss his hat
While trimming, pays a pint for that.

And he who can or will not pay,
Shall hence be sent half-trimm'd away,
For will he nill he, if in fault
He forfeit must in meal or malt.
But mark, who is already in drink,
The cannikin must never clink!

390 *Samuel Johnson (1709–84); lines printed on the 'toast list'
for a Shakespeare festival at Hull*

Each change of many-coloured life he drew;
Exhausted worlds, and then imagined new;
Existence saw him spurn her bounded reign,
And panting Time toiled after him in vain.

391 *Verses painted over the fireplace at the 'Six Ringers' inn,*
Silkstone, Yorkshire

> Customers came and I did trust them.
> I lost my liquor and my custom.
> To loose them both it grieved me sore,
> So I'm resolved to trust no more.
> Chalk is useful, say what you will,
> But chalk ner paid the malster's bill.
> I strive to keep a decent tap
> For ready money, but no strap.

392 *On a window in the Plumbers' Arms, Skeldergate, York (the*
glazier inscribed his verse in a diamond as here)

> A
> glazer I
> Am and I
> work for my
> bred and many
> fine window in my
> time have I made
> I with my dimond have
> Cut out the Glass and
> in a Corner Cist many
> a prity lass 1789

393 *A sweep's sign in Darlington, Co. Durham*

> Richard Bolam is my well known name,
> For sweeping chimneys extoll'd by fame;
> From a cottage to a castle, I will attend
> The shortest notice, from each friend.
> With my machine and attendant by my side,
> I'll sweep your chimneys either strait or wide.

391 strap] credit

394 *Verses on the war memorial fountain, Lofthouse, Yorkshire*

> If you want to be healthy, wealthy and stout,
> Use plenty of cold water inside and out.
> Let animal and Man drink freely.
> A pint of cold water three times a day
> Is the surest way to keep doctor away.
> Whoso thirsteth let him come hither and drink.

395 *On the village cross at Sprotborough, Yorkshire*

> Whoso is hungry and list well eate,
> Let him come to Sprotborough to his meate;
> And for a night and a day
> His horse shall have both corne and hay,
> And no man shall aske him when he goeth away.

396 *A riddle on the steeple of St Nicholas's Church (now Cathedral), Newcastle upon Tyne*

> My Altitude high, my Body foure square,
> My Foot in the Grave, my Head in the Ayre,
> My Eyes in my sides, five Tongues in my Wombe,
> Thirteen Heads upon my Body, four Images alone;
> I can direct you where the Winde doth stay,
> And I Tune Gods Precepts thrice a Day.
> I am seen where I am not, I am heard where eye is not,
> Tell me now what I am, and see that you misse not.

397 *Under a portrait of John Kaye's wife, Woodsome Hall, Yorkshire*

Vita Uxoris Honestae

> To live at home in housewyverie
> To order well my famylye,
> To see they lyve not Idyillye,
> To bring upe childrene vertuislye,
> To relyeve poor foulk willinglye,
> This is my care with modestye,
> To live my lyfe in honestye—

398 *Inscriptions on Sheffield cutlery (one couplet to each piece)*

> Sheffield made, both haft and blade;
> London for your life, show me such a knife.

*

> Sharpen me well and keep me clean,
> And I'll cut my way through fat and lean.

*

> I'm a Sheffield blade, 'tis true;
> Pray what sort of blade are you?

*

> To carve your meate is my intent;
> Use me, but let me not be lent.

*

> I'll wait upon you at the table,
> And doe what service I am able.

399 *On a piece of Sunderland ware*

> There is an hour of peaceful rest
> To mourning wanderers given;
> There's a tear for souls distrest,
> A balm for every wounded breast—
> 'Tis found above in Heaven.

400 *A verse on a Sunderland ware mug*

> The sailor tossed on stormy seas,
> Though far his bark may roam,
> Still hears a voice in every breeze
> That wakens thoughts of home;
> He thinks upon his distant friends,
> His wife, his humble cot;
> And from his inmost heart ascends
> His prayer, For-get-me-not.

401 *Verses in memory of Lord Nelson, on a 'frog' mug, Newcastle pottery*

> Remember whilst his mortal part has rest
> Th' immortal lives in every Briton's breast;
> Tho' short his Span of Life, recording fame
> Inscribes a deathless Volume to his Name;
> Mourn not for me, 'tis vain, chase grief away,
> Compleat my work and crown the glorious day;
> Behold! 'tis done, his parting spirit flew,
> And lighting rests, brave Collingwood, with you.

402 *A verse on a Sunderland ware pint mug*

> Glide on my bark, the summer's tide
> Is gently flowing by thy side;
> Around thy prow the waters bright,
> In circling rounds of broken light,
> Are glit'ring as if Ocean gave,
> Her countless gems to deck the wave.

403 *Verses on a handbill, distributed (nineteenth century) by Messrs Smith and Son, rag and paper merchants, Leeds*

> Messrs. Smith with most respectful feeling,
> Beg leave to inform you what they deal in
> They have not come your purse to try,
> Yourself shall sell and they will buy.
>
> So please look up that useless lumber,
> Which long you may have left to slumber
> We buy old boots, shoes, and stockings,
> Jackets, trousers, and smock-frockings.
>
> Towels, cloth, and cast off linen,
> Cords, cashmeres & worn-out woolens,
> Old gowns, caps, bonnets, torn to tatters,
> If fine or coarse, it never matters.

Bed-ticking, fustians, velveteens,
Stuffs, worsted, cord, or bombazines
Old worn-out handkerchiefs, or shawls,
Umbrellas, or parasols.

Sheep-netting, canvassing, or carpeting,
Whatever else you have pray bring,
And of the weight we will convince you,
And pay in ready money the utmost value.

We will purchase floor cloths, dusty rags,
Old ropes, sacking, and old bags,
Both cow and horse hair, broken glass,
Wine bottles, pewter, or old brass.

Old saucepans, boilers, copper kettles,
Pewter spoons, & other metals,
Old coins, silver, or ancient buttons,
Old copper, lead, or doctors' bottles.

Skins, whether worn by hare or rabbit,
However small your stock we'll have it
We will buy old rags, however rotten,
If made of woollen, hemp, or cotton.

We'll buy old iron, cast or wrought,
And pay the chink when it is bought,
If you have any bones to sell,
Their value in a trice we'll tell.

NB So over your dwellings give a glance
You never will have a better chance;
Our price is good, our weight is just,
And mind we never ask for trust,
So please look up if but a handful,
And for the same we shall be thankful.

404   *In the visitors' book at Mount Grace, Northallerton,
Yorkshire*

Ye pilgrims to the Mount called Grace,
    Who still may wend your way,
    Be sure that when you take your leave,

403 chink] cash

With grace you go your way:
So come with grace, and go with grace,
   And still Grace will remain,
When next you make a call this way,
   Consider this refrain.

405   *A sonnet by the Revd Richard Wilton, rector of*
Londesborough, Yorkshire

On my Parish Register Chest

In the scant compass of this iron chest
   Lie the brief records of three hundred years,
   The mute memorials of their smiles and tears:
Here side by side ten generations rest,
As with Time's iron hand together prest:
   A catalogue of names all that appears—
   Faded their joys, forgotten are their fears,
And all the eager hopes they once possessed.
With mournful mind I turn the yellow pages,
   Read the dim notice of a long-past wedding,
     How one was born, and overleaf was buried:
Thus swift and silent pass successive ages,
   Like autumn trees their leaves for ever shedding,
     Which into vast Eternity are hurried.

406   *Epitaph for Amos Street, huntsman, d. 1777; Birstall,*
Yorkshire

   This is to the memory of old Amos,
   Who was when alive for hunting famous;
   But now his chases are all o'er,
   And here he's earth'd of years four score.
   Upon this tomb he's often sat
   And tried to read his epitaph;
   And thou who dost so at this moment
   Shall ere long like him be dormant.

407 *An epitaph for Ned Allan, weaver and celebrated local*
fisherman, of Holystone, Northumberland; early nineteenth
century; by Robert Hunter, the village schoolmaster

Here lies old Ned in his cold bed,
For hunting otters famed,
A faithful friend lies by his side,
And 'Tug 'em' he was named.
Sport and rejoice ye finny tribes
That glide in Coquet river,
Your deadly foe no more you'll see
For he is gone forever.

The amphibious otter now secure,
On Coquet's peaceful shore,
May roam at large for Ned and Tug
Will never harm him more.
Up Swindon burn he may return,
When salmon time comes on;
For poor old Ned in his cold bed
Sleeps sound at Holystone.

408 *For Jeremiah Found; the church at Welton, Yorkshire*

. . . . . . has eight times married been;
But now old age has caught him in his cage,
And he lies under the grass so green.

409 *On the north wall of the church at Silkstone, Yorkshire; to*
Charles Greaves (who worked underground for many years);
from Dibdin's 'Tom Bowling'

His form was of the manliest beauty,
His heart was kind and soft;
Faithful below, he did his duty,
But now he's gone aloft.

410 *Once in All Saints' Church, Newcastle upon Tyne*

> Here lies Robert Wallas,
>   The King of good fellows,
> Clerk of All Hallows,
>   And a maker of Bellows.
> He bellows did make to the day of his death,
> But he that made bellows could never make breath.

411 *A seventeenth-century epitaph, for Josias Shute, Giggleswick, Yorkshire*

> Heer's y^t wise Charmer whose Sweet Ayres to Hear
> Each Soule delighted so to dwell i' th' Eare:
> Whose Life and Doctrine's Combin'd Harmony
> Familiarized St. Paul's Extasy:
> But now (from growing Evills) mounted high
> (Change but the Soule her Seat from Ear to th' Ey)
> This bright Starr still doth Lead wise men to Christ
> Through this dark Bochim, and aegyptian Myst
> Nay heer (what himself doth in Heav'n behoulde)
> Ev'n Blessed visions doth his Booke unfoulde.

412 *At Darrington, Yorkshire; for Alexander Blair of Aberdeen, d. 1671*

To the memory of that Just and Judicious Dealer, that piously well disposed Gentleman Mr. Alexander Blair of Aberdeen in Scotland Citizen and Merchant Taylor of London, and Merchant Factor to several parts in France and Scotland Who died the 28th of July 1671 in the 50th year of his age, by an Apoplexy, suddenly falling from his horse, of which he dyed three days after, to the great grief of his disconsolate widdow Mrs. Isabella Bruce, now Blair, who hath fixed
This Stone for his Remembrance.

> Here sleeps obscurely (till that Glorious Day
> Shall disenvelop, his Ecclipsed Clay)
> A sincere soul whom though death did divest
> Of life so soon surprised in an Arrest,
> Yet left him time to put in Bail, and by

411 Bochim] Old Testament place-name, 'the weeping ones' (Judges 2: 4–5)

A three days' respite, well prepared to die
Nor may we deem, he was with more hast hurld
Than with Good speed from this preposterous World
Where by his peaceful converse he did antedate
A pre-fruition of his present State.
For Why? His life was one continued act
Of kindness both in circumstance and Fact
Whose best devotion did consist in Deeds
Not in Gay blossomed Flowers but fruitful seeds
Sown with a liberal hand and chearful Heart
Seldom more prone to purchase than t'impart
Friends, kindred, neighbours, (if decayd or poor)
Kindly consider'd from his stock and store,
As though those earthly Blessings which heaven sent
Were in a literal sense, not given, but lent
These he returned, so largely at his Death
As if he ment to re-imburse his Breath
And live again remembered in the Grave
By those fair Legacies he freely Gave
Rest then blest Blair! Blest in thy blood and name
Blest in thy well born Consort, and the fame
Of Pious Deeds, Rest here, till that most Just
Judge, shall redeem and raise thee from the dust.

413   *A verse on hatchments and their mottoes; Allerton, Yorkshire*

Where'er a hatchment we discern
    (A truth before ne'er started),
The motto makes us surely learn
    The sex of the departed.
If 'tis the husband sleeps, he deems
    Death's day a *felix dies*
Of unaccustomed quiet dreams,
    And cries '*In caelo quies!*'
But if the wife, she from the tomb
    Wounds Parthian-like *post tergum*,
Hints to her spouse his future doom,
    And, threatening, cries '*Resurgam!*'

414 *In Beverley Minster, Yorkshire*

Mysterious was my cause of Death,
In the Prime of Life I fell;
For days I Lived yet ne'er had breath
The secret of my fate to tell.
Farewell my child and husband dear,
By cruel hands I leave you,
Now that I'm dead and sleeping here
My Murderer may deceive you.
Though I am dead, yet I shall live,
I must my Murderer meet,
And then in Evidence, shall give
My cause of death complete.
Forgive my child and husband dear,
That cruel Man of blood;
He soon for murder must appear
Before the Son of God.

415 *Epitaph for John Knott of Sheffield*

Here lies a man that was Knott born,
His father was Knott before him,
He lived Knott and did Knott die,
Yet underneath this stone doth lie
    Knott christened,
    Knott begot,
    And here he lies
    And yet was Knott.

416 *An epitaph in a Yorkshire churchyard*

Underneath this stone doth lie,
Back to back, my wife and I.
When the last trump sounds so shrill,
If she gets up I'll lie still.

417　*An epitaph for Catherine Alsopp, a Sheffield washerwoman, who hanged herself, 7 August 1905; it was composed by herself before her death*

Here lies a poor woman who always was tired;
She lived in a house where help was not hired,
Her last words on earth were: 'Dear friends, I am going,
Where washing ain't done, nor sweeping, nor sewing.
But everything there is exact to my wishes,
For where they don't eat, there's no washing of dishes
I'll be where loud anthems will always be ringing
But having no voice, I'll be clear of the singing.
Don't mourn for me now, don't mourn for me never,
I'm going to do nothing for ever and ever.'

418　*A children's Christmas wassail song from Huddersfield*

Here we come a-wassailing,
　Among the leaves so green;
Here we come a-singing,
　So fair to be seen.

Chorus

For it is in Christmas-time,
　Strangers travel far and near;
So God bless you and send you
　A Happy New Year.

We are not daily beggars,
　That beg from door to door,
But we are neighbours' children,
　Whom you have seen before,

Call up the butler of this house,
　Put on his golden ring,
Let him bring us a glass of beer,
　And the better we shall sing.

We have got a little purse,
　Made of stretching leather skin,
We want a little of your money
　To line it well within.

Bring us out a table,
  And spread it with a cloth;
Bring out a mouldy cheese,
  Also your Christmas loaf.

God bless the master of this house,
  Likewise the mistress too,
And all the little children
  That round the table go.

Good master and mistress,
  While you're sitting by the fire,
Pray think of us poor children
  Who are wandering in the mire.

419 *A Yorkshire New Year's Eve song*

To-night it is the New Year's night, to-morrow is the day,
And we are come for our right, and for our ray,
As we used to do in old King Henry's day,
  Sing fellows, sing, hag-man ha!

If you go the baconflick, cut me a good bit;
Cut, cut, and low, beware of your maw;
Cut, cut, and round, beware of your thumb,
That me and my merry men may have some.
  Sing fellows, etc.

If you go to the black ark, bring me ten marks;
Ten marks, ten pound, throw it down upon the ground,
That me and my merry men may have some,
  Sing fellows, etc.

420 *A 'Stang-Riding' song, Northallerton, Yorkshire*

Hey Derry! Hey Derry! Hey Derry Dan!
It's neither for your cause nor my cause that I ride the stang;
But it is for Tom—for banging his deary,

mouldy cheese] ?green cheese

419 ray] ?money   hag-man ha] Hogmanay, New Year's Eve   baconflick]
flitch, side of bacon   ark] box

420 ride the stang] be carried round the streets on a pole or ladder (see note)

If you'll stay a few minutes I'll tell you all clearly.
One night he came home with a very red face,
I suppose he was drunk as is often the case:
Be that as it may; but when he got in,
He knocked his wife down with a new rolling pin.
She jumped up again, and knocked off his hat,
And he up with the pestle, and felled her quite flat.
She ran out to the yard and shouted for life,
And he swore he would kill her with a great gully knife.
So all you good people that live in this row,
I'd have you take warning, for this is our law;
And if any of your husbands you wives do bang,
Come to me and my congregation, and we'll Ride the Stang.

421   *Silkstone, Yorkshire, and Dublin; a comparison, by John
Ford (?), a 'Village bard' of Silkstone, d. 1897 aged 80*

Two famous places I record,
    And match one for the other;
Old Silkstone's one of these, I trow,
    And Dublin is the other.

Each place produces, as you know,
    A stock of famous fuel:
Of this, some's put into your grate,
    And some into your gruel.

The former spreads its influence round
    And warms your icy feet;
The latter warms the inner man,
    Especially when it's neat.

The former's found beneath the soil,
    In hill or dale or hummock;
The latter is from grain distilled,
    And put inside the stomach.

But from that little snug retreat
    Into the head it wanders,
Making its dupes look soft like geese,
    And waddle just like ganders.

I do not ask to which you cling,
   The latter or the former;
But I prefer the coal, though some
   Declare that whisky's warmer.

422   *A popular rhyme on some places in Co. Durham and*
      Northumberland

Cuckenheugh there's gear enough, Collierheugh there's mair,
for I've lost the key of the Bounders, I'm ruin'd for ever mair.
Ross for rabbits, and Elwick for kail,
Of a' the towns eer I saw Howick for ale,
Howick for ale, and Kyloe for scrubbers,
Of a' the towns eer I saw Lowick for robbers,
Lowick for robbers, Buckton for breed,
Of a' the towns eer I saw Holy Island for need,
Holy Island for need, and Grindon for kye,
Of a' the towns eer I saw Doddington for rye.
Doddington for rye, Bowingdon for rigs,
Of a' the towns eer I saw Barmoor for whigs,
Barmoor for whigs, Tweedmouth for doors,
Of a' the towns eer I saw Ancroft for whores,
Ancroft for whores, and Spittal for fishers,
Of a' the towns eer I saw Berrington for dishes.

423   *A fragment on the witch Molly Cass; Yorkshire*

Foor seear sha war a queer au'd lass,
Ez meean ez muck, ez bou'd ez brass;
Ah meean t'au'd witch, au'd Molly Cass,
'At lived nigh t'mill at Leeming.
Noo fooak will clack, when pass't that way
Noo fooak will clack, Ah've heeard 'em saay
At t'dark o' neet, when pass't that waay,
Tha fan' it ommaist leet ez daay,
Sike leets war awlus gleaming;
An' sum held ti't 'at mair 'an yance
Wiv her feet fra t'grund they'd seean her prance,
Loup hoos heigh up, wi' t'Divil dance.

Bounders] ?boundaries   scrubbers] ?wooden harrows   breed] bread
kye] cattle   rigs] ?tricks, or flashy clothes   dishes] ?dishers (a local word
meaning 'dish-makers')

423 seear] sure   loup] leap   hoos heigh] house-high

424 *A sonnet on the Yorkshire legend of the 'Gabriel Ratchet' or 'Wild Hunt' tradition; by 'Mr Holland' of Sheffield, c.1860*

Oft have I heard my honoured mother say,
   How she has listened to the Gabriel hounds—
   Those strange unearthly and mysterious sounds,
Which on the ear through murkiest darkness fell;
And how, entranced by superstitious spell,
   The trembling villager not seldom heard,
   In the quaint noise of the nocturnal bird
Of death premonished, some sick neighbour's knell.
I, too, remember once at midnight dark,
   How these sky-yelpers startled me and stirred
   My fancy so, I could have then averred
A mimic pack of beagles low did bark.
   Nor wondered I that rustic fear should trace
A spectral huntsman doomed to that long moonless chase.

425 *The song of the 'Cauld Lad of Hilton'; Yorkshire*

       Wae's me! wae's me!
       The acorn is not yet
       Fallen from the tree,
       That's to grow the wood,
       That's to make the cradle,
       That's to rock the bairn,
       That's to grow to a man,
       That's to lay me.

426 *On Elphi the Dwarf, Farndale, Yorkshire; verses written into a cook book, and signed 'J.L. 1699'*

       Elphi bandy legs,
       Bent an wide apart,
       Neea yan i' this deeal
       Awns a kinder heart.
       Elphi great heead
       Greatest ivver seen,
       Neea yan i' this deeal
       Awns a breeter een.

426 neea yan] no one   deeal] dale

Elphi little chap,
Thoff he was so small
War big wi' deeds o' kindness,
Drink tiv him yan an all.
Him 'at fails ti drain dry,
Be it mug or glass
Binnot woth a pescod
Nor a buss fra ony lass.

427   *Lines written by Mr Pratt of Askrigg, Yorkshire, during a*
        great snowstorm; December 1784

I rise about ten to hear who's alive;
My breakfast I get; order dinner at five;
I go out to Robert to know how my Nags are,
His account, tho' its short, it pleases my ear;
The boys I saw busy in shovelling the snow,
To Turf and Coal Houses for lasses to go;
I call upon James to visit the vault,
And saw no Bins empty, so I found no fault;
The kitchen I entered, and found many pies,
Which Graham told me were made for the boys;
I met with Ianson, he of *Camden* did talk
That he would beat *Serjeant* at every stroke,
We both did agree, and were not afraid,
For *Camden* is stout and *Serjeant* a jade.
I walked in the gallery with all my might,
I came back again, and sat down to write
Till the clock it struck four; I rose all alive,
Got myself washed, clean shirt on by five:
To six year old mutton fat and good I sat down,
For which many Peers would have given a crown;
Then Tom brought a Moorcock, the last of this year,
A bird of great flavour I hereby declare.
After apples and wine appear on the table,
I eat up my apples and drink whilst I'm able;
Then send in for Batty to know how my stock fares,
He enters with countenance all full of cares,
His story is frightful, such a storm he ne'er saw,
The drifts are much deeper than oldest men know,
Men with shovels and spades were two hours a day

pescod] peascod
427 *Camden, Serjeant*] horses in a race

In cutting a road to come at the hay;
With other dismal accounts of what has been done
Day by day since the storm first begun;
At last he concludes my stock are all hearty
(I am glad for to hear), he goes to his party,
I order them ale to cheer up their spirits,
A quantum suffecit, due to their merits.
I prose on till ten, when Thomas appears
With slippers and candle to light me upstairs;
I get into bed; he tucks me up tight,
But seldom, or ever, bids me good-night;
So I sleep, slumber, and about sprawl,
Till nine the next morning he gives me a call.

428   *A Yorkshire song about 'Mother Shipton' and her prophecies;*
      c.1770

Of all the pretty pantomimes,
That have been seen or sung in rhime,
Since famous Johnny Rich's times,
    There's none like Mother Shipton.

She pleases folks of every class,
She makes her swans and ducklings pass;
She shows her hog, she shows her ass,
    Oh, charming Mother Shipton!

Near to the famous dropping well,
She first drew breath, as records tell,
And had good beer and ale to sell,
    As ever tongue was tipt on;

Her dropping well itself is seen,
Quaint goblins hobble round their queen,
And little fairies tread the green,
    Call'd forth by Mother Shipton.

429　*The Yorkshire legend of Semerwater*

> In ancient times, as story tells,
> The saints would often leave their cells,
> And stroll about, but hide their quality,
> To try good people's hospitality.
> It happened on a summer's day,
> As authors of the legend say,
> A tired hermit—a saint by trade—
> Taking his tour in masquerade
> Disguised in tatter'd habits, hied
> To an ancient town on Raydalside;
> Where, in the stroller's canting strain,
> He begged from door to door in vain;
> Tried every tone might pity win,
> But not a soul would let him in.
> Our wandering saint in woeful state,
> Treated at this ungodly rate,
> Having through all the city pass'd,
> To a small cottage came at last,
> Where dwelt a good old honest pair,
> Who, though they had but homely fare,
> They kindly did this saint invite
> To their poor hut to pass the night;
> And then the hospitable sire
> Bid his good dame to mend the fire,
> While he from out the chimney took
> A flitch of bacon from the hook,
> And freely from the fattest side
> Cut out large slices to be fried;
> Then stepp'd aside to fetch him drink,
> Fill'd a large jug up to the brink,
> And saw it fairly twice drained off,
> Yet (what was wonderful—don't scoff!)
> 'Twas still replenish'd to the top,
> As if he ne'er had touched a drop.
> The good old couple were amaz'd,
> And often on each other gaz'd;
> Then softly turned aside to view
> Whether the lights were turning blue.
> The gentle pilgrim was soon aware,
> And told his mission in coming there:
> 'Good folks, you need not be afraid,

I'm but a saint,' the hermit said.
'No hurt shall come to you or yours;
But for this pack of churlish boors,
Not fit to live on Christian ground,
They and their cattle shall be drown'd,
While you shall prosper in the land.'
At this the saint stretched forth his hand—
'Save this little house! Semerwater sink!
Where they gave me meat and drink.'
The waters rose, the earth sunk down,
The seething floods submerged the town;
The gen'rous couple there did thrive,
And near the lake aye long did live,
Until at good old age they died,
And slept in peace by Semerside.

430   *A song sung at the end of the Mummers' Play of St George and the Dragon; from near Sheffield*

Come all ye jolly mummers
  That *mum* in Christmas time,
Come join with us in chorus;
  Come join with us in rime.
      And a mumming we will go, we'll go,
      And a mumming we will go,
      With a white cockade all in our hats
      We'll go to the gallant show.

It's of St. George's valour
  So loudly let us sing;
An honour to his country
  And a credit to his king.
      And a mumming we will go, we'll go,
      And a mumming we will go;
      We'll face all sorts of weather,
      Both rain, cold, wet, and snow.

It's of the King of Egypt
  That came to seek his son;
It's of the King of Egypt
  That made his sword so *wan*.
      And a mumming, &c.

430 wan] grim, dreadful

It's of the black Morocco dog
    That fought the fiery battle;
It's of the black Morocco dog
    That made his sword to rattle.
        And a mumming we will go, we'll go,
        And a mumming we will go,
        With a white cockade all in our hats
        We'll go to the gallant show.

431 *Verses for a young people's round game, Sheffield district; the
    disconsolate one chooses the young man whom she loves best,
    and then they sing the final verse*

        Sally, Sally Slarter,
        Sitting by the water,
        Crying out and weeping
        For a young man.
        Rise, Sally, rise,
        Dry up your eyes;
        Turn to the east,
        Turn to the west,
        Turn to the young man
        That you love the best.

                    *

        So now you've got married,
            I hope you'll enjoy
        Your sons and your daughters;
            So kiss and good-bye.

432 *An 'Old Border Rhyme' about the rivers Tweed and Till*

        Quoth Tweed to Till,
        What gars ye rin sae still,
        Quoth Till to Tweed,
        Sae still's I rin and sae fast's ye gae,
        Whar ye droon ae man I droon twae.

            431 slarter] grubby, or wet
            432 gars] makes

243

433 *A nursery rhyme from near Sheffield*

> There was a man who had a lad;
> He put him in a pea swad.
> The pea swad it was so green;
> He put him in a silver pin.
> The silver pin it was so fine,
> He put him in a glass of wine.
> The glass of wine it was so good,
> He put him in a log of wood.
> The log of wood it was so thick,
> He put him in a candlestick.
> The candlestick it was so nasty,
> He put him in an apple pasty.
> The apple pasty was so hot,
> He put him in a porridge pot.
> The porridge pot it was so wide,
> He put him in an old house side,
> And there he lived and there he died,
> And nobody either laughed or cried.

434 *A Darlington rhyme*

> When I was a little girl, about seven years old,
> I hadn't got a petticoat, to cover me from the cold;
> So I went into Darlington, that pretty little town,
> And there I bought a petticoat, a cloak, and a gown.
> I went into the woods and built me a kirk,
> And all the birds of the air, they helped me to work;
> The hawk with his long claws, pulled down the stones,
> The dove, with her rough bill, brought me them home:
> The parrot was the clergyman, the peacock was the clerk,
> The bullfinch played the organ, and we made merry work.

435 *A North-country charm to see one's future husband*

> The even ash-leaf in my left hand,
> The first man I meet shall be my husband.
> The even ash-leaf in my glove,

433 swad] pod

The first I meet shall be my love.
The even ash-leaf in my breast,
The first man I meet's whom I love best.
The even ash-leaf in my hand,
The first I meet shall be my man.
Even ash, even ash, I pluck thee,
This night my true love for to see;
Neither in his rick nor in his rear,
But in the clothes he does every day wear.
Find even ash or four-leaved clover,
An' you'll see your true love before the day's over.

436   *A charm to see one's future husband in a dream; Yorkshire,
North Riding*

> New moon! new moon! I hail thee,
> This night my true love for to see:
> Not in his best nor worst array,
> But in his apparel for every day;
> That I to-morrow may him ken,
> From among all other men.

437   *A charm against cramp; northern counties of England*

> The devil is tying a knot in my leg,
> Matthew, Mark, Luke, and John unloose it I beg;
> Crosses three we make to ease us,
> Two for the thieves, and one for Christ Jesus.

438   *A charm to exorcize spirits; Yorkshire*

> Jesus, a name high over all,
> O'er earth, and air, and sea,
> Before thy name the angels fall,
> And devils fear and flee.

    435 rick] best   rear] worst

439   *Verses on March and April weather, the 'Borrowing Days';*
       North of England and Scotland

(i)   March said to Averil,
               I see three hoggs on yonder hill;
               An' if ye'll lend me dayis three,
               I'll find a way to gar them dee.
               The first o' them was wind an' weet;
               The second o' them was snaw an' sleet;
               The third o' them was sic a freeze,
               It froze the birds' nebs to the trees.
               When the three days were past and gane,
               The silly hoggs cam' hirplin hame.

(ii)   March borrowed from April
               Three days, and they were ill:
               The first of them was wan and weet,
               The second it is snaw and sleet,
               The third of them is peel-a-bane,
               And freezes the wee bird's neb to the stane.

440   *An anonymous English translation of Latin verses on*
       'Drunken Barnaby', by Richard Brathwaite, 1588–1673;
       Yorkshire

               Then to Rippon, I appear there
               To sell horses, if they're dear there;
               If they're cheap, I use to buy them,
               And i' th' country profit by them:
               When to quicken 'em I tell ye,
               I put quick eels into their belly.

439 hoggs] yearling sheep   gar] make   dee] die   nebs] bills   hirplin]
stumbling

441 *A dialect poem by Joseph B. Eccles, a nineteenth-century*
Yorkshire local poet

Deein be Inches

A'm deein be inches tha knaws weel enuf,
    But net e'en a fig duz ta care;
A'm a get aght road az sooin az I like—
    Ma cumpany I knaw tha can spare.
Goa fetch me that bottle ov fizzick daan stairs,
    An bring me that noggin ov gin;
I really feel ready ta faint inta t'earth—
    Tha knaws what a state I am in.

I cuddn't quite finish them two mutton chops,
    A'm az weak az wumman can be;
I hav all soarts ov pains flyin right thro' ma boans,
    But then tha's noa pity fer me.
A'l try and get t'doctor to give me a chainge—
    Sich pain I noa longer can bide;
A mun hev sum owd port ta strenthen me up,
    An a drop ov gud brandy beside.

Av hed a stiff neck and saand e ma heaad,
    An felt dizzy times aght ov mind;
But then its noa use, a kind wurd or thought
    Tha nivver wonce hez e thee mind;
Wen I sit daan an groan tha stands like a stoop
    An nivver wonce tries fer ma sake
To walk a bit faster, though du what I will
    Tha knaws 'at A'm all on a ake.

P'ray keep aght that draft—I feel all on a sweat;
    A'm suar at A'm wastin ta nowt;
I sal hav them cowd shivvers az suar az A'm wick—
    Tha can't have a morsel ov thowt.
Shut that door, an goa get spooin an t'glass,
    And mix up a drop nice an strong;
It's time tha did summat fer't sake ov thee wife
    A'm fear'd tha wean't hev me soa long.

aght road] out of the way   saand] sound, noise   stoop] post   wick] alive

A've waited for gruel this haar an a hawf,
    Summat strenthnin iz what I require;
A'm faintin awaay, yet az trew az I liv,
    Tha's nivver put t'pan onta t'fire.
I sal fade like a cannel et bottom ov t'stick,
    Fer want ov attention an care;
Be quick wi that glass, an bring me sum toast,
    I feel fit ta sink through ma chair.

It's a queer piece ov bizziness (sed John tull hizsen);
    It's cappin what wimmin can du;
Shoo's been cryin aght fer this last twenty years,
    An sayin at shoo woddn't get through;
Yet shoo eats an shoo drinks all 'at cums e her waay,
    An lewks weel and strong az can be;
Wal hear A'm hauf pined, an get nowt but crusts,
    It's noan her at's deein, it's ME.

442   *The diarist Abraham de Pryme on the hermit William of
Lindholme; Hatfield, Yorkshire*

Within an humble, lonesome cell,
He free from care and noise does dwell;
No pomp, no pride, no cursed strife,
Disturbs the quiet of his life.
A truss or two of straw his bed,
His arms the pillow for his head;
His hunger makes his bread go down,
Although it be both stale and brown.
A purling brook that runs hard by
Affords him drink whene'er he's dry,
In short, a garden and a spring
Do all life's necessaries bring.

443   *On a Sunderland ware butter dish*

When first I was a foremast man
I often did pretend,
That if e'er I got promoted

---

441 tull hizsen] to himself   cappin] astonishing   pined] starved

I would be a seaman's friend,
Then in a little time I was
Promoted to a mate,
But I then like all others
Soon forgot my former state.
When I became a Captain
I thought myself a king,
And very soon I did forget
The foremast man I'd been.

444 'The Fisher Lad of Whitby'; Yorkshire

My love he was a fisher-lad, and when he came ashore
He always steer'd to me, to greet me at the door;
For he knew I loved him well, as any one could see,
And O but I was fain when he came a courting to me.

It was one lovely morning, one morning in May,
He took me in his boat to sail out on the bay;
Then he told me of his love, as he sat by my side,
And he said that in a month he would make me his bride.

That very afternoon a man of war came in the bay;
And the press-gang came along and took my lad away;
Put irons on his hands, and irons on his feet,
And they carried him aboard, to fight in the fleet.

My father often talks of the perils of the main,
And my mother says she hopes he will come back again:
But I know he never will, for in my dreams I see
His body lying low at the bottom of the sea.

The ships come sailing in, and the ships they sail away,
And the sailors sing their merry songs out on the bay;
But for me, my heart is breaking, and I only wish to be,
Lying low with my lover deep down in the sea.

When the house is all still, and every one asleep,
I sit upon my bed, and bitterly I weep;
And I think of my lover away down in the sea,
For he never, never more, will come again to me.

445   *A 'Border ballad', by 'Crawhall'*

Wae's me—God wot—
But the beggarlie Scot
Through the 'bateable land has prickit his waie
An' ravaged wi' fire
Peel, hau'din' an' byre—
Ooor nowte, sheep, an' galloways a' tae'n awae:
But—by hagbut an' sword—ere he's back owre the Border,
We'll be het on his trod an' aye set him in order.

Nae bastles or peels
Are safe frae thae deils,
Gin the collies be oot, or the Laird's awae—
The bit bairnies an' wives
Gang i' dreid o' their lives.
For they scumfish them oot wi' the smoutherin' strae:
Then—spear up the lowe—ca' oor lads thegither,
An' we'll follow them hot-trod owre the heather.

Weel graith'd—sair on mettle—
Oor harness in fettle—
The Reivers we sicht far ayont 'the Wa'.
Gin we bring them to bay
Nae 'saufey' we'll pay
Weel fangit—syne hangit, we'se see them a'—
Then—on lads, on—for the trod is hot,
As oot owre the heather we prod the Scot.

We'll harass them sairly—
Nae 'hoo' gi'e for parley,
Noo the spur's i' the dish 'fore their hungrie wames,
To your slogans gie mouth
An' we'll sune lead them south—
Gra'merce—gin we cross them—we'll crap their kames:
Then—keep the lowe bleezin' lads—ca' to the frae—
Syne we're up wi' the lifters we'll gar them pay.

'bateable land] borderland   peel] peel tower   nowte] cattle   gallo-
ways] small Galloway horses   hagbut] hackbut, harquebus, early kind of
portable gun   trod] track   bastles] bastilles, towers   scumfish]
choke   strae] straw   spear] rouse   lowe] beacon-fire   graith'd]
prepared   saufey] blackmail   fangit] taken   crap] crop   kames]
combs   gar] make

Fae to fae—steel to steel—
Noo the donnert loons reel
An' catiff—cry 'hoo'—but it's a' in vain:
Sec a clatter o' thwacks
Fa's on sallets an' jacks,
Till we've lifted the lifters as weel's oor ain:
Then, wi' fyce to the crupper they'll ride a gaie mile,
To their dance frae the woodie at 'Merrie Carlisle'.

446 *Two election ballads sung at Eslington, Northumberland;*
(i) was by Elizabeth Wyndham (better known as 'Betty
Wundrum')

(i)   Liddle for Me!

Tune: 'Jigging for Me'

By the margin of Tyne as I saunter'd along,
I heard an old woman lilt up a new song,
As she sat near a cot, with a child on her knee,
And the burthen was—'Liddell, brave Liddell for me!'

Chorus—
O Liddell, sweet Liddell, brave Liddell for me,
O Liddell, sweet Liddell, brave Liddell for me,
For a Parliament man he will suit to a T—
The bright star of Eslington—Liddell for me!

O Liddell and Bell are now running a heat,
The prize to the winner—a Parliament seat;
And Liddell's the man that will suit to a T—
The bright star of Eslington—Liddell for me!
                    O Liddell, sweet Liddell, &c.

Matt. Bell's a good shot, and can stand a good drink,
At the cry of the hounds he'll run off in a blink.
May the next fox he chases run into the sea,
And he follow after it—Liddell for me!
                    O Liddell, sweet Liddell, &c.

    445 donnert] stupefied   woodie] gallows

O Liddell cares little about a fox chase,
But Liddell has goodness and Liddell has grace,
And Liddell I'll love till the day that I dee—
The bright star of Eslington—Liddell for me!
    O Liddell, sweet Liddell, &c.

May Liddell succeed with his aim in the end,
For Liddell has been our supporter and friend;
At a tale of distress the tear starts in his e'e—
The bright star of Eslington—Liddell for me!
    O Liddell, sweet Liddell, &c.

Now the old wife arose, and entered her cot,
And more of this favourite song I heard not;
But her lilting made such an impression on me,
That all the way home I sang—Liddell for me!
    O Liddell, sweet Liddell, &c.

(ii)   For Bell

Matt. Bell and Kenn'd Worth
Tune: 'Sing hey diddle diddle, the cat and the fiddle'

Sing hey diddle diddle,
 Here's young Mister Liddell,
To Parliament wishes to go;
 Then give us your voices,
 And that will rejoice us,
How say you, freeholders?—No, no!

He's smart and he's natty,
 He's tall and he's pretty,
Of very first water a beau;
 At court and at gala,
 He's sure without fellow,
How say you, freeholders?—No, no!

At waltz and quadrille,
 He's quite sans pareil:
On fiddle he draws a good bow.
 Then send him to London;
 That we mayn't be undone;
How say you, freeholders?—No, no!

No, no, Mr. Liddell,
Tho' you dance and can fiddle,
You won't do for us of the north;
Tho' your coat's the first fashion,
And your style very dashing,
We like better Matt. Bell, and kenn'd Worth.

VIII

NORTH-WEST ENGLAND

Of Scawfell Pike I clomt the height;
　　And when I got upon it,
With all my soul, with all my might,
　　I wished I hadn't done it.

My blythe companion lay at ease,
　　No heights had he to scale!
And smoked the pipe of utter peace,
　　Reclining down the vale.

Woe to the man on clambering bent!
　　He finds but falls and strains,
And mists, and much bewilderment,
　　And divers aches and pains.

But well for him who, in the vale,
　　Reclining smokes in peace;
No strains are his, no heights to scale,
　　Body and mind at ease.

I scrambled down; my limbs, though sound,
　　Were most severely shaken;
Oft when I thought I'd reached smooth ground,
　　I found I was mistaken!

Let he who wills go climb the hills,
　　My taste with his don't tally;
Let he who wills go climb the hills,
　　But I'll stay in the valley!

448 *Framed papers at Hoghton Towers, Lancashire; c.1571*

The Blessed Conscience

Apollo with his radiant beams,
　　Inflamed the air so fair,
Phaeton with his fiery teams
　　The heat of war did bear.
The day was hot, the evening cool,
　　And pleasures did abound;

And meads, with many a crystal pool,
　　Did yield a joyful sound.

This fragrant time to pleasures prest
　　Myself for to solace.
I walked forth as I thought best,
　　Into a private place.
And as I went myself alone,
　　There came to my presence
A friend, who seemed to make great moan,
　　And said, 'Go, get you hence.'

'Alas, good sir, what is the cause
　　You this have said to me?'
'Indeed,' he said, 'the princes laws
　　Will bear no more with thee:
For Bishop Younge will summon thee
　　You must to his presence;
For in this land you cannot live
　　And keep your conscience.'

'I am told I must not ride.
　　What is my best to do?'
'Good sir, here you must not abide,
　　Unless to church you go;
Or else to Preston you must wend,
　　For here is no residence;
For in this land you have no friend
　　To keep your conscience.'

Then did I think it was the best
　　For me in time to provide;
For Bishop Younge would me molest
　　If here I should abide.
Then did I cause my men prepare,
　　A shipp for my defence;
For in this land I could not fare
　　And keep my conscience.

When my ship that it was hired
　　My men return'd again;
The time was almost full expired,
　　That here I should remain;
To Preston town I should have gone
　　To make recognizance;
For other help perceived I none,
　　But keep my conscience.

To lovely Lea I then me hied,
   And Hoghton bade farewell;
It was more time for me to ride,
   Than longer there to dwell.
I durst not trust my dearest friend,
   But secretly stole hence,
To take the fortune God would send
   And keep my conscience.

When to the sea I came until
   And passed by the gate,
My cattle all, with voices shrill,
   As if they mourned my fate,
Did leap and roar, as if they had
   Understood my diligence;
It seemed my cause they understood,
   Thro' God's good providence.

At Hoghton high which was a bower
   Of sports and lordly pleasure.
I wept; and left that lofty tower
   Which was my chiefest treasure.
To save my soul and lose the rest
   It was my true pretence;
Like frightened bird I left my nest
   To keep my conscience.

Thus took I there my leave, alas,
   And rode to the sea-side:
Into the ship I hied apace,
   Which did for me abide.
With sighs I sailed from Merry England,
   I asked of none licence
Therefore my estate fell from my hand
   And was forfeit to my prince.

Thus Merry England have I left
   And crossed the raging sea,
Whereof the waves have me bereft
   Of my so dear country.
With sturdy storms and blustering blast,
   We were in great suspense;
Full sixteen days and nights they last,
   And all for my conscience.

until] unto   diligence] ?persistent devotion

When on the shore I was arrived,
　Through France I took my way;
And unto Antwerp I me hied,
　In hope to make my stay.
When to the city I did come,
　I thought that my absense
Would to my men be cumbersome,
　Though they made no offence.

At Hoghton where I used to rest,
　Of men I had great store,
Full twenty gentlemen at least,
　Of yeomen good three-score.
And of them all brought but two
　With me, when I came thence;
I left them all, the world knows how
　To keep my conscience.

But when my men came to me still,
　Lord, how rejoiced I,
To see them with so good a will
　To leave their own country.
Both friends and kin they did forsake,
　And all for my presence,
Alive or dead, amends I'll make,
　And give them recompense.

But fortune had me so bereft,
　Of all my goods and lands,
That for my men was nothing left
　But at my brethren's hands.
Then did I thirst the truth to prove
　Whilst I was in absence,
That I might try their constant love,
　And keep my conscience.

When to my brethren I had sent,
　The welcome that they made
Was false, reports to me present
　Which made my conscience sad.
My brethren all did thus me cross,
　And little regard my fall.
Save only one that rued my loss—
　That is Richard of Park Hall.

He was the comfort that I had:
   I proved his diligence,
He was as just, as they were bad,
   Which cheered my conscience.
When this report of them I heard,
   My heart was sore with grief,
In that my purpose was so marr'd,
   My men should want relief.

Good cause had I to love my men,
   And them to recompense;
Their lives they ventured, I know when,
   And left their dear parents.
Then to come home straightway I meant,
   My men for to relieve;
My brethren sought this to prevent,
   And sums of gold did give.

A thousand marks they offered them,
   To hinder my licence:
That I should not come home again,
   To keep my conscience.
But if that day I once had seen,
   My lands to have again
And that my prince had changed been
   I would not have me stay'n.

. . . .

I should my men so well have paid,
   Thro' God's good providence,
That they should ne'er have been afraid
   To lose their due expense.

But now my life is at an end,
   And Death is at the door,
That grisly ghost his bow doth bend,
   And through my body gore:
Which Nature now must yield to clay,
   And Death will take me hence:
And now I shall go where I may
   Enjoy my conscience.

Fair England, now ten times adieu,
   And friends that therein dwell;
Farewell, my brother Richard true

Whom I did love so well.
Farewell, farewell, good people all,
   And learn experience:
Love not to much the golden ball,
   But keep your conscience.

All ye who now this song shall hear,
   Help me for to bewail
The wight, who scarcely had his peer,
   Till Death did him assail.
His life a mirror was to all,
   His death without offence;
'Confessor,' then, let us him call.
   O blessèd conscience.

449   *An old Lancashire riddle*

The Goose, the Calf, the little Bee,
Are great on Earth I prove to thee,
And rule the great affairs of Man,
Explain this riddle if thou can.

450   *Verses on or about a chapel of ease, with wine merchants'*
vaults below, at Kendal, Westmorland

There's a Spirit above and a spirit below
A Spirit of love and a spirit of woe;
The Spirit above is the Spirit divine,
And the spirit below is the spirit of wine.

451   *Kendal church, Westmorland; inscription on the fifth bell*

In wedlock bands,
All ye who join with hands,
   Your hearts unite;
So shall our tuneful tongues combine
   To laud the nuptial rite.

452   *An alehouse sign at Troutbeck, near Ambleside*

> Thou mortal man that lives by bread,
> What made thy face to look so red?
>
> Thou silly fop, that looks so pale,
> 'Tis red with Tommy Burkett's ale.

453   *Inscription on a Liverpool ware jug*

> At last it pleased His Majesty
> To give peace to the Nation,
> And honest hearts
> From foreign parts
> Came home for consolation,
> Like lightning—for I felt new life
> Now safe from all alarms
> I rushed and found my Friend and Wife
> Locked in each others Arms,
> Yet fancy not
> I bore my lot
> Tame like a lubber—No
> For seeing I was finely tricked
> Plump to the devil I boldly kick'd
> My Poll and my Partner Joe.

454   *On a six-gallon Liverpool ware jug*

> Here's luck in the bottom dear Jane only see,
> My dream and my Coffee in a Wedding agree,
> But ah! my dear sister what fate me befall,
> I fear I can wait for no wedding at all.

455   *On a 'Farmer's Arms' pitcher, Liverpool ware*

> Let mighty and great
> Roll in splendour and state,
> I envy them not, I declare it;
> I eat my own lamb,
> My chicken and ham,

I shear my own sheep and I wear it.
I have lawns, I have bowers,
I have fruits, I have flowers,
The lark is my morning alarmer;
So you jolly dogs now
Here's to God bless the Plow,
Long life and content to the Farmer.

456 *Rossendale Forest, Lancashire; an oath once taken by every inhabitant, at the age of 12*

You shall true Leige-man be,
Unto the King's Majestie:
Unto the beasts of the Forest you shall no hurt do,
Nor to anything that doth belong thereunto;
The offences of others you shall not conceal,
But, to the utmost of your power, you shall them reveal
Unto the Officers of the Forest,
Or to them who may see them redrest:
All these things you shall see done,
So help you GOD at his Holy Doom.

457 *On a piece of Liverpool masonic ware*

We help the poor in time of need,
The naked clothe, the Hungry feed.
'Tis our foundation stone.
We build upon the noblest plan,
Where Friendship rivets man to man
And makes us all as one.

458 *At 'Sunderland Point', Lancashire; an inscription for 'Samboo', a black slave who died there in 1736*

Full sixty years the angry Winter's Wave,
Has thundering dashed this bleak and barren Shore
Since SAMBOO's Head laid in this lonely GRAVE,
Lies still and ne'er will hear their turmoil more.

Full many a sandbird chirps upon the Sod
And many a Moonlight Elfin round him trips,
Full many a Summer's Sunbeam warms the Clod,
And many a teeming Cloud upon him drips;

But still he sleeps—till the awakening Sounds
Of the Archangel's Trump new life impart,
Then the GREAT JUDGE his Approbation founds
Not on Man's COLOR, but his WORTH OF HEART.

459   *Tomb of Thomas Morley, d. 1566; Staining, Lancashire*

Man by lying downe in his bedde to reste,
Signifieth layed in grave by suggeste,
Man by sleepinge in his cowche by nyghte,
Betokeneth the corps in grave withowte spirite,
And by rysinge again from reste and sleepe,
Betokeneth resurrection of bodie & soule to meete,
When atropos divideth bodie and soule a sonder
Th' one to the arthe thother to heaven w^{th}owte encomb^r
God graunte us his grace to be readie to passe
at the hower of deathe with him in spirite to solace
That we maye have o^r eares attente to heare ye trumpes sound
Sayinge, Arise yee dedde and come to the doome
To the blessed, Joifull, and to the cursed ach and woe.
and to the electe, heaven, and to the reprobate inferno.

460   *Epitaph on a wrestler; a gravestone in a churchyard near*
       Wigton, Cumberland

Here lies a man beneath this stone
Who often threw but never was thrown.
Before him his antagonists fell
As many a broken bone can tell.
Death cried: 'I'll try this man of strength,'
And laid him here, at his full length.

459 Atropos] the third of the Greek Fates; she severed the thread of life   ach] ache

461　*An inscription to John Richardson, architect, born 1774,
died aged over 90; the Soutergate, Kendal*

My earthly house has fallen to decay,
The base was shaken, and the walls gave way;
The pillars that had borne its weight for more
Than fourscore years, were mouldered at the core;
The rafters crumbled, and the light was faint
That crept in at the windows old and quaint;
While seam and crevice in the tottering shell
For years let in the wind, when down it fell;
The roof-tree, strong and sound, being last
To topple beneath the resistless blast.
Then, past repairs, I looked for no new plan
Whereby to have rebuilt the outward man;
But calmly waited, with the world at peace,
Nor would, when death approached, renew the lease;
But humbly sought for my departing soul,
Beyond the grave, eternally a place,
Where it might still the grand creations trace
Of God, the first great *Architect* of all.

462　*Holy Trinity Church, Kendal; epitaph for Raulph Tirer,
d. 1627*

London bredd me, Westminster fedd me,
Cambridge sped me, my Sister wed me,
Study taught me, Living sought me,
Learning brought me, Kendal caught me,
Labour pressed me, sicknes distressed me,
Death oppressed me, and grave possessed me,
God first gave me, Christ did save me,
Earth did crave me, and heaven would have me.

463　*Epitaph for Alice Bateman, d. 1637 aged 26, leaving three
daughters; Kendal*

Shall we entrust a grave with such a guest,
Or thus confine her to a marble chest,
Who though the Indies met in one smale roome,

Th'are short in treasure of this pretious tombe,
Well borne, and bred, brought up to feare and care,
Marriage, which makes up women, made her rare,
Matron and maide with all choyse virtues grac'st.
Louving and lov'd of all, a soule so chast,
Ne're rigg'd for heaven, with whom none dare
Venture their states with her in bliss to share,
She liveing virtues pattern, the poores releife,
Her husband's cheifest joy, now dead, his greife.

464 *Epitaph for Mary Bolton, d. 1822 aged 7, in Bolton parish church, Lancashire*

> She had no fault save what travellers give the moon,
> Her life was bright, but died, alas! too soon.

465 *Epitaph for the first Lord Wharton (d. 1568); at Kirkby Stephen, Westmorland*

> Here I Thomas Wharton do lie,
>   With Lucifer under my head;
> And Nelly my wife hard by,
>   And Nancy as cold as lead;
> Oh, how can I speak without dread!
>   Who could my sad fortune abide,
> With one devil under my head,
>   And another laid close on each side!

466 *Epitaph in Holm Cultram Abbey, Cumberland*

> Feby. VII. 1655.
> JOHN CHAMBER.
>
> Till death brought him
> Here mayntained still the
> Custom cleare: the
> Church, the wood and parish

rigg'd] ?set sail

465 Lucifer] the stone helmet, with a bull's crest, on the tomb   Nelly, Nancy]
Eleanor and Anne, Lord Wharton's first and second wives

Right, He did defend with all
His might. Kept constant
Holy Sabbath dayes, and
Did frequent the Church
Alwayes. Gave alms
Freely to the poore, who
Dayly sought it at his door
And purchased land as
Much and more than all
His elders did before.
He had foure children
With two wives, they dy-
ed young, the one wife
Survives: None better of
His rank could be for
Liberall Hospitallite.

467 *Verses by the incumbent (d. 1878) at Rivington, Lancashire (see the note)*

  Who has not heard of Steeple-Jack
  That lion-hearted Saxon?
  Though I'm not he, he was my sire
  For I am Steeple Jackson.

468 *Part of an epitaph for two sailors, in Skelton churchyard, Cumberland*

  Tho' Boreas' blasts, and Neptune's waves,
   Have toss'd us to and fro;
  In spite of both, by God's decree,
   We anchor here below.
  Though here we safe in harbour lye,
   With many of our fleet,
  We shall one day set sail again,
   Our admiral, CHRIST, to meet.

---

468 Boreas] the north wind

469   *Inscription for the workmen who lost their lives by accidents during the works on the Lancaster–Carlisle railway (Shap District); 1845*

> Like crowded forest trees we stand
> And some are marked to fall,
> The axe will smite at God's command,
> And soon shall smite us all.
> No present health can life ensure
> For yet an hour to come,
> No human power our life secure
> And save us from the tomb.

470   *A watchman's song from Kendal*

> Ho, watchman, ho!
> Twelve is the clock!
> God keep our town
> From fire and brand,
> And hostile hand;
> Twelve is the clock!

471   *Part of an epistle describing the Preston 'Guild' celebrations of 1782; by the Revd Thomas Wilson, headmaster of Clitheroe Grammar School*

... The Recorder attracted the eyes of the town,
With his wig of three tails and the blush of his gown.
Joy sparkled and smiled in the face of the Mayor,
And he marched through the streets with right worshipful air.
Whilst dignity shone in the steps of each Bailiff,
With looks of command and the pomp of a Caliph.
New scour'd was the Mace, and so bright, I could see't,
By the help of a glass, half the length of a street.
'Twas glorious to see how the men of all trades,
With faces clean wash'd, wore their flaming cockades.
With a strut of true consequence, every Profession
Did honour to Preston throughout the procession.
The gentlemen, coupled in pair after pair,
Cock'd their hats, and look'd fierce, when reviewed by the fair.

I'd the pleasure to see our old grandmother Eve;
But how Adam was tempted I cannot conceive,
For her face and her air seem'd more fit for laughter,
And I'm sure she scarce e'er had so ugly a daughter.
I cannot perceive, on perusing her face,
The remains of one dimple, or trait of one grace;
And, if truth must be spoken, our grandfather Adam
Was stupid, and awkward, and clumsy as madam.
But I cannot describe or sufficiently praise
The beauties that beamed with astonishing blaze;
They were rich constellations—a galaxy bright—
A host of pure angels—too much for the sight.
There were Lancashire Witches, whom Venus still arms
With the magic of eyes, and profusion of charms—
Who bind us with spells, and display all their art
To wind their soft fetters in wreathes round the heart.
Each eye is prepared, and well tutored, no doubt,
As love, death, and darts are flying about;
Each shot is successful, well-aimed at its man,
And all look as killing as ever they can.
Amidst their parading such glances were sent
That sighs were excited wherever they went:
Gowns, caps, and ruffles, performed well their part,
While nets, lawns, and gauzes are spread for the heart.
Even matrons of eighty, with years bowed down,
Stand straight as an arrow, and skip through the town;
Each dame her old age and infirmities scorns,
Skips light o'er the pavement, in spite of her corns.
Her flagging curls wave with a diligent care,
Her baldness relieved with a purchase of hair.
All the world is at Preston, the multitude spreads
So thick through each street, 'tis a pavement of heads,
Whilst feasting and dancing and music and noise
Are the soul of a Guild and the chief of its joys. . . .

472   *'Marriage' verse used by Salathiel Cross (d. late eighteenth
      century); Carlisle*

> Behind this hedge, in frosty weather
> I join this wench and rogue together
> Let none but Jove, who rules the thunder
> Then part this wench and rogue asunder.

473 *Lancashire 'Weather Rhymes'*

> If red the sun begins his race
> Expect that rain will fall apace.

*

> The evening red, the morning grey
> Are certain signs of one fair day.

*

> If woolly fleeces spread the heavenly way,
> No rain, be sure, disturbs the summer's day.

*

> In the waning of the moon,
> A cloudy morn—fair afternoon.

*

> When clouds appear like rocks and towers,
> The earth's refreshed by frequent showers.

*

> When Pendle wears its woolly cap,
> The farmers all may take a nap.

474 *Lancashire; a charm 'to get drink within one hour'*

> Upon Good Friday I will fast while I may,
> Until I heare them knell
> Our Lord's own bell.
> Lord in his messe
> With his twelve Apostles good;—
> What hath he in his hand?
> Ligh in leath wand:
> What hath he in his other hand?
> Heaven's doore keys.
> Steck, Steck Hell door,
> Let Chrizun child
> Goe to its mother mild.
> What is yonder that casts a light so farrandly?
> Mine own dear Sonne that's naild to the tree.

> 474 steck] shut   farrandly] brightly

He is naild sore by the head and hand;
And Holy harne Panne.
Well is that man
That Friday spell can,
His child to learne:—
A cross of Blue and another of Red,
As Good Lord was to the Roode.
Gabriel laid him down to sleep
Upon the ground of Holy weepe:—
Good Lord came walking by,
Sleepest thou, wakest thou, Gabriel?
No, Lord, I am sted with stick and stake,
That I can neither sleepe nor wake.
Rise up, Gabriel, and go with me,
The stick nor the stake shall never deere thee.
Sweet Jesus. Our Lord. Amen.

475 *Verses by the philosopher David Hume (1711–76) that he
wrote on a window of the Bush Inn, Carlisle*

Here chicks in eggs for breakfast sprawl,
Here godless boys God's glories squall,
Here Scotsmen's heads do guard the wall,
But Corby's walks atone for all.

476 *A traditional verse on the church at Winwick, Lancashire,
with a 'modern' addition*

The church at little Winwick,
    It stands upon a sod,
And when a maid is married there,
    The steeple gives a nod.

*

Alas! how many ages,
    Their rapid flight have flown,
Since on that high and lofty spire
    There's moved a single stone.

---

474 harne panne] brain   sted] anchored   deere] threaten

477   *A 'favourite of our grandsires'; a ballad from Radcliffe,*
Lancashire

Radcliffe Otter Hunt

I am a bold otter, as you shall hear,
   I've rambled the country all round;
I valued no dogs far or near,
   In the water, nor yet on the ground.

I valued no dogs, far or near;
   But I roved thro' the country so wide,
Till I came to a river so clear
   That did Clifton and Prestwich divide.

As thro' the wild country I rambled,
   I lived at extravagant rate,
On eels, chubs, and gudgeons I feasted;
   The fishermen all did me hate.

Yet still up the rivers I went,
   Where the fishes my stomach did cheer;
Till a challenge from Radcliffe they sent me,
   They quickly would stop my career.

Next morning these dogs did assemble;
   Jack Allen, he swore I must die.
It made me full sorely to tremble
   To hear those stout hounds in full cry.

It was near Agecroft Bridge I oft went,
   Where with me they'd had many a round;
So closely they stuck to the scent.
   That they forced me to take to fresh ground.

Jack Allen, the darling of hunters,
   And Ploughman, the glory of hounds
You may search all the country over,
   Their equals are not to be found.

Although I my country did leave,
   It was sorely against my own will;
They pursued me with courage so brave,
   That they proved a match for my skill.

Again thro' the country I rambled;
    To the Earl of Wilton's I came,
Where I made bold his fish-pond to enter,
    And there I found plenty of game.

But the Earl being now at his hall,
    He swore that my life they must end;
So straight for Tom Thorpe he did call,
    And for Squire Lomas' hounds they did send.

Then the dogs and the huntsmen arrived,
    Thinking my poor life for to end;
But to gain my old ground I contrived,
    Where I could myself better defend.

At length by misfortune I ventured
    Again up the river to steer,
Where into a tunnel I entered,
    Not thinking my death was so near.

But those dogs from old Radcliffe they came,
    And into my hold did me cry;
The hunters they all did the same,
    And they swore they would take me or die.

'Twas on the next morning so early
    They forced me from my retreat;
Then into the river I dived,
    Thinking all their sharp schemes to defeat.

But those dogs did soon force me out,
    Because that my strength it did fail;
Tom Damport, that tailor so stout,
    He quickly laid hold of my tail.

Then into a bag they did put me,
    And up on their backs did me fling;
And because that in safety they got me,
    They made all the valleys to ring.

Then right for old Radcliffe did steer,
    And soon at Bob Hampson's did call;
And hundreds of people were there
    To drink and rejoice at my fall.

The same afternoon they contrived
    With me more diversion to have;
Put me into a pit, where I dived,
    Just like a stout otter so brave.

And yet I remained so stout,
    Though they swam me for three hours or more;
The dogs they could not force me out,
    Till with stones they did pelt me full sore.

Thus forcing me out of the water,
    Because that my strength it did fail;
And then in a few minutes after,
    Jack Ogden laid hold of my tail.

And so now they had got me secure,
    They right to the 'Anchor' did steer;
But my lot was too hard to endure,
    And my death was approaching too near.

Next morning to Whitefield they took me,
    To swim as before I had done;
When out of the bag they did put me,
    Alas! my poor life it was gone.

And so now this bold otter you've killed,
    You may go to Bob Hampson's and sing,
Drink a health to all true-hearted hunters,
    Success to our country and King.

478 *An 'Impromptu' from a Blackburn newspaper, 20 February
     1811, 'on hearing nearly twenty beautiful girls had recently
     met a tea-party, unaccompanied by one male creature'*

    'Tis strange that twenty Blackburn belles,
        All ting'd with youth's delicious glow;
    All form'd with nature's beauteous swells,
        Should sip their tea without one beau;
    Yes, strange indeed that twenty pair
        Of pouting lips should sweetly move,
    And not one youthful swain be there
        To sigh, or even talk of love.

As in a glass, concenter'd rays
  Will soon the lightest fabric fire,
So such a group would form a blaze
  That might each beau with dread inspire;
If one fine girl can warm the heart,
  And this we daily ascertain;
The heat that twenty would impart,
  Might dry up liver, heart and brain.

Then Blackburn swains, 'twas wisely done,
  To fly from such a mass of charms;
For he who gazes on the sun
  'Tis ten to one his vision harms.
Nay, e'en the moths that play around
  The candle oft resign their breath;
So Beaux, where female charms abound,
  Must fly, or risk a scorching death.

479   *A courtship (?) ballad from Cumberland*

Jwohnny, Git Oot!

Git oot wid the', Jwohnny, thou's no'but a fash;
Thou'll come till thou raises a desperat clash,
Thou's here ivery day just to put yan aboot,
An' thou moiders yan terrably—Jwohnny, git oot!

What says t'e? I's bonnie? Whey! That's nowte 'at's new.
Thou's wantin' a sweetheart?—Thou's hed a gay few!
An' thou's cheatit them, yan efter t' t'udder, nèa doubt;
But I's nūt to be cheatit sèa—Jwohnny, git oot!

There's plenty o' lads i' beàth Lamplugh an' Dean
As yabble as thee, an' as weel to be seen;
An' I med tak' my pick amang o' there aboot—
Does t'é think I'd ha'e thee, than? Hut, Jwohnny, git oot!

What? Nūt yan amang them 'at likes mé sa weel?
Whey, min—there's Dick Walker an' Jonathan Peel
Foorsettin' mé ola's i't' lonnins aboot,
Beàth wantin' to sweetheart mé—Jwohnny, git oot!

479 fash] pest   clash] scandal   moiders] worries   yabble] able
med] might   min] man   foorsettin'] waylaying   ola's] always
lonnins] lanes

What?—Thou will hev a kiss?—Ah, but tak't if thou dar!
I tell the', I'll squeel, if thou tries to cǔ' nār.
Tak' care o' my collar—Thou byspel, I'll shoot.
Nay, thou sha'n't hev anudder—Noo Jwhonny, git oot!

Git oot wid the', Jwohnny—Thou's tew't me reet sair;
Thou's brocken my comb, an' thou's toozelt my hair.
I willn't be kiss't, thou unmannerly loot!
Was t'ere iver sec impidence! Jwohnny, git oot!

Git oot wid the', Jwohnny—I tell the', be deùn.
Does t'e think I'll tak' up wid Ann Dixon's oald sheùn?
Thou ma' gā till Ann Dixon, an' pu' hur aboot,
But thou s'alln't pu' me, sèa—Jwohnny, git oot!

Well! That's sent him off, an' I's sworry it hes;
He med ken a lass niver means hoaf 'at she says.
He's a reet canny fellow, howiver I floot,
An' it's growin o' wark to say Jwohnny, git oot!

480   *Verses by Robert Tannahill, a Paisley weaver working in
Bolton in 1800*

      Quoth gobbin Tom of Lancashire,
      To northern Jock a lowland drover,
      'Thoose are foin kaise thai'rt driving there,
      They've sure been fed on English clover.'
      'Foin kaise?' quoth Jock, 'ye bleth'ring hash,
      Deil draw your nose as lang's a sow's!
      That talk o yours is queer-like trash;
      Foin kaise! poor go·k! their names are koose.'

---

byspel] 'by-word'   shoot] shout   tew't] disarranged   sheùn] shoon, shoes
growin o' wark] getting harder and harder

480 gobbin] rustic, ignorant

IX

SAMPLES FROM SCOTLAND, WALES, AND ELSEWHERE

481   *On Giles Cor(e)y, executed as a wizard, late seventeenth
        century; a New England 'ditty' of the time*

Giles Cory was a wizzard strong,
A stubborn wretch was he;
And fitt was he to hang on high
Upon ye Locust Tree.

So when before ye Magistrates
For tryall he did come,
He would no true confession make,
But was compleately dumbe.

'Giles Corey' said ye Magistrate.
'What hast thou heare to pleade
To these who now accuse thy soule
Of Crymes and horrid deed?'

Giles Corey, he sayde not a word:
No single word spake he.
'Giles Corey' sayth ye Magistrate,
'We'll press it out of thee.'

They got them then a heavy beam;
They layde it on his breast;
They loaded it with heavy stones;
And hard upon him prest.

'More weight,' now sayd this wretched man:
'More weight,' again he cryed.
And he did no confession make;
But wickedlie he dyed.

482   *A Berwickshire rainbow rhyme*

Rainbow, rainbow, haud awa' hame,
A' yer bairns are dead but ane,
And it lies sick at yon grey stane,
And will be dead ere you win hame.
Gang owre Drumaw and yont the lea,
And down the side o' yonder sea;
Your bairn lies greeting like to die,
And the big teardrop's in his e'e.

483 *Epitaph for Dr McCulloch; Bothwell churchyard,*
Lanarkshire, Scotland

> There lies interred beneath this sod,
> A sycophantish man of God,
> Who taught an easy way to Heaven,
> Which to the rich was always given.
> If he gets in he'll look and stare,
> To find some out that he put there.

484 *On the tombstone of Margaret Scott, in Dalkeith churchyard,*
Midlothian, Scotland; she died in 1738 aged 125 years

> Stop, passenger, until my life you read:
> The living may get knowledge by the dead.
> Five times five years I lived a virgin's life:
> Ten times five years I was a virtuous wife:
> Ten times five years I lived a widow chaste;
> Now, weary'd of this mortal life, I rest,
> Between my cradle and my grave have been
> Eight mighty kings of Scotland and a queen.
> Four times five years the Commonwealth I saw;
> Ten times the subjects rose against the law.
> Twice did I see old Prelacy pull'd down;
> And twice the cloak was humbled by the gown.
> An end of Stuart's race I saw: nay, more!
> My native country sold for English ore.
> Such desolations in my life have been,
> I have an end of all perfection seen.

485 *Girls' yarrow-gathering verse for May-Day evening;*
Nielston, Renfrewshire

> Yarrow, fair yarrow!
> I hope before this time tomorrow
> That you will show me
> Who my true love shall be;
> The colour of his hair,
> The clothes that he'll wear,
> And the words that he'll speak,
> When he comes to court me.

486 *Robert Burns (1759–96); lines he inscribed on a window at the Queensberry Arms, Sanquhar, Dumfriesshire, Scotland*

> Ye gods! ye gave to me a wife
>   Out of your grace and favour,
> To be a comfort to my life;
>   And I was glad to have her.
> But if your providence divine
>   For other ends design her,
> To obey your will at any time,
>   I'm ready to resign her.

487 *Robert Burns; epitaph for James Smith*

> Lament him, Mauchline husbands a',
>   He aften did assist ye;
> For had ye staid hale weeks awa,
>   Your wives they ne'er had miss'd ye.
>
> Ye Mauchline bairns, as on ye pass
>   To school in bands thegither,
> O tread ye lightly on his grass,—
>   Perhaps he was your father!

488 *The 'Queen Anne' game; (i) from Belfast; compare (ii) from Swaffham, Norfolk*

(i) Lady Queen Anne she sits on a stand,
She is fair as a lily, she is white as a swan;
A pair of green gloves all over her hand,
She is the fairest lady in all the land.
Come taste my lily, come smell my rose,
Which of my babes do you choose?
I choose not one, but I choose them all,
So please, Miss Nell, give up the ball.

The ball is ours, it is not yours,
We will go to the woods and gather flowers;
We will get pins to pin our clothes,
You will get nails to nail your toes.

(ii)   Queen Anne, Queen Anne, she sits in the sun,
As fair as a lily, as brown as a bun;
We've brought you three letters, pray can you read one?
I can't read one without I read all,
So pray —— deliver the ball.

You old gipsy, sit in the sun,
And we fair ladies go and come;
The ball is mine, and none o' thine,
And so good-morning, Valentine.

489   *From Fochabers, Morayshire*

Hear all! let me at her;
    Hear all! let me go;
Hear all! let me at her,
    When my mammy will or no.

—— has ta'en a notion
    For to go and sail the sea;
There he's left his own dear ——,
    Weeping on the Greenland sea.

Hold your tongue, my own dear ——,
    Take your baby on your knee.
Drink his health, my jolly sailors,
    I'll come back and marry thee.

I will buy thee beads and ear-rings,
I will buy thee diamond stones,
I will buy thee silken ribbons,
    When thy baby's dead and gone.

—— says she'll wear the ribbons,
—— says she'll wer them a'—
—— says she'll wear the ribbons
    When her baby's dead and gone.

490   *A New Year's Eve weather rhyme, said to be from the
        Highlands of Scotland*

> If New Year's eve night-wind blow *south*,
> It betokeneth warmth and growth;
> If *west*, much milk, and fish in the sea;
> If *north*, much cold, and storms there will be;
> If *east*, the trees will bear much fruit
> If *north-east*, flee it man and brute.

491   *A Scottish charm to preserve the house from danger at night*

> Who sains the house the night,
> They that sains it ilk a night.
> Saint Bryde and her brate,
> Saint Colme and his hat,
> Saint Michael and his spear,
> Keep this house from the weir;
> From running thief,
> And burning thief,
> And from a' ill rea[f],
> That be the gate can gae,
> And from an ill wight,
> That be the gate can light;
> Nine reeds about the house,
> Keep it all the night.
> What is that what I see
> So red, so bright, beyond the sea?
> 'Tis he was pierc'd through the hands,
> Through the feet, through the throat,
> Through the tongue,
> Through the liver and the lung;
> Well is them that well may,
> Fast on Good Friday.

491 sains] safeguards   brate] apron   weir] ?war   reaf] reif, plundering
reeds] roods, crosses

492   *Weather and the seasons of life; a Scottish verse*

> West wind to the bairn
>   When ga'an for its name,
> And rain to the corpse
>   Carried to its lang hame;
> A bonny blue sky
>   To welcome the bride,
> As she gangs to the kirk
>   Wi' the sun on her side.

493   *By the Lanarkshire poet Joseph Hawcroft; 1878*

In a Manx Glen

Here, once more seated, where the dewy leaves
  And sunbeams mingle,
I, musing, fancy every ripple grieves,
  That I'm still single.

They murmur of the joys of years ago,
  When I, poor dreamer,
The dice of fate would venture not to throw,
  On board the steamer.

The dimpled sea, soft air, and bonny sky—
  They might have aided;
My friends have taken that course—why did I
  Not do as they did?

Nor yet, through many a happy moonlight walk,
  Comes the suggestion,
Through the sweet current of our 'spoony' talk,
  To pop the question.

'The happy "Yes" her sweet lips shall not pass,
  Nor kiss exquisite,'
I said, 'Until the glen at Ballaglass
  We chance to visit.'

And soon we rambled there one glorious morn—
  I, Tom, and Harry;
Buoyed up with hope how could I feel forlorn?
  With me was Carry!

We gathered flowers, sang songs, and filled the glen
  With joyous laughter;
I lived on love, and could not foresee, then,
  The dread hereafter.

By Fate beguiled, I took the river side;
  Deeds piscatorial
Induced me to forget my longed-for bride.
  Ah! sad memorial

Of that sad time is this loud mountain stream;
  For when I wended
My way back to my friends I found my dream
  Too rudely ended.

Dire was the blow: my darling, blithe and fair,
  Engaged to Harry!
I sighed aloud, and said, with anguished air,
  'Deceitful Carry!'

To which, in playful mood, she then replied,
  'I knew your wishes;
But, when next time you want to win a bride,
  Neglect the fishes!'

494   *Verses for New Year's morning; the Isle of Man*

Again we assemble, a merry New Year,
To wish each one of the family here,
Whether man, woman, or girl, or boy,
That long life, and happiness, all may enjoy;
May they of potatoes and herrings have plenty,
With butter and cheese, and each other dainty;
And may their sleep never, by night or day,
Disturbed be by even the tooth of a flea;
Until at the Quaaltagh again we appear,
To wish you, as now, all a happy New Year.

494   Quaaltagh] Manx word referring to 'first footing'

495 *A New Year's Day song; Pembroke Dock, Wales*

Rise up a New Year's mornin',
The cocks is all a-crowin';
And if you think it is too soon,
Rise up and look at the stars and moon,
And then you'll see it's dawnin'.
Rise up, the master of the house,
With gold upon your toes,
And open you the back-door,
And out the Old Year goes.
Rise up, the mistress of the house,
With gold upon your chin,
And open you the front-door,
And turn the New Year in:
For I'm come here with a free good will
To give you some New Year's water.

The roads is very dirty,
My shoes is very thin;
I have a little pocket
To put a penny in.

Two or three ha'pence, if you please,
Two or three ha'pence, if you please,
To buy some ink and paper.

496 *South Pembrokeshire; a children's song as they visit with the 'New Year's Water'*

Here we bring new water from the well so clear,
For to worship God with, this happy new year;
Sing levy dew, sing levy dew, the water and the wine,
With seven bright gold wires, and bugles that do shine;
Sing reign of fair maid, with gold upon her toe,
Open you the west door, and turn the old year go,
Sing reign of fair maid, with gold upon her chin,
Open you the east door, and let the New Year in.

---

496 levy dew] ?Welsh *llef ar Dduw*, call upon God

497 *Verses from a sailors' song*

I'm only a sailor man—tradesman would I were,
For I've ever rued the day I became a tar;
Rued the rambling notion, ever the decoy
Unto such an awful life. Board of Trade, ahoy!

I snubb'd skipper for bad grub, rotten flour to eat,
Hard tack full of weevils; how demon chandlers cheat!
Salt junk like mahogany, scurvying man and boy.
Says he, 'Where's your remedy?' Board of Trade, ahoy!

Can ye wonder mutiny, lubber-like, will work,
In our mercantile marine, cramm'd with measly pork?
Is it wonderful that men lose their native joy,
With provisions maggoty? Board of Trade, ahoy!

Oh had we a crew to stand by when we're ashore,
Show this horrid stuff that pigs even would abhor!
Sue the swindling dealer who'd our health destroy.
What say ye, oh sailor friends? Board of Trade, ahoy!

Dutchmen here before the mast, and behind it too!
Dutchmen mate and carpenter, Dutchmen most the crew!
Foreigners to man our ships, horrible employ!
What's old England coming to? Board of Trade, ahoy!

498 *Verses from the anti-turnpike riots; Pembrokeshire, 1843*

Rebecca and her Daughters

Where is Rebecca?—that daughter of my story!
Where is her dwelling? Oh where is her haunt?
Her name and her exploits will be complete in history
With famed Amazonians or great 'John of Gaunt.'
Dwells she mid mountains, almost inaccessible,
Hid in some cavern or grotto secure,
Does she inhabit—this miscreant Jezebel,
Halls of the rich, or the cots of the poor?
With exquisite necklace of hemp we'd bedeck her
Could we but capture the dreadful Rebecca!

snubb'd] scolded, rebuked   junk] lumps of meat
498 Amazonians] Amazons, legendary women warriors

Who is Rebecca? She seems hydra-headed
Or Argus-like—more than two eyes at command,
The mother of hundreds—the great unknown—dreaded
By peace-loving subjects in Cambria's land.
Unknown her sex too—they may be discovered
To all our bewildered astonishments soon
To be, Mother Hubbard, who lived in a cupboard,
Great Joan of Arc's ghost or the man in the moon.
'Twould puzzle the brains of a Johnson or Secker
To make out thy epicene nature—Rebecca!

Who are thy daughters? in *parties* we meet them,
Which proves them of ages quite fit to *come out*,
Some *Balls* it appears were preparing to greet them,
Which soon would have ended of course in a *rout*.
They are not musicians, though capital dancers,
So puzzled they seem to encounter each *bar*;
But—Shade of Terpsichore! call for the *lancers*,
How fastly they'll step out with matchless éclat;
The wonderful prophet who flourished in Mecca
No heaven could boast like thy daughters, Rebecca!

What are your politics? Some people say for you—
Travelling System you always will aid,
And 'twould appear the far happiest day for you,
Throwing *wide open the road to free trade*.
You cannot with Whigs take up any position,
If what I assert here is known as a fact;
That you give decided and stern opposition
To all that *may hinge on the new Postage Act*.
The State is in danger, and nothing can check her
From ruin with politics like yours—Rebecca.

Farewell, Rebecca! cease mischievous planning,
Whoever you might be—Maid, Spirit or Man;
Lest haply your days should be ended by hanging,
And sure you're averse to that sad *New Gate* plan.
Oh no! to the drop you may never be carted,
No end so untimely e'er happen to you:
But change, and be honest, and when you're departed
May have from the Sexton, the *Toll* that is due.
My muse is at fault—I may pinch and may peck her
But all to no purpose—Good-bye then, Rebecca!

Argus] hundred-eyed Greek demigod   Terpsichore] Muse of dancing

499   *Verses sent to the toll-collector at 'Llandowor'*
      (Llanddowror?), Carmarthen, Wales, by the anti-turnpikers

Habe omnes
The Days of Vengeance!!!

By blood and fire Christ strikes the blow,
And London falls like Jericho:
Behold the monsters die around,
Whose grave-diggers may not be found.
   Erin go Bragh
Pour Dieu et mon Droit.
O'Connell shines some people say,
Who admits none, except they pay
           The Piper.

500   *W. B. Yeats; 'To be Carved on a Stone at Thoor Ballylee',*
      Co. Clare, Ireland; (i), as published; (ii), an earlier draft

(i)   I, the poet William Yeats,
      With old mill boards and sea-green slates,
      And smithy work from the Gort forge,
      Restored this tower for my wife George;
      And may these characters remain
      When all is ruin once again.

(ii) I, the poet, William Yeats,
      With common sedge and broken slates
      And smithy work from the Gort forge,
      Restored this tower for my wife George;
      And on my heirs I lay a curse
      If they should alter for the worse,
      From fashion or an empty mind,
      What Raftery built and Scott designed.

499 Erin go Bragh] Ireland for ever

501   *Lines on the burial of the leg of Henry Paget, Marquis of*
Anglesey; it was shot off at the battle of Waterloo, and buried
at Hougomont, Belgium

Here lies—and let no saucy knave
   Presume to sneer and laugh,
To learn, that, mouldering in this grave,
   Is laid—a British calf.

For he who writes these lines, is sure
   That those who read the whole,
Will find such laugh were premature,
   For here, too, lies—a sole.

And here five little ones repose—
   Twin-born with other five—
Unheeded by their brother toes,
   Who all are now alive.

A leg and foot—to speak more plain—
   Rest here, of one commanding;
Who, though his wits he might retain,
   Lost half his understanding.

Who—when the guns, with murder fraught,
   Poured bullets thick as hail—
Could only in this way be brought
   To give the foe leg bail.

Who, now, in England, just as gay
   As in the battle brave,
Goes to the rout, review, or play,
   With one foot in the grave.

Fortune in vain here shewed her spite,
   For he will still be found,
Should England's sons engage in fight,
   Resolv'd to stand her ground.

But Fortune's pardon I must beg—
   She wished not to disarm;
And when she lopped the hero's leg,
   She did not seek his h-arm:

And but indulged a harmless whim,
  Since he could walk with one,
She thought two legs were lost on him
  Who never deigned to run.

502   *Byron; beneath (i), written in the 'Travellers' Book' of the*
     Macri family at Athens, Byron in 1810 inserted (ii)

(i)   Fair Albion, smiling, sees her son depart
        To trace the birth and nursery of art:
        Noble his object, glorious is his aim;
        He comes to Athens, and he writes his name.

(ii)   The modest bard, like many a bard unknown,
        Rhymes on our names, but wisely hides his own;
        But yet, whoe'er he be, to say no worse,
        His name would bring more credit than his verse.

503   *'Rough bush poetry' inscribed on the wall of the musterers'*
     hut at Glenthorne sheep station, Canterbury, New Zealand

The musterers of Coleridge
In 1921
Set out to muster Glenthorne
Where the wild merinos run.
They reached the Harper river,
Which was running deep and fast,
And they gamely struggled over,
But McPherson, he came last.
Now Frenchy was the packman,
And he drove the b—— team
Where the waters were the deepest
And the rocks could not be seen.
The leaders, they went out of sight
In a six foot drop or more,
And McPherson got the wind up
And jumped back on the shore.

---

503 muster] round up (the hill sheep at)   merino] a breed of sheep, of which
some have reverted to the wild state

Joe Casey held the butter,
He was sitting on the side,
And the dray tipped up and threw him
Into the raging tide.
But he went in nice and graceful
For he made a splendid dive,
But never a man expected him
To come to the top alive.
He struck out on the breast-stroke,
But the current was too strong—
It swept him underneath the dray
And carried him along.
But he struck out game as ever
And at last he reached the shore,
After swimming through the Harper
As he'd never swum before.

504　*R. L. Stevenson (1850–94); inscribed on his tomb in
Samoa (see note)*

Requiem

Under the wide and starry sky,
Dig the grave and let me lie.
Glad did I live and gladly die,
    And I laid me down with a will.

This be the verse you grave for me:
Here he lies where he longed to be;
Home is the sailor, home from sea,
    And the hunter home from the hill.

X

VERSES ON SOME MOVABLE OR UNLOCATED OBJECTS

505 *On a match-box; from Scott's* Lady of the Lake

The boat had touch'd the silver strand,
Just as the Hunter left his stand,
And stood conceal'd amid the brake,
To view this lady of the lake.

506 *A verse on a patch-box*

Thou hast no faults
Or none that I can spy.
Thou art all sweetness,
or, all blindness I.

507 *Lines upon a looking-glass 'which bears the likeness of Nell Gwynn and King Charles, modelled in wax'*

Glass antique, 'twixt thee and Nell
Draw we here a parallel.
She, like thee, was forced to bear
All reflections, foul or fair;
   Thou art deep and bright within,
   Depths as bright belonged to Gwynn;
   Thou art very frail as well,
   Frail as flesh is—so was Nell.

Thou, her glass, art silver-lined,
She too had a silver mind;
Thine is fresh to this far day,
Hers till death ne'er wore away;
   Thou dost to thy surface win
   Wandering glances, so did Gwynn;
   Eyes on thee long love to dwell,
   So men's eyes would do on Nell.

Life-like forms in thee are sought,
Such the forms the actress wrought;
Truth unfailing rests in you,
Nell, whate'er she was, was true;
   Clear as virtue, dull as sin,
   Thou art oft, as oft was Gwynn;

Breathe on thee, and drops will swell—
Bright tears dimmed the eyes of Nell.

Thine's a frame to charm the sight,
Framed was she to give delight.
Waxen forms here truly show
Charles above and Nell below;
  But between them, chin with chin,
  Stuart stands as low as Gwynn,—
  Paired, yet parted—meant to tell
  Charles was *opposite* to Nell.

Round the glass wherein her face
Smil'd so oft, her 'arms' we trace;
Thou, her mirror, hast the pair,
Lion here, and leopard there.
  She had part in these;—akin
  To the lion-heart was Gwynn;
  And the leopard's beauty fell,
  With its spots, to bounding Nell.

Oft inspected, ne'er seen through,
Thou art firm, if brittle too;
So her will, on good intent,
Might be broken, never bent.
  What the glass was, when therein
  Beamed the face of glad Nell Gwynn,
  Was that face, by beauty's spell,
  To the honest soul of Nell!

508 *A sampler dated 16 June 1825*

Vital spark of heavenly flame
Quit oh quit this mortal frame
Trembling hoping lingring flying
Oh the pain the bliss of dying
Cease from nature cease from strife
And let me languish into life.

509   *Samplers from the Fitzwilliam Museum, Cambridge*

(i)   *Inscribed 'EB', early eighteenth century*

Behold the grave the tombstone rowld away
And angels sit where one more glorious lay
No wonder the bright angels mark the place
From whence that risen sun began his race.

*

See how the Lillies flourish white and fare
See how the Ravens fed from Heaven are
Then neer distrust thy God for cloth and bread
Whilst Lillies flourish and the Ravens fed.

(ii)   *'1736 Alice Ruddock aged 13 years'*

Life is happy hear the birds
Early as the morning breaks
Every sweet toned throat of silver
Into songs of gladness breaks.

(iii)   *'Harriet Plastin. Her Work. Aged 10 years 1814'*

Fragrant the rose is but it fades in Time
The violet sweet but quickly past the prime
White lilies hang their Head and soon decay
And whiter snow in Minutes wasts away
Such and so withring are our early joys
Which Time or Sickness speedily destroys.

510   *An eighteenth-century sampler verse*

Look well to what you in hand,
For larnin is better than house and land,
When land is gone and money spent,
Then larnin is most excellent.

509   early joys] ?earthly joys

511 *Other sampler verses*

(i)
Worked by Ann Wood, aged 8 (1817)

With cheerful mind we yield to men
The higher honours of the pen
    The needle's our chief care,
In this we chiefly wish to shine
How far the art's already mine
    This sampler does declare.

(ii)
Unsigned and undated (seventeenth century)

When I was young I little thought
That wit must be so dearly bought
But now experience tells me how
If I would thrive then I must bow
And bend unto another's will That
I might learn both art and skill To
Get My Living With My
Hands That So I M
ight Be Free From Ba
nd[s] And My Own Dam
e that I may be And free from all suc
h slavery. Avoid vaine pastime fle
youthfull pleasure Let moderatio
n allways be thy measure And so pr
osed unto the heavenly treasure.

(iii)
The Ten Commandments

Signed 'Dorothy Greame her sampler 1734'

Thou Shall Have No other Gods But Me
Nor to no Image Bow Thy Knee
Take Not The Name of God in Vain
Do not the Sabbath Day Profane
O Love Thy Father and Mother Too
And See That Thou No Murder Do
From Vile Adultry Keep Thee Clean
Steal Not although Thy Share Be Mean
Falls Witness Bear Thou Not Of That
Which Is The Neighbours Do Not Covet.

pr/osed] proceed

(iv)   The Converted Indian's Prayer

Worked by Mary Eyre, 1833

In de dark wood no Indian nigh
Den me look heaven and send up cry.
  Upon my knee so low,
Dal god so high a shiny place.
See me in night with teary face.
  My priest do tell me so.

He send his angel take me care
He comes his self and hear my prayer.
  If Indian heart do pray.

(v)   Heavenly Love

Worked 'With The Hair of Mr Thomas Vickery By Elizabeth,
His Daughter, 1782'

Christs Arms Do Still Stand Open To Receive
All Weary Prodigals That Sin Do Leave
For Them He Left His Father's Blest Abode
Made Son Of Man To Make Man Son Of God
To cure Their wounds He Lives Elixier bled
And Died A Death To Rise Them from The Dead.

512 *A sampler verse recorded in Cornwall; 'Elizabeth Cornish*
     done this work in the nine year of her age 18 . .'

I sit by the fire in the dark Winter night,
Where the cat cleans her face with her foot in delight;
And the winds all a-cold with rude clatter and din
Shake the windows like robbers who want to come in.

513 *Border inscription on an embroidery of Pomona, the Roman*
     goddess of fruit-trees; worked by Lady Cory in 1907 (?)

I am the ancient apple green
As once I was so am I now
For evermore a hope unseen

511 Dal] ?till   Lives] ?life's

Betwixt the blossom and the bough
Ah! Where's the river's hidden gold
And where the windy grave of Troy?
Yet come I as I came of old
From all the heat of Summer's joy.

514   *On a gallon jug*

Come, my old friend, and take a pot,
But mark me what I say;
Whilst thou drink'st thy neighbour's health,
Drink not thy own away.

For it too often is the case,
Whilst we sit o'er a pot,
And while we drink our neighbour's health,
Our own is quite forgot.

515   *On Edward III's gold noble coin, after the battle of Sluys
(1340)*

Foure things our noble sheweth to me,
King, ship and sword and power of the sea.

516   *A posy in a napkin, c.1650*

Receive with hand and keep with heart
This simple gift of my good will,
And from thy love do never start
But in heart do love hearty still.
In riches is no trust
And beauty will decay,
And I shall [n]ever faithful love
Till death take me away.

In my heart this have I thought
And with my hand this have I wrought.

517 *An inscription for a watch*

> Could but our tempers move like this machine,
> Not urg'd by passion nor delay'd by spleen;
> And true to Nature's regulating power,
> By virtuous acts distinguish every hour:
> Then health and joy would follow, as they ought,
> The laws of motion and the laws of thought;
> Sweet health to pass the present moments o'er,
> And everlasting joy, when time shall be no more.

518 *On the door of a long-case clock by Thomas Lister; c.1730*

> Lo! Here I stand by you, upright
> To give you warning, day and night;
> For ev'ry tick that I do give
> Cuts short the Time you have to live.
> Therefore a warning take by me,
> To serve thy God as I serve thee:
> Each day and night be on thy guard,
> And thou shalt have a just reward.

519 *Verses on watch-papers (the first is dated 1730)*

(i)
> With me while present may thy lovely eyes
> Be never turned upon this golden toy,
> Think every pleasing hour too swiftly flies,
> And measure time by joy succeeding joy,
> But when the cares that interrupt our bliss
> To me not always will thy sight allow,
> Then oft with kind impatience look on this,
> Then every minute count, as I do now.

(ii)
> Little monitor, impart
> Some instruction to the heart.
> Show the busy and the gay
> Life is hasting swift away.
> Follies can not long endure,
> Life is short and death is sure.
> Happy those who wisely learn
> Truth from error to discern.

(iii)
> Little monitor! by thee
> Let me learn what I should be;
> Learn this round of Life to fill,
> Useful and progressive still.
> When I wind thee up at night,
> Mark each fault and set thee right,
> Let me search my bosom too,
> And my daily thoughts review;
> Mark each movement of my mind,
> Nor be easy when I find
> Latent errors rise to view,
> Till all be regular and true.

520 *On an eighteenth-century watch-paper*

> Time is—the present moment well employ.
> Time was—is past—thou canst not it enjoy.
> Time future—is not, and may never be.
> Time present is the only time for thee.

521 *A watch-paper verse; probably nineteenth century*

> Onward
> Perpetually moving—
> These hands are proving
> How soft the hours steal by . . .
> This monitory pulse-like beating
> Is oftentimes, methinks, repeating:
> 'Swift, swift, the hours do fly!'
> Reader, be ready! Perhaps before
> These hands have made
> One revolution more
> Life's spring is snapt.
> You die!

522 *Pencilled in a book, date unknown*

> Here lies old Jones,
> Who all his life collected bones
> Till death, that grim and bony spectre,
> That all-amazing bone-collector,
> Boned old Jones so neat and tidy,
> That here he lies all bona fide.

523 *Lines 'often written in a book' to remind borrowers to
return it*

> Thys boke is one and GODES kors ys anoder:
> They that take the on, GOD gefe them the toder.

524 *A verse by John M'Creery dated 2 November 1810*

Inscription for my Daughters' Hour-glass

> Mark the golden grains that pass
> Brightly thro' this channell'd glass,
> Measuring by their ceaseless fall
> Heaven's most precious gift to all!
> Busy, till its sand be done,
> See the shining current run;
> But, th' allotted numbers shed,
> Another hour of life hath fled!
> Its task perform'd, its travail past,
> Like mortal man it rests at last!—
> Yet let some hand invert its frame
> And all its powers return the same,
> Whilst any golden grains remain
> 'Twill work its little hour again.—
> But who shall turn the glass for man,
> When all his golden grains have ran?
> Who shall collect his scatter'd sand,
> Dispers'd by time's unsparing hand?—
> Never can one grain be found,
> Howe'er we anxious search around!
>
> Then, daughters, since this truth is plain,
> That Time once gone ne'er comes again.
> Improv'd bid every moment pass—
> See how the sand rolls down your glass.

525 *An inscription on the fly-leaf of a Bible*

> Could we with ink the ocean fill,
> Were ev'ry stalk on earth a quill,
> And were the skies of parchment made,

And ev'ry man a scribe by trade,
To tell the love of God alone
    Would drain the ocean dry.
Nor could a scroll contain the whole,
    Though stretched from sky to sky.

526   *Edmund Waller (1606–87)*

(i) 'written in My Lady Speke's singing-book'

Her fair eyes, if they could see
What themselves have wrought in me,
Would at least with pardon look
On this scribbling in her book:
If that she the writer scorn,
This may from the rest be torn,
With the ruin of a part,
But the image of her graces
Fills my heart and leaves no spaces.

(ii) 'under a lady's picture'

Some ages hence, for it must not decay,
The doubtful wonderers at this piece, will say
Such Helen was! and who can blame the boy
That in so bright a flame consumed his Troy?
But had like virtue shined in that fair Greek,
The amorous shepherd had not dared to seek
Or hope for pity; but with silent moan,
And better fate, had perished alone.

527   *A will in verse, inscribed in a copy of Sir Philip Monkton's*
      Memoirs; c.1670

This is my last will
I insist on it still
So sneer on and welcome,
And e'en laugh your fill,
I, William Hickington,
Poet, of Pocklington,
Do give and bequeathe
As free as I breathe
To thee, Mary Saram

The Queen of my Haram,
My Cash and Cattle
With every Chattel.
Come heat or come cold,
To have and to hold
Sans hindrance or strife
Tho' thou are not my wife,
As witness my hand
Just here as I stand,
This twelfth of July
In the Year seventy.

528   *Jonathan Swift (1667–1745); verses written in a lady's
ivory table-book, 1698*

Peruse my leaves thro' ev'ry part,
And think thou seest my owner's heart,
Scrawl'd o'er with trifles thus, and quite
As hard, as senseless, and as light;
Expos'd to ev'ry coxcomb's eyes,
But hid with Caution from the wise.
Here you may read (*Dear charming saint*)
Beneath (*A new receipt for paint*):
Here in beau-spelling (*tru tel deth*),
There in her own (*for an el breth*).
Here (*lovely nymph pronounce my doom*),
There (*a safe way to use perfume*);
Here a page fill'd with billets-doux;
On t'other side (*laid out for shoes*):
(*Madam, I die without your grace*),
(Item, *for half a yard of lace*).
Who that had wit would place it here,
For ev'ry peeping fop to jeer?
In power of spittle, and a clout,
Whene'er he please to blot it out;
And then, to heighten the disgrace,
Clap his own nonsense in the place.
Whoe'er expects to hold his part
In such a book, and such a heart,
If he be wealthy, and a fool,
Is in all points the fittest tool;
Of whom it may be justly said,
He's a gold pencil tipp'd with lead.

529 *Verses by Byron (?) worked in pins on a pin-cushion*

> Hail to this teeming age of strife
> Hail lovely miniature of life.

530 *Verses written into her pocket-book by the first Mrs Grimaldi, with a wish that they might be inscribed on her grave*

> Earth walks on Earth like glittering gold;
> Earth says to Earth, we are but mould;
> Earth builds on Earth castles and towers;
> Earth says to Earth, all shall be ours.

531 *Matthew Arnold (1822–88); poems inscribed in copies,*

(i) of Emerson's *Essays*

> 'O monstrous, dead, unprofitable world,
> That thou canst hear, and hearing, hold thy way!
> A voice oracular hath peal'd to-day,
> To-day a hero's banner is unfurl'd;
>
> Hast thou no lip for welcome?'—So I said.
> Man after man, the world smiled and pass'd by;
> A smile of wistful incredulity
> As though one spake of life unto the dead—
>
> Scornful, and strange, and sorrowful, and full
> Of bitter knowledge. Yet the will is free;
> Strong is the soul, and wise, and beautiful;
>
> The seeds of godlike power are in us still;
> Gods are we, bards, saints, heroes, if we will!—
> Dumb judges, answer, truth or mockery?

(ii) of Bishop Butler's *Sermons*

> Affections, Instincts, Principles, and Powers,
> Impulse and Reason, Freedom and Control—
> So men, unravelling God's harmonious whole,
> Rend in a thousand shreds this life of ours.

Vain labour! Deep and broad, where none may see,
Spring the foundations of that shadowy throne
Where man's one nature, queen-like, sits alone,
Centred in a majestic unity;

And rays her powers, like sister-islands seen
Linking their coral arms under the sea,
Or cluster'd peaks with plunging gulfs between

Spann'd by aërial arches all of gold,
Whereo'er the chariot wheels of life are roll'd
In cloudy circles to eternity.

532　*George Meredith (1828–1909); lines inscribed by him in a
presentation copy of his poems, 1851*

'Poems', says the title:
And for a book 'tis vital
　　As is a head on shoulders.
Yet many shoulders going,
And many a book worth knowing,
　　Would be to all beholders,
More solemn & more sightly
Decapitated lightly.
Nor would the book be read less,
If I should make it headless.

533　*Austin Dobson (1840–1921); verses for a copy of Herrick's
poems*

Many days have come and gone,
Many suns have set and shone,
HERRICK, since thou sang'st of Wake,
Morris-dance and Barley-break;—
Many men have ceased from care,
Many maidens have been fair,
Since thou sang'st of JULIA's eyes,
JULIA's lawns and tiffanies;—
Many things are past: but thou,
GOLDEN-MOUTH, art singing now,
Singing clearly as of old,
And thy numbers are of gold!

533　lawns] fine linens　　　　tiffanies] thin gauzes

534 *'A common tavern notice'*

> All you that bring tobacco here
> Must pay for pipes as well as beer;
> And you that stand before the fire,
> I pray sit down by good desire,
> That other folks as well as you
> May see the fire, and feel it too.
> Since man to man is so unjust,
> I cannot tell what man to trust.
> My liquor's good, 'tis no man's sorrow,
> Pay to-day, I'll trust to-morrow.

535 *A horse's petition to his driver; 'A placard on the walls',*
     March 1885

> Up hill . . . .   whip me not;
> down hill . . . .   hurry me not;
> loose in stable . . . .   forget me not;
> of hay and corn . . . . .   rob me not;
> of clean water . . . .   stint me not;
> with sponge and brush   neglect me not;
> of soft, dry bed . . . . . .   deprive me not;
> tired or hot . . . .   leave me not.
> Sick or cold . . . .   chill me not;
> with bit or reins . . . . .   oh jerk me not;
> when you are angry . .   strike me not.

536 *A flower calendar*

Feb. 2. The Snow-drop in purest white arraie
         First rears her head on Candlemas daie.

14. While the Crocus hastens to the shrine
     Of Primrose love on Saint Valentine.

Mar. 25. Then comes the Daffodil beside
          Our Ladye's Smock at our Ladye Tide.

April 23. About Saint George when blue is worn,
           The blue Harebells the fields adorn.

SOME MOVABLE OR UNLOCATED OBJECTS

May 3.   While on the day of the Holy Cross,
The Crowfoot gilds the flowerie grasse.

June 11.   When Barnaby bright smiles night and day,
Poor Ragged Robin blooms in the hay.

24.   The Scarlet Lychnis, the garden's pride,
Flames at Saint John the Baptist's tyde.

July 15.   Against Saint Swithin's hastie showers
The Lily white reigns the Queen of the flowers.

20.   And Poppies a sanguine mantle spread,
For the blood of the Dragon St. Margaret shed.

22.   Then under the wanton Rose agen
That blushes for penitent Magdalen.

Aug. 1.   Till Lammas-day called August's wheel,
When the long corn stinks of Camomile.

15.   When Mary left us here below,
The Virgin's Bower begins to blow.

24.   And yet anon the full Sun-flower blew,
And became a star for Bartholomew.

Sep. 14.   The Passion-flower long has blowed,
To betoken us signs of the Holy Rood.

29.   The Michaelmas Daisie among dead weeds
Blooms for Saint Michael's valorous deeds.

Oct. 28.   And seems the last of flowers that stood
Till the feast of St. Simon and St. Jude.

Nov. 1.   Save Mushrooms and the Fungus race
That grow as All-hallow-tide takes place.

25.   Soon the evergreen Laurel alone is seen,
When Catherine crowns all learned men.

Dec. 25.   Then Ivy and Holly-berries are seen,
And Yule-Clog and Wassail come round again.

hay] hedge   Yule-clog] Yule-log

537 *An old ceiling dial; unlocated*

> See the little day-star moving,
> Life and time are worth improving,
> Seize the moments, while they stay,
>   Seize and use them
>   Lest you lose them,
> And lament the wasted day.

538 *Epitaph for a potter; place unrecorded*

> Here in this grave lies Catherine Gray,
> Changed to a senseless lump of clay;
> By earth and clay she got her pelf,
> And now she's turned to clay herself.
>
> Ye weeping friends, let me advise,
> Abate your tears and dry your eyes;
> Who knows, but in the course of years,
> In some tall pitcher or brown pan,
> She in her shop may be again.

539 *A sampler by Mary Cameron, Aberdeen*

> O may I stand before the Lamb,
> when earth and seas are fled,
> And hear the Judge pronounce my name,
> with blessings on my head.

NOTES AND SOURCES

(The numbers in square brackets [ ] indicate an earlier note where the full title, etc., of the source is given.)

I. LONDON

1. W. H. Hutton, *Hampton Court* (1897), p. 177.
2. A. S. Foord, *Springs, Streams and Spas of London* (1910), p. 261.
3. G. E. Evans, *Kensington* (1975), p. 31.
4. H. B. Wheatley, *The Adelphi and its Site* (1885), p. 14. S. Edel, *London's Riverside* (1975), p. 167, gives the rhyme as *Adam/madam*; the correct spelling, but somewhat impairing the epigram. When first built, Adelphi pre-empted a long and prominent stretch of Thames-side.
5. A. J. C. Hare, *Walks in London* (1894), ii. 44.
6. W. Gaunt, *Kensington* (1958), p. 26.
7. M. Brentnall, *The Old Customs and Ceremonies of London* (1975), p. 99. 'Sculler' refers to the annual Tom Doggett 'Coat and Badge' race on the river.
8. H. P. Maskell, *Taverns of Old England* (1927), p. 149.
9. C. Knight, *London* (rev. E. Walford, *c.* 1878), iv. 381. Noted elsewhere as 'on a clockdial'.
10. Hare [5], i. 59. The original emblems of the Knights Templars were a lamb, and a horse with two riders (to signify poverty). At a certain time, when the horse was repainted, the two men were in error restored as wings. Hence the ironies.
11. *Complete Works*, ed. C. H. Herford and P. and E. Simpson, vol. viii (1947), p. 657. Phoebus Apollo was the Greek god of poetry. At his oracle at Delphi the priestess prophesied from a *tripos*.
12. W. H. Moore, *The Old China Book* (1904), p. 132; the lines are from Shakespeare's *Tempest* (IV. i. 152–6) with divergences from the established text. They appear also on the cliff-face at Swanage, Dorset (information from Professor R. D. Robinson).
13. K. Ullyett, *Watch Collecting* (1970), p. 94.
14. D. Hawkins, *Avalon on Sedgemoor* (1973), p. 205. This remarkable early calculator, once on exhibition in the village museum at Street, Somerset, was later found, derelict, in a local factory, and restored.
15. F. Arnold, *History of Streatham* (1886), p. 68. *Susannah* is from the Hebrew for 'lily', *Margarite* from the Greek for 'pearl'; cf. no. 136.
16. Herford and Simpson [11], viii. 77.
17. E. Parker, *Highways and Byways in Surrey* (1908), p. 438.
18. *Notes and Queries* [*N. & Q.*], 4 Aug. 1855.

19. J. F. Curwen, *Kirkbie-Kendall* (1900), p. 15.

20. *Poems*, ed. G. C. Moore-Smith (1923; 1968 reprint), p. 53. '. . . to be fastned upon the Church door.'

21. N. Moore, *Church of St Bartholomew the Great* (1892), pp. 59–60.

22. *Poems*, ed. C. Ricks (1969); (i) p. 1233, (ii) p. 1317.

23. P. W. Berriman Tippetts, *History of the Worshipful Company of Glaziers* (n.d., *c*.1919), p. 55. Composed by J. B. Tippetts, clerk to the company 1887–98.

24. *Poems and Fables of John Dryden*, ed. J. Kinsley (1962), pp. 488–9.

25. J. Timbs, *Curiosities of London* (1855); 1868 edn., p. 182.

26. Hare [5], 1879 edn., ii. 355.

27. Canon Thompson, *Southwark Cathedral* (1910), p. 176.

28. P. Norman, *London Signs and Inscriptions* (1893), p. 56.

29. E. A. Downman, *English Pottery and Porcelain* (1918), p. 70. Also recorded on a set of pewter plates (H. Masse, *Chats on Old Pewter* (1971), p. 111. Lines 3–4 are noted in *Country Life*, 5 April 1984, p. 903, and ll. 5–6 elsewhere.

30. Hare [26], i. 301.

31. *Selected Prose and Poetry*, ed. A. M. C. Latham (1965), p. 59.

32. *Poems*, ed. J. Beer (1974), p. 357.

33. J. Aubrey Rees, *The Grocery Trade, its History and Romance* (1910), ii. 386–7.

34. Fitzwilliam Museum, Cambridge. Brislington is near Bristol.

35. W. Hone, *Everyday Book*, vol. i (1838), 16 April.

36. Id., *Year Book* (1838), 26 September.

37. J. H. Macmichael, *Charing Cross* (1906), pp. 75–6. The 'Figure' was George I, who became king in 1714.

38. A. W. Hutton, *Bow Church, Cheapside* (1908), pp. 9–10. 'Bell and the dragon' is a play on Bel and the dragon, the Babylonian idols in the book of that name in the Apocrypha.

39. R. Kemp, *Some Notes on the Ward of Aldgate* (1904), p. 20.

40. Hone [35], 5 September.

41. R. Davey, *Pageant of London* (1906), i. 98. 'Dance over my Lady Lee' is said to refer to the bridge over that tributary of the Thames at London. Possibly a sixteenth-century song; Davey heard it sung by children c.1906.

42. Ibid. 251–2. Stated to be taken from a fifteenth-century MS; the language sounds northern. St John the Baptist's Day is Midsummer Day, 24 June.

43. Timbs [25], p. 48. As he uttered these verses the clerk rang his handbell (see l. 7).

44. J. C. Cox, *Sanctuaries and Sanctuary Seekers* (1911), pp. 72–4; taken by Cox from a paper in the Domestic State Papers, Public Record Office.

45. M. Davitt, *Leaves from a Prison Diary* (1885), i. 159.

46. Ibid. 161.

47. J. Glyde, *New Suffolk Garland* (1866), pp. 258–61; reminiscent of the dialect of Sam Weller in Dickens's *Pickwick Papers*.

48. Poetical Works, ed. D. Bush (1966), p. 169: 'the idea of putting the sonnet on his door was only a poetic device'.

II. SOUTH-EAST ENGLAND

49. *Poems*, ed. H. Davis (1966), p. 653.

50. W. Jerrold, *Highways and Byways in Middlesex* (1909), p. 76.

51. E. B. Chancellor, *History and Antiquities of Richmond* (1894), pp. 231–2.

52. Ibid. p. 231.

53. Hone [35], 2 May.

54. E. V. Lucas, *Highways and Byways in Sussex* (1935), p. 93.

55. J. Timbs, *Abbeys, Castles and Ancient Halls of England and Wales* (n.d.), ii. 297. Battle of Hastings, fought on 14 October, St Callistus' Day.

56. H. S. Lecky, *The King's Ships* (1913), ii. 30. Anson circumnavigated the globe in 1740–2. The *Centurion* was later moored at Greenwich. The lion eventually 'crumbled to pieces'.

57. R. Pocock (ed.), *History of Gravesend and Milton* (1797), p. 133.

58. J. S. Bright, *History of Dorking* (1884), p. 100.

59. J. Tavenor-Perry, *Memorials of Old Middlesex* (1909), p. 34.

60. A. Hussey, *Chronicles of Wingham* (1896), p. 97. The source does not make clear whether these verses were actually inscribed. They were composed by the parish clerk Henry Sancroft.

61. C. S. Orwin and S. Williams, *History of Wye Church and Wye College* (n.d., c.1923), p. 49.

62. Lucas [54], pp. 402–3.

63. G. S. Steinman, *History of Croydon* (1833), p. 211.

64. H. Smetham, *History of Strood* (1899), p. 15. Chimney money was a tax imposed briefly during the 1670s and 1680s.

65. Lucas [54], pp. 56–7.

66. Tavenor-Perry [59], p. 42. Recorded as beside a bas-relief of the gamekeeper with dog and gun. *Tray* was a common name for a dog.

67. J. Thorne, *Handbook to the Environs of London* (1876), i. 147.

68. E. T. Evans, *History of Hendon* (1890), p. 167, where it is recorded that 'the lines . . . have been erased'.

69. Parker [17], p. 367. Cf. no. 278.

70. Chancellor [51], pp. 316–17.

71. C. H. Fielding, *Memorials of Malling and its Valley* (1893), p. 33.

72. A. J. C. Hare, *Sussex* (1894), p. 4.

73. P. H. Ditchfield, *The Parish Clerk* (1907), p. 98.

74. T. D. W. Dearn, *Weald of Kent* (1814), p. 63.

75. P. H. Ditchfield, *City Companies of London* (1904), p. 218; recorded as by Bishop Redyngton.

76. H. M. Vibart, *Addiscombe* (1894), pp. 271–2.

77. J. A. Brown, *Chronicles of Greenford Parva* (n.d., *c.* 1891), p. 92.

78. W. T. Vincent, *Records of the Woolwich District* (n.d., *c.* 1886), pp. 814–6.

79. P. Lucas, *Heathfield Memorials* (1910), pp. 60–2. The proper names are those of various actors of the time.

80. G. F. Northall, *English Folk Rhymes* (1892), p. 564. *Goliere* is a convivial chorus, connected with *goliard*, jester, buffoon.

81. R. Bell, *Ancient Poems, Ballads and Songs of the Peasantry of England* (1857), p. 205. Sung to the tune of 'Lilli burlero', the 'chorus of whistlers' whistling the refrain melody. 'Very ancient'. Burns is said to have based his 'Carle of Killyburn Braes' on this song.

82. *N. & Q.*, 26 February 1853.

83. W. C. Hazlitt, *Popular Antiquities of Great Britain* (1870), i. 4. Recorded also for Devon and elsewhere. Cf. no. 162.

84. C. Fleet, *Glimpses of Our Ancestors in Sussex* (1878), pp. 100–1. *Hum cap*, (i) stanza 5, 'very strong beer' (OED), strong enough to make one's head ring. (ii) was 'frequently sung at Sussex sheep-shearing in former days'.

85. (i) Northall [80], p. 167; (ii) *Gentleman's Magazine*, Nov. 1868 (p. 858), 'a . . . no doubt very ancient custom'.

86. L. Melville, *Brighton* (1909), p. 127.

87. Ibid. 232; these verses are to some extent a skit on Horace, *Odes*, I. ix: 'Do you see how the lofty Mount Soracte stands white with snow . . . ?' *D'Orsay* must be the artist Count D'Orsay (1801–52), who for a long period was a leader of London fashion.

88. Fleet [84], pp. 143–4.

89. C. Hindley, *Life and Times of James Catnach* (1878), p. 238.

90. E. and M. A. Radford, *Encyclopaedia of Superstitions* (1948), 1975 edn., enlarged by C. Hole, p. 121. Cf. no. 175.

91. Supplied by Vera Ridley of Tunbridge Wells.

92. R. Inwards, *Weather Lore* (1893), p. 118; *N. & Q.*, 5 September 1874.

93. Radford [90], p. 325.

94. A. B. Gomme, *Traditional Games of England, Scotland and Ireland*, vol. i. (1894), pp. 156–7; cf. nos 301 and 364 (i). In line 2, 'thus' as in no. 301 is probably the original rather than 'dust(y)'.

95. Ibid. 321; cf. no. 364 (ii).

96. J. Brand, *Popular Antiquities*, ed. H. Ellis, vol. ii (1813), p. 614; the last line is a version of a well-known Catholic prayer.

III. SOUTH AND SOUTH-WEST ENGLAND

97. B. Jones, *Follies and Grottoes* (1953), 1974 edn., p. 311.

98. S. Heath, *The Cornish Riviera* (1911), p. 61.

99. A. Mee, *Dorset* (1939), p. 123. Possibly now gone, since it is not mentioned in later editions.

100. J. Polsue, *Parochial History of the County of Cornwall* (1867–73, reprinted 1975), iii. 289.

101. H. W. Timperley, *The Vale of Pewsey* (1954), p. 167.

102. Mee [99], p. 281.

103. J. Larwood and J. C. Hotten, *History of Signboards* (1866), p. 144; it is not clear that these verses were inscribed.

104. J. D. Champlin, *Chronicle of the Couch* (1886), p. 77; cf. T. F. Kirby, *Annals of Winchester College* (1892), pp. 39–40. Also recorded elsewhere as on the inn-sign of the 'Trusty Servant' inn, Minstead, Hampshire.

105. W. Money, *Popular History of Newbury* (1905), p. 94.

106. P. E. B. Porter, *Around and About Saltash* (1905), p. 143.

107. R. Hopkins, *Literary Landmarks of Devon and Cornwall* (1926), p. 181.

108. W. Crossing, *Folk Rhymes of Devon* (1911), p. 151.

109. R. C. Hope, *Legendary Lore of the Holy Wells of England* (1893), p. 67.

110. Northall [80], p. 295.

111. S. Baring-Gould, *A Book of Dartmoor* (1900), p. 248.

112. J. J. Daniell, *History of Chippenham* (1894), pp. 32–3.

113. *Poetical Works*, ed. H. S. Melford (1926), p. 397.

114. M. Harland, *Hannah More* (1900), p. 30.

115. Jones [97], p. 239.

116. R. S. Hawker, *Cornish Ballads* (1904), p. x.

117. Porter [106], p. 228.

118. Crossing [108], p. 14.

119. Polsue [100], ii. 117.

120. Ibid., iii. 13. Also recorded as on the tenor bell at Cleobury Mortimer, Shropshire.

121. H. B. Walters, *Church Bells of England* (1912), p. 345.

122. W. E. Colchester, *Hampshire Church Bells* (1920), pp. 66–7.

123. Ibid., 68. The source records that the 'sweet and clear' number 2 bell is cracked.

124. R. Hine, *History of Beaminster* (1914), p. 25. Almost identical verses, but omitting ll. 22–3, are recorded for Saltash parish church (Porter, [106], p. 290); also an abridged version in Brushford church (L. Meynell, *Exmoor* (1953), p. 118).

125. *Collected Poems* (1930 edn.), pp. 761–2.

126. J. Wesley Walker, *History of Maidenhead* (2nd edn, 1931), pp. 206–7.

127. B. H. Cunnington, *Records of the County of Wilts* (1932), pp. 48–9; recorded as in part by John Hulberd. In stanza 6 perhaps 'bookes' should be 'bootes'.

128. W. Money, *Collections for . . . the Parish of Speen, Berks* (1892), p. 45.

129. Polsue [100], ii, 18.

130. J. J. Hissey, *Across England in a Dogcart* (1891), p. 139.

131. Taken from a sampler in the Cambridge and County Folk Museum.

132. Polsue [100], iv. 105.

133. Ibid. 110.

134. F. Treves, *Highways and Byways in Dorset* (1906), p. 320.

135. R. Wightman, *The Wessex Heathland* (1953), p. 148.

136. G. Grigson, *Shell Country Alphabet* (1966), p. 53.

137. Treves [134], p. 211. Note the concealed rhyme and metre.

138. Polsue [100], i. 136.

139. K. Lindley, *Of Graves and Epitaphs* (1965), p. 140.

140. J. Stabb, *Some Old Devon Churches* (1911), ii. 72.

141. A. Colby, *Samplers Yesterday and Today* (1964): (i), p. 124; (ii), p. 252.

142. *Poetical Works*, ed. L. C. Martin (1956), p. 419.

143. Ibid. 284, 322, 323, 258.

144. (i) and (ii), A. E. Bray, *Borders of the Tamar and the Tavy* (3 vols, 1836), i. 334; (iii), *N. & Q.*, 5 April 1851 (with no. 171); (iv), Porter [106], p. 108. See Introduction, p. xvi, and cf. no. 309 and note.

145. Treves, [134], p. 33.

146. J. Vaughan, *Winchester Cathedral* (n.d., *c.*1920), p. 290.

147. *N. & Q.*, 11 July 1874.

148. S. Baring-Gould, *A Book of the West* (2 vols, 1899), ii. 323. This gives both English and Cornish versions of the epitaph.

149. Hine [124], pp. 285–6.

150. B. B. Woodward *et al.*, *General History of Hampshire* (3 vols, n.d.), ii. 339.

151. V. S. Lean, *Collectanea*, vol. i (1902), p. 213.

152. J. Timbs, [55], ii. 165–6. *Weary-all Hill*, near Glastonbury; *Pumparles*, thought to be 'Pons perilous', a bridge over the nearby River Brue.

153. Porter [106], p. 18.

154. E. M. Richardson, *Story of Purton* (1919), pp. 50–2.

155. A. F. Leach (ed.), *History of Bradfield College* (1900), p. 54.

156. A. F. Mockler-Ferryman, *Annals of Sandhurst* (1900), pp. 94–6. *Tam Marte quam Minerva* ('by the Gods of War and Wisdom, equally') is the Staff

College Motto. The quotations in stanza 7 are from an old Administration syllabus.

157. Text from A. Gillingham, then director of the school. *Helen of Troy*, the school's yacht.

158. G. R. Harvey, *Mullyon* (1875), pp. 125–8. Original title in Latin, and a note at the end in classical Greek. From this it appears that the author was one John Blackhouse (?), a Scot. *Bellini*, perhaps Vincenzo Bellini (1801–35), composer of tuneful operas.

159. Porter [106], p. 45.

160. Bell [81], p. 193: 'taken down . . . from the leader of a parish choir, who assigned it to a very remote . . . antiquity'. Said also to have been translated from the Cornish. The source glosses 'doat fig' as 'a fig newly gathered from the tree'.

161. Addison, *Spectator*, no. dcxiv, 1 November 1714. Addison takes it from Cowell's *Interpreter* (1607).

162. *Gentleman's Magazine*, May 1791, pp. 403–4. Cf. no. 83.

163. Baring-Gould [148], i. 85–7; 'now remembered only by very old men'. Taken down from an 80-year-old sexton, near Tiverton.

164. Northall [80], p. 188. Also in *N. & Q.*, 24 Jan. 1852.

165. Hone [35], Feb. 14. 'Collop Monday', the day before Shrove Tuesday, was when the remaining meat was cut into steaks or 'collops', and salted down for use after Lent.

166. *N. & Q.*, 11 August 1855. On 29 May, the word 'shig-shag' replaced 'April Fool' in similar festivities.

167. Gomme, [94], vol. ii (1898), p. 339. The song could begin 'Water(s)', 'Wallflowers', or 'Wild flowers'. Various versions occurred in many English localities. The girl's name would of course vary with the players.

168. Hazlitt [83], ii. 277.

169. T. F. T. Dyer, *Folklore of Plants* (1889), p. 285.

170. *Jubilee Congress of the Folklore Society, 1928* (1930), p. 195. *Udern-ill*, an udder ailment in cows.

171. From *N. & Q.*, 5 April 1851.

172. Northall [80], p. 139.

173. *Novels*, ed. M. E. Lawlis (1961), pp. 26–8.

174. Northall [80], p. 535. Cf. no. 381.

175. Bray [144], i. 326. Cf. no. 90.

176. Woodward [150], III, p. 232.

177. J. J. Hissey, *On Southern English Roads* (1896), p. 32.

178. (i), text supplied by A. L. Rowse; (ii), W. Andrews, *Literary Byways* (1898), p. 109; (iii), W. Hazlitt, *Dictionary of Faiths and Folklore* (2 vols, 1905), ii. 507.

179. G. E. Dartnell and E. H. Goddard, *Glossary of Words used in the County of Wiltshire* (1893), pp. 208–9. Cf. nos. 9, 10.

180. Lean [151], vol. ii, part i (1903), p. 134.

181. *Poetical Works* [142], p. 262.

IV. EASTERN ENGLAND

182. G. R. Clarke, *History and Description of the Town . . . of Ipswich* (1830), p. 207.

183. W. F. Rawnsley, *Highways and Byways in Lincolnshire* (1914), p. 321.

184. H. M. Doughty, *Chronicles of Theberton* (1910), p. 42.

185. Ibid. 223.

186. Northall [80], p. 29.

187. C. R. B. Barrett, *Essex* (1892), ii. 134.

188. H. A. Evans, *Highways and Byways in Northamptonshire and Rutland* (1918), p. 152.

189. R. L. Hine, *History of Hitchin* (1927):, i. 117.

190. *Verses and Translations* (1877), pp. 55–7. Bacon's original shop has been rebuilt, but the poem still stands inscribed, on a modern bronze plaque.

191. *Victoria County History, Cambridgeshire*, ii. 367. Lines 7–8, presumably omitted on the inscription, are added here from E. H. Pinto, *Wooden Bygones of Smoking and Snuff Taking* (1961), p. 33, where the verses are attributed to Isaac Hawkins Browne (1706–60).

192. Noted by the editor. The building has recently been demolished; the inscribed stone is to be placed in a village museum.

193. Lean [151], i. 102.

194. C. Bax, *Highways and Byways in Essex* (1939), p. 27.

195. W. Andrews, *Bygone Essex* (1892), pp. 152–3. Couples winning the flitch for 'quiet, peaceable, tender and loving cohabitation' sometimes made much money by selling slices to bystanders.

196. I. C. Hannah, *Heart of East Anglia* (n.d., c.1915), p. 253.

197. Bax [194], p. 137.

198. J. Glyde, *Norfolk Garland* (1872), p. 135.

199. Rawnsley [183], p. 144.

200. *N. & Q.*, 4 August 1855; 'an inventory of the effects that were in the cottage'.

201. Rawnsley [183], p. 235; part of a metrical version of Psalm 128.

202. J. W. Burrows, *Southend-on-Sea and District* (1909), p. 110.

203. C. F. D. Sperling, *Short History of the Borough of Sudbury* (1896), p. 205.

204. H. E. Norris, *History of St. Ives* (1889), p. 21.

205. Timbs [55], ii. 223–4. By Dr C. Mackay. The tradition of a vault at Newark Abbey which went under the river to a nunnery comes in Aubrey's *Brief Lives*.

206. H. Cobbe, *Luton Church* (1899), pp. 345–6.

207. Rawnsley [183], p. 424. Latin: 'Thus it is that all have gone; thus we are going, and you shall go and so shall they.'

208. *Poems and Fables* [24], p. 848. Kinsley, following Lintot (1712), has 'Barningham in Norfolk'.

209. *Suffolk Green Books*, xv (1910), 197.

210. Text supplied by H. H. Erskine-Hill.

211. Noted by the editor.

212. Norris [204], pp. 28–9.

213. J. J. Raven, *History of Suffolk* (1895), pp. 164–5. The source varies the rector's initial as here.

214. J. W. Clark, *Cambridge* (1908), p. 80.

215. Glyde [47], p. 295.

216. From the Ely Cathedral postcard of the monument.

217. P. H. Ditchfield, *English Villages* (1901), p. 244.

218. A. J. Foster, *The Ouse* (n.d. *c.* 1891), p. 77.

219. Noted by the editor.

220. P. C. Standing (ed.), *Memorials of Old Hertfordshire* (1905), pp. 165–7. Also in R. Chambers, *Book of Days* (1864 edn), i. 578–9.

221. E. C. Gurdon (ed.), *County Folklore, Suffolk* (1893), p. 64.

222. T. Wright, *Romance of the Lace Pillow* (1919): (i) p. 190; the final couplet was sung to any girl who looked up before she had counted twenty lace-pins. (ii), p. 192; the reference is to taking rushes to church on 'Rush-bearing Sunday'. (iii) pp. 182–3; for the legend of 'Mr Fox', see e.g. Katherine Briggs, *Dictionary of British Folk-Tales*, part II, *Folk Narratives*, ii. 446–50; cf. no. 297.

223. Bax [194], p. 238.

224. Clark [214], pp. 85–6. At a previous Commencement the ladies (now confined to the church chancel) were thought to have behaved frivolously.

225. L. E. Beedham, *Ruined and Deserted Churches* (1908), p. 94. These epigrams are recorded in several versions, e.g. C. Sayle, *Annals of the University of Cambridge* (1916), p. 92, where the events are dated 1715. The first epigram is attributed to Dr Trapp, the second to Sir William Brown.

226. Clark [214], p. 289.

227. Ibid. 288.

228. Gurdon [221], pp. 139–40. In stanza 4 perhaps 'doon' should be 'dom', i.e. 'doom' (meaning 'Now you're for it!').

229. Hannah [196], pp. 271–2. Line 2, Latin, 'Of which the contrary is false'.

230. E. Peacock, *Glossary of Words . . . in Manley and Corringham* (1889 edn), i. 184.

231. *The Suffolk Garland* (1818), p. 397.

232. W. A. Dutt, *The Norfolk and Suffolk Coast* (1909):, pp. 391–2. The closing couplet probably lists kinds of snares.

233. Supplied by F. R. Whitmarsh, whose informant was George Black; both of Grimsby. The *Howe* sailed on 'Friday the Thirteenth' (November 1931); see the article in the *Grimsby Evening Telegraph*, 9 December 1960.

234. Supplied by the above from the original broadsheet as sold by the author.

235. Dutt [232], p. 205.

236. Supplied by F. R. Whitmarsh from a Grimsby newspaper.

237. R. J. Olney, *Rural Society and County Government in Lincolnshire* (1979), pp. 60–1.

238. E. Porter, *Cambridgeshire Customs and Folklore* (1969), p. 92.

239. Radford [90], p. 152.

240. Northall [80], p. 483. The *weirling* is either the great grey shrike, known to shriek when it sees a hawk, or the red-backed shrike.

241. Lean [151], II. i. 202.

242. Ibid. 321.

243. Bell [81], pp. 170–1.

244. Inwards [92], p. 2. The echo of Pope in l. 11 suggests an eighteenth-century date.

245. Rawnsley [183], p. 428. Boston 'Stump' is hardly a steeple.

246. Lean [151], II. ii. 591. Cf. no. 492.

V. THE MIDLANDS

247. *The Torrington Diaries* (1970 reprint), ii. 33; a metrical version of Psalm 42: 1.

248. Ibid. i. 326.

249. G. K. Stanton, *Rambles and Researches among Worcestershire Churches* (2 vols, 1884, 1886), i. 38. Lines 5–7 (here printed as in Stanton) are really a rhyming quatrain.

250. P. H. Ditchfield, *Memorials of Old Oxfordshire* (1903), p. 166. Charles I is reputed to have played at Collins Green.

251. C. J. Ribton-Turner, *Shakespeare's Land* (1893), p. 98. Malone (1741–1812) published an eleven-volume edition of Shakespeare in 1790.

252. G. T. Wright, *Longstone Records, Derbyshire* (1906), p. 190. From the *Antiquary*, Jan. 1871.

253. A. Hayden, *Chats on English Earthenware* (1909), p. 366; the lines are from Butler's 'Hudibras' (I. i. 359–62).

254. M. F. Raphael, *Romance of English Almshouses* (1926), p. 193.

255. E. Brill, *The Cotswolds* (1955), p. 48.

256. A. Dryden, *Memorials of Old Warwickshire* (1908), pp. 33–4. The map measured about 18′ by 12′ 6″.

257. Ibid. 33; about 15′ by 12′. E. C. Pulbrook, *The English Countryside* (2nd edn, 1926), p. 1, records the map as sixteenth-century; it is in the Bodleian Library, Oxford.

258. C. Shorter, *Highways and Byways in Buckinghamshire* (1910), p. 318.

259. Ibid. 315.

260. Supplied by C. Bunn, Lostwithiel, Cornwall. Cf. no. 393.

261. Stanton [249], i. 19. The old manor house was largely destroyed by fire, *c.*1730.

262. Ibid. ii. 43.

263. (i) J. Hammond, *A Cornish Parish* (1897), p. 184 n.; (ii) E. Gutch, *County Folklore: East Riding of Yorkshire* (1912), p. 214.

264. Ditchfield [217], pp. 248–9; *grandsires, trip(p)les, bob*, are ways of ringing long peals on church bells.

265. Hone [36], April 10. The bells are named after events or personalities in the early-eighteenth-century wars against France.

266. Madden Collection, University Library, Cambridge.

267. Andrews [178], p. 106; the verses mimic the sounds made by the bells in these Derbyshire parishes.

268. Lean [151], i. 158–9. In (i) verse 5, perhaps 'pay' should be 'pay me'.

269. Hope [109], pp. 175–6.

270. E. J. Climenson, *History of Shiplake* (1894), p. 327.

271. Stanton [249], ii. 103.

272. Ibid. i. 104, 105.

273. Ibid. 229.

274. C. O. Moreton, *Waddesdon and Over Winchendon* (1929), p. 135.

275. J. H. Smith, *Brewood* (1874), p. 76.

276. *Poems*, ed. R. Dunlap (1970 edn.), p. 56. Stanzas 1 to 6 only are inscribed (see Carew, *Poems*, ed. A. Vincent (n.d.), p. 248).

277. J. Noake, *The Rambler in Worcestershire* (1854), p. 222. 'A derelict . . .', left a widow at age 26; or, for 26 years?

278. Dryden [256], p. 171. Cf. no. 69.

279. Smith [275], p. 85.

280. W. Andrews (ed.), *Bygone Northamptonshire* (1891), p. 175.

281. A. W. Coysh, *Historic English Inns* (1972), p. 165.

282. R. Gibbs, *The Buckinghamshire Miscellany* (1891), p. 305.

283. *Torrington Diaries* [247], i. 235. 1 August 1715 was the first anniversary of the accession of George I.

284. J. Pendleton, *History of Derbyshire* (1886), pp. 97–8.

285. *Reliquiae Hearnianae*, coll. P. Bliss (1857), i. 404.

286. Ditchfield [73], p. 95.

287. Shorter [258], pp. 28–9.

288. E. W. Badger, *Monumental Brasses of Warwickshire* (1895), p. 21.

289. C. Brown, *History of Nottinghamshire* (1891), p. 289.

290. Stanton [249], i. 38–9.

291. Noake [277], p. 187. *Invalids*; Captain Wambey may have been an officer at the Chelsea Pensioners' barracks.

292. F. Redfern, *History and Antiquities . . . of Uttoxeter* (2nd edn, 1886), p. 236; this records that ll. 7–8 were 'obliterated on the instructions of the incumbent, but preserved, as now printed, in local memory'. See also Introduction, p. x.

293. (i), H. Armitage, *Chantrey Land* (1910), p. 94; (ii), (iii), Stanton [249], ii. 30, 227.

294. J. J. Hissey, *The Road and the Inn* (1917), p. 167.

295. *Complete Poetical Works*, ed. J. J McGann (1980), i. 224–5.

296. L. Johnston, *Down English Lanes* (1933), p. 75.

297. Northall [80], p. 534. Cf. no. 222 (iii).

298. Wright [222], p. 191.

299. J. Noake, *Notes and Queries for Worcestershire* (1856), pp. 192–3. The girl puts her shoes under her pillow and goes to bed in silence.

300. T. F. T. Dyer, *British Popular Customs* (1876), p. 99.

301. Gomme [94], i. 157–8.

302. Northall [80], pp. 430–1.

303. Ibid. 240–1. Northall suggests that these verses were reworked by the Puritans. Also recorded in almost identical form from Hitchin, Herts. (Bell [81], pp. 166–7).

304. Stanton [249], ii. 53. Singers sometimes carried a 'hoberdy' lantern, a hollowed-out turnip with holes for eyes, nose, and mouth, and a lighted candle inside. St Clement, 23 November; St Catherine, 25 November.

305. W. S. Brassington, *Historic Worcestershire* (1894), p. 179.

306. Lean [151], i. 60.

307. J. Halliwell, *Popular Rhymes* (1849). p. 158.

308. Lean [151], i. 391.

309. Halliwell [307], p. 210. *Wood*, probably in the old sense, demented. W. Henderson, *Folklore of the Northern Counties* (1866), p. 136, gives l. 3 as 'The waters were mild of mood'. In a version from Devon, no. 144 (i), l. 3 runs 'The water was wild in the wood'. The three versions taken together suggest that the Halliwell reading is the least corrupt, and therefore that the verse is probably medieval in origin.

310. Andrews [280], p. 211.

311. R. Wilbraham, *Attempt at a Glossary of some Words used in Cheshire* (1826), p. 105.

312. Wright [222], p. 186. The gold-headed pins used to attach the lace are the 'golden girls'; counting the pins frequently started at nineteen.

313. Supplied by S. Bush.

314. A. C. Ainger, *Memories of Eton Sixty Years Ago* (1917), pp. 91–2.

315. From the Oxford magazine *Kingdom Come*, Nov. 1939.

316. A. Mackinnon, *The Oxford Amateurs* (1910), p. 108.

317. Ibid. 7–8; apparently a song from *The Christmas Prince* (1816 edn., p. 24), a series of lord-of-misrule entertainments at St John's College, Oxford, Christmas 1607–8.

318. A. Wood, *Life and Times* (ed. A. Clark, 1891), i. 351–2; still sung at Christmas at Queen's. The Latin, 'as many as are at the feast', 'I bring in the boar's head, rendering praise to the Lord', 'serve (it) with singing', 'in The Queen's (College) Hall'. A boar's head is part of the arms of the college.

319. Ibid. iii. 512–3. The Capitol was allegedly saved from capture (BC 371) by the cackling of the sacred geese.

Stanzas 4 and 5 are not now normally sung, and there are some other variations.

320. S. O. Addy, *Household Tales* (1895: 1973 reprint), pp. 108–9.

321. Stanton [249], i. 54.

322. J. H. Ingram, *North Midland Country* (1947–8), p. 44. The *OED* under *stow* sb.^{2} quotes a prose version of ll. 1–6 from Fuller's *Worthies* (1662), Derbyshire.

323. Stanton [249], i. 57.

324. *Journal of the Gypsy Lore Society*, 1969, pp. 25–7; a translation by Henry Sherriff of a Romany poem learnt from his grandfather.

325. M. W. Bailey, *Lincolnshire and the Fens* (1952), pp. 16–17. Bill Scrimshaw, buried in Claypole church, was known in the 1760s as a champion wrestler. The ballad was found by Bailey 'copied into a farmer's account book in a Nottinghamshire Village'.

326. A. Stapleton, *Religious Institutions of Old Nottingham* (third series, 1899), pp. 191–2.

VI. THE WELSH BORDERS

327. Lean [151], i. 231.

328. W. Andrews, *Bygone Cheshire* (1895), p. 96.

329. Bell [81], p. 49.

330. *Torrington Diaries* [247], i. 43.

331. *Works*, ed. F. E. Hutchinson (1941), p. 67.

332. Raphael [254], p. 97.

333. *N. & Q.*, 23 August 1856.

334. H. M. Timmins, *Nooks and Corners of Herefordshire* (1892), p. 47.

335. Fitzwilliam Museum, Cambridge.

336. P. Drabble, *Black Country* (1952), p. 78.

337. T. Blount, *Fragmenta Antiquitatis* (enlarged by J. Beckwith, 1815), p. 666. The grant was allegedly by William I; Jackson [346], p. 584 states that the language is sixteenth-century. In l. 6 the source has 'line' which is presumably a misprint for 'l(e)iue'.

338. A. Mee, *Shropshire* (1968 edn.) p. 121.

339. R. C. Skyring Walters, *Ancient Wells . . . of Gloucestershire* (1928), p. 132. Milton is said to have written some part of *Paradise Lost* here.

340. *N. & Q.*, 3 September 1853.

341. Timbs [55], i. 426.

342. P. Sulley, *Hundred of Wirral* (1889), pp. 210–11. Composed by the local rector.

343. G. Griffiths, *History of Tong, Shropshire* (1894), p. 99. Cf. nos. 124 and 389.

344. Lean [151], i. 182–4.

345. H. E. Forrest, *Old Churches of Shrewsbury* (1920), p. 130.

346. G. F. Jackson, *Shropshire Folklore* (ed. C. S. Burn, 1883), p. 612.

347. Forrest [345], p. 87.

348. Jackson [346], p. 575.

349. E. Hutton, *Highways and Byways in Gloucestershire* (1932), p. 424.

350. R. Granville, *History of the Granville Family* (1895), p. 123.

351. *Torrington Diaries* [247], i. 326.

352. W. H. Cooke, *Collections towards the History and Antiquities of the County of Herefordshire . . .* (1892), p. 153.

353. A. Ingham, *Cheshire . . .* (1920), p. 249.

354. A. G. Bradley, *In the Marches and Borderland of Wales* (1905), p. 140. A variant version, with two extra lines, is given in the *Dictionary of National Biography*, where it is stated that John Abel composed this epitaph himself when aged over 90.

355. J. Fisher, *History of Berkeley* (1864), p. 37.

356. H. Clairborne Dixon, *The Abbeys of Great Britain* (n.d., *c.* 1909), p. 130.

357. W. A. Sampson, *The Bristol Grammar School* (1912), pp. 105–6.

358. H. J. Massingham, *Shepherd's Country* (1938), pp. 153–4. *Helen* is correct in l. 9, but in l. 5 is presumably a mistake for *Hecuba*, Paris' mother.

359. Ingham [353], pp. 112–13. Cf. no. 304.

360. E. Barber and P. H. Ditchfield, *Memorials of Old Cheshire* (1910), p. 240.

361. Ibid. 242.

362. Gomme [94], i. 175.

363. Ibid. i. 51.

364. (i), ibid. 156, Cf. no. 301. (ii), Northall [80], p. 376.

365. Brand [96], i. 6–7. The words omitted in stanzas 2 and 3 were names of horses. Filpail is a cow.

366. Hope [109], p. 150; there was a tradition at Bath that the ancient British King Bladud (father of King Lear), reduced by leprosy to being a swineherd, noticed that the Bath springs cured disease in his pigs. See *N. & Q.*, 2nd Series, ix. 45.

367. Halliwell [307], pp. 196–7; inhabitants of Shropshire, and especially Shrewsbury, were said to misplace the letter H when speaking.

368. T. Darlington, *Folk-Speech of South Cheshire* (1887), p. 288. Cf. no. 433.

369. E. M. Leather, *Folklore of Herefordshire* (1912), pp. 229, 230. Answers: (i), the moon; (ii), a gun.

370. Jackson [346], pp. 573–4. Answers: (i), a cock; (ii), a thimble.

371. Leather [369], p. 62. 'This' was half of a hard-boiled egg.

372. Jackson [346], p. 179. Compare nos. 371–2 with nos. 299 and 435–6.

373. *Cambrian Quarterly Magazine*, 1831, pp. 70–1.

374. Lean [151], i. 100.

375. Cooke [352], p. 102; 'from a scarce pamphlet of the time'.

376. Jackson [346], p. 560. Composed, communally, by villagers in the shoemaker's shop: 'we all on us maden a bit on it, and when we thoughten on anything we putten it down'.

377. Ibid. 70–1.

378. Ibid. 110.

379. J. Duncomb, *Collections Towards the History and Antiquities of the County of Hereford*, vol. ii (1812), pp. 198–200. Tedstone Delamere is a few miles west of Worcester.

380. Ingham [353], p. 107.

381. V. Robie, *Bypaths in Collecting* (1913), pp. 264–5. Cf. no. 174.

VII. NORTH-EAST ENGLAND

382. J. R. F. Prince, *Silkstone* (1922), p. 58.

383. Jones [97], p. 363.

384. R. Heape, *Dates on Old Buildings in Rochdale and District* (1910), p. 22.

385. G. B. Wood, *Yorkshire Villages* (1971), p. 175.

386. Prince [382], p. 59. *Faith, Angel, Grace*, were perhaps names of women once working at the inn.

387. *N. & Q.*, 5 April 1856.

388. Andrews [178], p. 94.

389. Halliwell [307], pp. 255–6. 'Who will or cannot miss his hat', perhaps the customer who always thinks it is lost, or who fusses to keep it in sight.

390. Andrews [178], p. 111.

391. Prince [382], p. 59.

392. I. P. Pressly, *A York Miscellany* (n.d., c. 1938), p. 220.

393. W. H. D. Longstaffe, *History . . . of Darlington* (1909), p. 336. Cf. no. 260.

394. Wood [385], pp. 62–3.

395. Ibid. 107.

396. Text from Jonson, *Complete Works* [11], viii. 443; see also *Gentleman's Magazine*, 1866, p. 408. Herford and Simpson in effect indicate that the verses are not by Jonson.

397. D. F. E. Sykes, *History of Huddersfield* (1898), p. 198. Latin title: 'the life of a virtuous wife'.

398. R. E. Leader, *Sheffield in the Eighteenth Century* (1901), p. 64.

399. J. F. Blacker, *Nineteenth Century English Ceramic Art* (n.d., *c.*1911), pp. 395–6.

400. Robie [381], p. 262.

401. Blacker [399], pp. 395–6.

402. Ibid. 396.

403. Supplied by R. Palmer. On the ballad sheet the first line begins simply 'M. . . . with'; with minor variations, the verses were used by other Leeds merchants in both the nineteenth and twentieth centuries.

404. T. Parkinson, *Legends and Traditions of Yorkshire* (vol. ii, 1889), p. 121.

405. W. A. Cutting, *Glimpses about Gayton* (1889), p. 184.

406. J. Mayhall, *Annals of Yorkshire* (2 vols, n.d.), i. 156.

407. P. A. Graham, *Highways and Byways in Northumbria* (1920), p. 322.

408. Wood [385], p. 198.

409. Prince [382], p. 23.

410. R. J. Charleton, *Newcastle Town* (1885), p. 186.

411. J. S. Fletcher, *Picturesque History of Yorkshire* (3 vols, 1901), iii. 162.

412. Id., *Memorials of a Yorkshire Parish* (1917), pp. 72–3.

413. R. Stewart-Brown, *History of the Manor and Township of Allerton* (1911), p. 196. The Latin runs: 'joyful day', 'there is peace in Heaven', 'behind one's back' (i.e. as a parting shot), 'I shall rise again'.

414. Fletcher [411], ii. 99–100.

415. J. J. Hissey, *Leisurely Tour in England* (1913), p. 376.

416. Hissey [177], p. 79.

417. E. Jameson, *1000 Curiosities of Britain* (1937), p. 35. Left written out by Catherine Alsopp in pencil on a scrap of paper.

418. Northall [80], pp. 206–7.

419. Ibid. 182.

420. E. Gutch, *County Folk-lore: North Riding, . . .* (1901), pp. 334–5. 'Stang-riding' was widespread over England as a practice to hold bullying husbands up to ridicule. The rider might be the culprit himself, or an effigy, or (as here) another man who proclaimed the real culprit's name.

421. Prince [382], pp. 114–15.

422. Lean [151], i. 166.

423. R. Blakeborough, *Wit . . . of the North Riding of Yorkshire* (1898), p. 111.

424. C. Hardwick, *Traditions, Superstitions, and Folklore (chiefly Lancashire and the North of England)* (1872), p. 154.

425. Halliwell [307], p. 189. The 'Cauld Lad' is of course a ghost.

426. G. Home, *Evolution of an English Town (Pickering, Yorks)* (1915), p. 208.

427. E. T. Evans, *Askrigg* (1890), pp. 26–7.

428. Parkinson [404] (vol. i, 1888), pp. 156–7.

429. Hope [109], pp. 182–3. Cf. the legend of Baucis and Philemon, Ovid, *Metamorphoses* viii.

430. S. O. Addy, *Glossary of Words . . . in Sheffield* (1888), p. 153. Addy records that the mummers' play performed in villages around Sheffield was called 'The Peace Egg'; it was printed in a chapbook, but without this closing song.

431. Ibid. 198.

432. J. Christie, *Northumberland* (1893), p. 57.

433. Addy [320], p. 147.

434. Longstaffe [393], p. 335; modified to suit many other towns also.

435. Henderson [309], 1879 edn., pp. 110–11. An 'even' ash-leaf lacks the single leaflet at the end of the leaf-stalk.

436. Gutch [420], p. 42.

437. Henderson [435], p. 155.

438. Addy [320], p. 141.

439. Inwards [92], p. 22. Legends of March borrowing days (for bad weather) from April are found elsewhere in England and Scotland, and also in Spain. *Silly* doubtless has the archaic sense of 'guileless' (an indication of the age of the verse).

440. *Ripon Millenary Record* (1892), part ii, p. 64.

441. W. Andrews, *Modern Yorkshire Poets* (1885), pp. 9–10.

442. Parkinson [404], p. 120.

443. W. C. Mitchell, *History of Sunderland* (1919; 1972 reprint), p. 151.

444. C. F. Forshaw (ed.), *Holroyd's Collection of Yorkshire Ballads* (1892), pp. 86–7.

445. D. D. Dixon, *Whittingham Vale* (1895), p. 192.

446. Ibid. 106–7. The spelling *Liddle* in the title is as printed by Dixon.

VIII. NORTH-WEST ENGLAND

447. E. Bogg, *A Thousand Miles of Wandering Along the Roman Wall* (1898), p. 206.

448. G. C. Miller, *Hoghton Tower . . .* (1954), pp. 29–32. Possibly by Roger

Anderson, butler to Thomas Hoghton. *Bishop Younge* was doubtless Thomas Young, Archbishop of York 1561–8, a zealous Protestant.

449. W. E. A. Axon, *Lancashire Gleanings* (1883), p. 122. Answer: quill-pens, parchment, and wax.

450. H. A. L. Rice, *Lake Country Towns* (1974), p. 62 (in ll. 1–2 only the capital S is explicit as to which spirit is which).

451. Brand [96], ii. 83.

452. Larwood and Hotten [103], p. 40.

453. G. Chandler, *Liverpool* (1957), pp. 339–40.

454. Ibid. 340.

455. Robie [381], p. 263. This verse is probably part of a complex tradition: in Shakespeare's *As You Like It* (III. ii. 64–8) there is a corresponding passage about the joys of the country labourer's life, and the title or first line of a similar song for the country gentleman ('I have parks', etc.) may be found in Hardy's *Tess of the D'Urbervilles*, chapter 49.

456. T. Newbigging, *History of the Forest of Rossendale* (c. 1867); 2nd edn. (1893), p. 59. The forest lies between Bacup and Burnley.

457. Robie [381], p. 257.

458. H. C. Collins, *Lancashire Plain and Seaboard* (1953), p. 144.

459. A. Povah, *Annals of the Parishes of St Olave Hart Street and Allhallows Staining* (1894), p. 74.

460. W. R. Mitchell, *Men of Lakeland* (1966), p. 122.

461. Curwen [19], p. 143.

462. Ibid. 251; l. 2 probably means that the vicar had married according to his sister's advice.

463. E. Bellasis, *Westmorland Church Notes* (1889), ii. 5–6; l. 3 echoes Marlowe, *Jew of Malta*, I. i. 34: 'infinite riches in a little room'.

464. J. C. Scholes, *History of Bolton* (1892), p. 197.

465. R. S. Ferguson, *History of Westmorland* (1894), p. 288; English version of a Latin epitaph done by Chancellor Burn when a schoolmaster at Orton, Westmorland.

466. W. Baxter, *Description of Holm Cultram Abbey* (1917), pp. 24–5. Note the concealed metre and rhymes throughout.

467. M. Lefebure, *The English Lake District* (1964), p. 159. The local steeplejack refused to repair the church spire, so Mr Jackson climbed up himself.

468. W. Hutchinson, *History of the County of Cumberland* (1794; 1974 reprint), I. 516. Recorded in the source as 'by Mr Richardson of Blencowe'.

469. Bellasis [463], p. 271.

470. Curwen [19], p. 116.

471. W. Dobson and J. Harland, *A History of Preston Guild* (n.d.), p. 58.

472. J. W. Brown, *Round Carlisle Cross* (Fourth Series, 1924), p. 150.

473. J. Harland and T. T. Wilkinson, *Lancashire Legends* (1873; Scolar Press reprint, 1973), pp. 188–9.

474. Id., *Lancashire Folk-Lore* (1882), p. 73; l. 7 may mean 'a wand light to hold'.

475. Brown [472], p. 102.

476. Northall [80], p. 39.

477. W. Nicholls, *History and Traditions of Radcliffe* (n.d., c. 1910), pp. 212–15.

478. G. C. Miller, *Blackburn: the Evolution of a Cotton Town* (1951), p. 235.

479. A. C. Gibson, *Folk Speech of Cumberland* (1869), pp. 40–2.

480. Axon [449], p. 207.

IX. SAMPLES FROM SCOTLAND, WALES AND ELSEWHERE

481. W. K. Baker, *Acton* (2nd edn., n.d.), p. 64.

482. Henderson [435], p. 24.

483. G. Henderson and J. J. Waddell, *By Bothwell Banks* (1904), p. 73.

484. *N. & Q.*, 27 September 1851; there are allusions to the revolutions of the 1640s, and 1688; and to the Union of the English and Scottish Parliaments in 1707.

485. D. Pride, *History of the Parish of Nielston* (1910), p. 144. A girl placed the yarrow under her pillow and repeated this verse before sleeping.

486. Andrews [178], p. 98.

487. *Poems and Songs*, ed. J. Kinsley (1958), p. 469. Mauchline is a small town in Ayrshire; the epitaph was presumably not inscribed on Smith's tombstone.

488. Both from Gomme [94], ii. 92–3, who suggests that *stand* in (i) l. 1 should be 'sedan'.

489. Ibid. 428–9.

490. Hone [35], January 1. Also recorded for Devon (Crossing [108], p. 145).

491. *N. & Q.*, 4 August 1855.

492. Lean [151], vol. II, part i, p. 103; for ll. 3–4, cf. no. 246.

493. W. E. A. Axon, *Cheshire Gleanings* (1884), pp. 204–5.

494. Northall [80], p. 185.

495. S. Peters, *History of Pembroke Dock* (1905), pp. 133–4.

496. E. Laws, *History of the Little England Beyond Wales* (1888), p. 407.

497. W. C. Russell, *Sailors' Language* (1893), p. x.

498. H. T. Evans, *Rebecca and Her Daughters* (1910), pp. 37–8. In South Wales in 1843–4 toll-gates were attacked by men disguised as women, who called themselves 'Rebecca and her daughters' because of Genesis 24:60, where Rebecca is told 'let thy seed possess the gate of those which hate them'.

499. Ibid. 196. An interesting social contrast with the previous verses. The Latin *Habe omnes* seems to mean 'Take them all!' The Irish patriot leader Daniel

O'Connell organized enormous public meetings in Ireland in 1843, the year of these riots.

500. (i), *Collected Poems* (1933), p. 214; (ii), Mary Hanley and Liam Miller, *Thoor Ballylee: home of William Butler Yeats* (rev. edn. 1977), p. 16. Liam Miller drew my attention to this version. Reprinted by permission of A. P. Watt Ltd. on behalf of Michael B. Yeats and Macmillan, London Ltd.

501. Clarke [182], pp. 446–7.

502. McGann [295], i. 279. In earlier editions recorded as 'in the Travellers' Book at Orchomenos'.

503. P. Newton, *High Country Journey* (1952), pp. 105–6.

504. *Collected Poems*, ed. J. A. Smith (1971), p. 130 and 479 n. The poem is inscribed on the Stevenson Memorial in St Giles's Cathedral, Edinburgh, and also on Stevenson's tomb on Mount Vaea, Samoa (see D. Daiches, *R. L. Stevenson and his World* (1973), p. 110).

X. VERSES ON SOME MOVABLE OR UNLOCATED OBJECTS

505. A. J. Cruse, *Match-box Labels of the World* (1946), p. 48.

506. Supplied by Mrs Ursula Vaughan Williams.

507. Timbs [55], ii. 509–10. Timbs records that the mirror (or its frame) had two likenesses of Charles II and also of Nell Gwynn. She used the lion and leopard for a crest.

508. Worked by Mary Ainsley; original in the possession of Margery Hyslop, Trumpington, Cambridge.

509. All from the Fitzwilliam Museum, Cambridge, by permission of the Curator.

510. N. H. Moore, *The Lace Book* (1905), p. 180.

511. A. Sebba, *Samplers—Five Centuries of a Gentle Craft* (1979); title page and pp. 46, 54, 106, 59.

512. From the magazine *Old Cornwall*, vol. v (1960), no. 11, p. 467.

513. M. Gostelow, *A World of Embroidery* (1975), p. 91; the original is in the National Museum, Wellington, NZ.

514. N. H. Moore, *Old China Book* (1904), p. 118.

515. A. de Selincourt, *The Channel Shore* (1953), p. 167.

516. Lord Hylton, *Notes on the History of the Parish of Kilmersdon* (1910), p. 146. Presumably 'never' in l. 7 should be 'ever'.

517. *N. & Q.*, 9 August 1856; recorded there as in 'Scots' Magazine, October 1747'.

518. K. Ullyett, *In Quest of Clocks* (1950), p. 63.

519. (i), N. H. Moore, *Old Clock Book* (1912), p. 35; (ii), E. J. Wood, *Curiosities of Clocks and Watches* (1866; 1973 facsimile), which records that Lord George Lyttelton sent these verses to Lucy Cavendish; (iii), *N. & Q.*, 1 August 1874.

520. Ullyett [13], p. 94.

521. Ibid. 95.

522. Hissey [294], p. 130. Cf. no. 294.

523. Timbs [55], i. 449.

524. Hone [35], November 2. Doubtless too long to have been inscribed.

525. *N. & Q.*, 2 April 1853. Cf. John 21:25, 'even the world itself could not contain the books that should be written'. In l. 5 'alone' perhaps should be 'above'.

526. *Poems*, ed. G. T. Drury (1893?), ii. 1.

527. Pressly [392], pp. 83–4.

528. *Satires and Personal Writings*, ed. W. A. Eddy (1932), p. 451.

529. T. Hughes, *English Domestic Needlework* (1961), p. 176.

530. Dickens, *Sketches by Boz* (1836), 'Memoirs of Joseph Grimaldi', chapter 7. Recorded also in the churchyard at Melrose, at St Ambrose Church, Ombersley, Bromsgrove, and other places. Joseph Grimaldi (1779–1837) was a famous clown.

531. *Poetical Works*, ed. C. B. Tinker and H. F. Lowry (1963 edn.), pp. 5–6. Allott, *Complete Poems* (1979 edn.), p. 43, has 'Where'er' in l. 13 of the Butler sonnet.

532. *Poems*, ed. P. B. Bartlett (1978), ii. 1020.

533. *Collected Poems* (1897), p. 433.

534. C. Hindley, *Tavern Anecdotes and Sayings* (1875), p. 307.

535. Lean [151], i. 449.

536. Ibid. i. 407; not linked by Lean to any specific locality.

537. Robie [381], p. 556.

538. W. T. Marchant, *In Praise of Ale* (1888), p. 593.

539. Fitzwilliam Museum, Cambridge, by permission of the Curator.

While every effort has been made to trace the copyright holder, we may have failed in a few cases, and apologize for any inadvertent omission.

INDEX OF LOCALITIES

The references are to poem numbers
(The county locations are according to the pre-1974 divisions)

INDEX OF FIRST LINES

The references are to poem numbers

339

INDEX OF FIRST LINES

INDEX OF FIRST LINES

INDEX OF FIRST LINES